More Praise for *Multiple Pathways to the Student Brain*

"This groundbreaking 'how-to manual' for brain-compatible teaching applies solid neuro-science to real-life classroom situations and stud███████████████ hugely ███████ practical insights into lesson planning and classroom tea████████████████████████

      —Dan Moody, professor, department███████████████████████████ western ███████████████████████ ista, CA

"Steeped in valid research, this practical guide provides a plethora of educational strategies to enhance students' learning experiences and accelerate academic achievement."

      —Cindy Lee Seiger, retired teacher, Lebanon, PA

Multiple Pathways to the Student Brain

Energizing and Enhancing Instruction

Janet Nay Zadina

JB JOSSEY-BASS™

A Wiley Brand

Published by Jossey-Bass
A Wiley Imprint
One Montgomery Street, Suite 1200, San Francisco, CA 94104-4594—www.josseybass.com

Jossey-Bass books and products are available through most bookstores. To contact Jossey-Bass directly call our Customer Care Department within the U.S. at 800-956-7739, outside the U.S. at 317-572-3986, or fax 317-572-4002.

Wiley publishes in a variety of print and electronic formats and by print-on-demand. Some material included with standard print versions of this book may not be included in e-books or in print-on-demand. If this book refers to media such as a CD or DVD that is not included in the version you purchased, you may download this material at http://booksupport.wiley.com. For more information about Wiley products, visit www.wiley.com.

Library of Congress Cataloging-in-Publication Data has been applied for and is on file with the Library of Congress.
ISBN 978-1-118-56761-6 (pbk.); ISBN 978-1-118-58486-6 (ebk); ISBN 978-1-118-58488-0 (ebk)

Printed in the United States of America
FIRST EDITION
PB Printing   10 9 8 7 6 5 4 3 2

Contents

This book is dedicated to all the wonderful teachers
who have attended my presentations,
shared their feedback and expertise,
and inspired me.
Keep up the great work!

and

To Jim Zadina,
who has inspired and supported me
in both careers—teaching and science.

Acknowledgments

Huge thanks to Marjorie McAneny at Jossey-Bass for inviting me to write this book. Margie, you have been a pleasure to work with and so supportive. Thanks also to Tracy Gallagher who was always helpful in answering questions along the way. Heartfelt appreciation goes to editor Bev Miller for her outstanding attention to detail and thoughtful queries.

I could never have made this book deadline without the amazing support of Pat Kidder. Pat worked diligently and expertly on the references, permissions, and lists of suggested reading at the end of every chapter—a huge task—while at the same time keeping me on track with my speaking schedule and the many other ways she enables me to devote so much time to the work that I do. Pat, I couldn't ask for a nicer, more enjoyable, or more talented assistant.

I am greatly indebted to the wonderful teachers who volunteered to review chapters as a kindness to me. Thanks to Maxine Anchondo, Ella Baccouche, Amy Baskin, Mary C. Belknap, Floyd Brigdon, Lainey Brottem, Desbra Canavan, Shirl Cook, Lacie Crone, Kathleen Gable, Amy Garcia, Sandra Graff, Wendy Hagman, Beverly Hearn, Dan Moody, Vicki Moulson, Grace Quagliariello, Darwin Risdon, Robert Searson, Cindy Seiger, Sue Selde, Karen Shipman, Zelda Smith, Ursula Sohns, Karen Solis, Jan Sundmark, Susan Szabo, Bill Thompson, Annette Wall, Donnell

Wolff, Rosie Woodruff, and Telford Work. They thoughtfully provided perspectives from many content areas and grade levels. The book is much better thanks to their tough love and thoughtful insights. I thank the two anonymous reviewers provided by Jossey-Bass for their contributions.

I couldn't have devoted as much time to this book while engaging in my speaking schedule without the support of Rachel McLaughlin. Thanks to my friends, colleagues, and mentors for the wonderful discussions about teaching and learning, as well as their friendship: April Whatley Bedford, Renee Casbergue, Deborah Christie, Denise DeFelice, Judith Kieff, Marina Morbiducci, and Gayle Nolan. I also thank those who provide me with a welcome relief from work and much-needed support, including Karen and Tom Blanchard, Jim and June Blount, Percy Doiron and Marcia Warner, Ross and Claudine Foushee, Lisa Irwin, Jeff LaJess, Patti Vallee and Bob Schick, and Victor Vazquez (RIP).

A special thank-you goes to my family: Jason Nay, Alex Nay, Jeff and Kathy Nay, Anne and Steve Capes, and my husband, Jim, to whom I dedicate this book.

Preface

I believe I was born a teacher. One of my earliest memories was being in home quarantine in third grade with scarlet fever and receiving letters from my classmates. I got out a red pen and graded the letters, correcting all errors. Oh my! Playing school was my favorite pastime, and my mom recalls my favorite phrase as, "Now just think about that!" What else could I become?

One of the most common questions I get is how I went from being a high school teacher to a neuroscientist. It was an arduous and exhilarating journey of a lifetime.

Right after I earned my BS in education, I became a high school English teacher and was given the remedial classes (as they were called then). I discovered that my students couldn't read. I immediately started night school in a master's program and wanted to specialize in older learners with reading problems. However, no such program existed at the time. The reading professor in the master's program at the University of New Orleans (then part of Louisiana State University) allowed me to do independent study on reading difficulties in older children. After earning my master's in English education with a specialty in reading, I continued course work to earn a reading specialist certificate and taught high school for many years in varied demographics. I also taught adults in night classes.

As I continued to study dyslexia (reading difficulty), I became very discouraged. The research wasn't going anywhere, and students continued to struggle. I began teaching reading and English at a community college and engaging in course work beyond my master's. One day I saw a newspaper article about a scientist, Christiana Leonard, who did brain scans of college students with dyslexia and realized suddenly that there was a new window into this disorder. I recall standing in my living room and announcing that I was going to do that work. How? I didn't know.

That scientist came to speak at Tulane's medical school, and by some fluke in e-mail, I found out about it and showed up at the grand rounds to hear her speak. Afterward I approached her, and she and the local researcher, Anne Foundas, were happy to find out that I was a reading specialist. At lunch, we discussed an eventual possibility of my doing a dissertation on dyslexia in Dr. Foundas's lab, where she was investigating stuttering, another language disorder.

While the process of reaching that dream was long and arduous, in short, I enrolled in the University of New Orleans doctoral program where, at first, the professors were skeptical, thinking learning and the brain was old left brain/right brain discussions now seen as neuromyths. I persisted studying that on my own while pursuing a more traditional program and maintained connections with researchers in the medical school lab who were interested in allowing me to pursue my dissertation in conjunction with them if I proved myself. Eventually my education professors understood where I was going with my research and enthusiastically jumped on board. As a result of my literature review on scientific studies of dyslexia, the language lab in the Department of Neurology at Tulane Medical School allowed me to attend lab meetings.

I continued to take the steps toward a dissertation on the neuroanatomy of dyslexia, meeting the requirements of the education program, working alongside neuroscience graduate students at Tulane, and learning everything I needed to know about the brain, scans, and brain measurements. I was hired as a research assistant and moved from teaching to full-time lab and dissertation work. I gave brain scans to college students with and without dyslexia and measured regions of the brain related to language to look for neuroanatomical risk factors.

After earning my PhD with a joint committee from the University of New Orleans College of Education and Tulane Department of Neurology, I was awarded a three-year postdoctoral fellowship in cognitive neuroscience at Tulane's medical school in the department of neurology. I continued to research dyslexia and began a major project on stuttering using magnetic resonance imaging (MRI) brain scans. Then Hurricane Katrina hit New Orleans, destroying the scanners and scattering the lab across the country. We were seven brains short of finishing the three-year stuttering project. At the 2005 Society for Neuroscience conference that fall, I went from poster to poster begging for brains. Robert Dougherty, a scientist from Stanford who had conducted similar language tests on his volunteers, gave us the brains we needed to finish the project, enabling the doctoral students to finish and graduate.

With our lab in upheaval and MRI research at a standstill, I continued my speaking career as an educational neuroscientist seeking to bridge the gap between science and education. At this point the speaking engagements became full time and led to my eventually receiving a prestigious annual award given by the Society for Neuroscience: the Science Educator Award presented to "an outstanding neuroscientist who has made a significant impact in informing the public about neuroscience." This huge honor mitigated my loss of research due to Hurricane Katrina.

This book stems from my decade of speaking to teachers all over the world about how the brain learns and what this means in the classroom. At the time I graduated, I was the only person, so far as I knew, using the term *educational neuroscience*. No programs existed to do what I had done: earning credentials and experience in both fields. The term used at that time was *brain based*, which had a bad reputation in the scientific field. Myths about the brain were being perpetuated, and presenters were training teachers by getting them excited with a few brain terms and presenting a mixture of credible and noncredible information. I set about to change that lack of credibility in my new field.

Because I had a background in reading extensively in the scientific literature, I was able to distinguish the credible from the noncredible. As a teacher, I could see how many of our practices were in line with what the research was showing. I wanted to be sure that we kept the valuable practices and discarded practices that seemed to fly in the face of the research.

As the dribble of research on learning turned into a flood, I looked for a simple and meaningful way to organize the information so that it could be discussed and used. Eventually I developed the *multiple pathways model*, which allows teachers to discuss pathways involved in learning and make sense of them in context.

Because teachers were craving credible information about the brain and strategies that align with what we are learning, I wrote this book. It is designed for all teachers at all levels—from elementary school through college—who want to learn the underlying science as well as for those who are interested solely in the strategies that would be in alignment with recent research.

To me, teaching is an art *and* a science. Good teachers have an instinct for learners, so you will find much of this information validating. I hope that you find this book inspiring, informative, and empowering. You have inspired and motivated me. Keep up the great work!

Multiple Pathways to the Student Brain

Introduction

I don't think there is a profession more noble than teaching. All teachers can think of students whose lives were changed as a result of their impact. In some cases, we know that we have even saved a life by altering the course of someone's life or changing his or her worldview. As if that were not enough, we now know that what we teachers do can change our students' brains, affecting the rest of their life in many ways.

As knowledge about the brain proliferates, educators look for ways to apply this information to their practice. Unfortunately, many myths about the application of brain research to education abound. These can be perpetuated by well-meaning but inadequately informed presenters repeating what they have heard, but making mistakes in the translation or not knowing how to evaluate the scientific literature or put it into perspective. Some well-meaning scientists who present to educators about the application of research to education have never been in a K–12 classroom or taught struggling learners, so the "What does it mean to us?" part is missing. What is needed is the ability to see research through the eyes of a teacher and teaching through the eyes of a researcher—experience and credentials in both fields to create a credible bridge between scientific research and educational practice. That is my aim in writing this book.

We are beyond the point where we ask whether neuroscience can inform education to the new position of blended information coming from multiple research sources that inform each other and education. This book addresses mind (metacognition), brain (neuroscience), and behavior (psychology, neuroscience, and education) to achieve the best possible practices based on new research. I call this new synthesis *educational neuroscience*. This integration of research and resources from multiple fields creates a synergy, with advances in one field contributing to an understanding in another field. Whereas neuroscience may enlighten us about an underlying process affecting reading, for example, education research may help us apply that information.

I wrote this book at the request of a multitude of teachers who have attended my presentations and asked for additional information about the brain and appropriate teaching strategies. To avoid untenable leaps from basic research to classroom application, I bridge the basic science (*What does the research say?*) to some general implications for the field of education (*What does this mean for educators?*). Then I make some leaps into classroom practices (what I refer to as *leaping into the classroom*) with strategies that align themselves with the literature and the implications. I do not assume a direct link between the research and the teacher strategies, as those generally have not been proven to be linked. I felt it was essential to discuss strategies in this book because teachers want this information. I also needed to provide examples to put the role of strategies in proper perspective to counteract the untenable links that were being made. We have to create a credible *bridge* between research and strategies. Therefore, I have divided the main topics in the chapters into three sections: "What Does the Research Say?" "What Does This Mean for Educators?" and "Leaping into the Classroom."

THREE TYPES OF INFORMATION

Because so many of you love learning about the anatomy and science of learning, I explore the topics in the chapters beginning with, "What Does the Research Say?" and present some basic brain anatomy and interactions relevant to the pathway. I then look at recent studies that exemplify some new directions and findings. Of course, since an entire book could be written on each pathway, this is not meant to be a comprehensive review of the fast-changing literature, but rather a sampling of interesting findings that illustrate the complexity of the learning process and suggest some new directions.

The next section, "What Does This Mean for Educators?" draws some general conclusions about the direction of education from the research. This is a broader look directed toward overall policy and curriculum in general.

Then we make a leap into the classroom in "Leaping into the Classroom." In this section I draw on my teaching experience and that of my colleagues to suggest some sample strategies that align with the research. Let me stress that brain research does not "prove" that we should do this. However, if the research suggests, for example, a relationship between brain activation and finger representation, we may encourage educators to allow children to use their fingers when counting, or when research shows the effects in the brain on learning coming from a feeling of threat, we can remind teachers that sarcasm is not an appropriate tool to use with children. There is no proven direct link, but it just makes sense. We refine our practices based on what we are learning, just as we refine them based on our personal experience.

THE MULTIPLE PATHWAYS MODEL

I developed the *multiple pathways model* as a means of making sense of this ever-increasing new research on learning. The model puts the research into arbitrary "pathways" involved in learning so that we can think and talk about various aspects of the research in an orderly way. Too often presentations about the brain consist of a list of bullet points of random information. This information needs to be placed in a bigger context related to other information about the brain and to education.

In order to think about, discuss, and apply large amounts of new information, the information needed to be categorized in a meaningful way. The challenge is that the brain is complex and processes are integrated across multiple brain areas. It was therefore very hard to talk about one process in depth without referring to other brain areas and processing pathways. How could I categorize this information in a simple and useful manner?

I began by listing some major pathways in the brain involved in learning as the major categories for the model. Many concepts could have been placed in any number of these pathways. For example, music is auditory, emotional, and, for some, a language. Stress is an emotion that affects working memory and higher-order thinking skills. We need a way to talk about these factors one at a time *and* have a simple schematic so that we can see if we are addressing as many pathways as possible in our curriculum and lessons.

I use the term *pathway* not to represent a single structure but rather as a network of activation. Sometimes the network has the strongest activation in one area, such as the frontal lobe "pathway" (the site of higher-order thinking skills), but it interacts with multiple other pathways in the brain. By discussing it as a pathway, we can talk about the functions and nature of a component of this network and how it integrates with other pathways and with learning theory and practice. This does not imply that only one pathway is active in a student at any time. Multiple pathways are active every moment. The goal of the multiple pathways model is to make us aware of the many pathways that are involved in learning and then to address as many as possible in one lesson plan.

The multiple pathways model, unlike the learning styles model, has a synergistic effect: learning one way to compensate may help a student, but learning multiple pathways of compensation will create a synergy, with the whole greater than the sum of its parts. For example, teachers often think of diversifying instruction as visual, auditory, and kinesthetic. That is only one pathway in this book—the sensory motor pathway. When designing lessons, we also want to think about developing the student's frontal lobe and improving memory and attention, making learning rewarding, and acknowledging the emotional component. We want to address multiple pathways.

The concept of multiple pathways has three components:

1. *Multiple pathways in the brain:* We examine many brain processes powerfully involved in learning. For example, we examine the reward pathway in the brain to see how we can better motivate and engage students and examine the attentional network for helping students with this underlying process.

2. *Multiple pathways of teaching:* We must diversify our instruction to reach diverse students. One way to do this is by thinking and talking about multiple pathways of instruction and offering students multiple pathways for practice and assessment.

3. *Multiple pathways of knowledge about learning:* The research behind this book draws on multiple pathways of research: neuroscience, psychology, medicine, and education. These multiple pathways of research are blended into the information and strategies in this book.

CONTENT OF THIS BOOK

In order to orchestrate optimal learning, we must have an understanding of how the brain learns and what is required prior to the introduction of new information. Chapter 1 sets the stage for learning prior to the introduction of content. Understanding the difference in the brain between thinking and learning is critical to designing appropriate learning activities. Then we examine what students are bringing to the learning experience.

The next four chapters cover what I call the *invisible pathways* for learning. They underlie visible ("visible" meaning measured in the classroom) processes such as reading and math. Chapter 2 looks at sensory input and output, often referred to as visual, auditory, and kinesthetic. Students do not necessarily see and hear what we think they do; hence, these processes are invisible to us but greatly affect learning outcomes. How do students receive our content (sensory input)? Why do students seem to take it in but have a problem with expressing what they know (sensory output)?

Sensory input and output are affected by and in turn affect emotion, the topic of chapter 3. You might think that emotion, for example, is a visible pathway because you see it expressed, say, in anger. However, perhaps it is fear that is acted out as anger. Perhaps it is trauma. Emotion is critical to learning, and this chapter explores the biology and impact of emotion, along with strategies for addressing emotions that have a negative impact on learning and increasing emotions that enhance learning.

Some behaviors are rewarding to the brain, providing a sense of pleasure and making it more likely that the behavior will persist—motivation. Chapter 4 explores the science of reward, along with suggestions for tapping into this powerful pathway in the brain.

Chapter 5 examines a pathway seldom discussed when addressing math deficits or reading comprehension difficulty, yet it is probably the culprit in most instances: attention and working memory. These invisible processes are critical to academic achievement. However, many instructional materials and tests fly in the face of what we know about this and create poor performance in many cases. This chapter explains the relationship of attentional mechanisms to working memory and the impact on learning. This is followed by an explanation of how the brain moves information from temporary storage in working memory to long-term storage—that is, learning.

Next we turn to the visible pathways—visible in the sense that we can measure the performance in these pathways in the classroom. These are the pathways that have long been understood, or I should say misunderstood, as *the* pathways—reading, writing, and arithmetic, for example. Yes, reading is an invisible process, but we see the visible production associated with it. However, what manifests as poor reading may stem from invisible pathways, such as attention or working memory capacity. Chapter 6 addresses the complexity of language, second language, reading, and math in the brain in order to provide an understanding of how we can diversify strategies to address the multiple way students can be impaired in any of these skills.

Chapter 7 addresses one of the most critical aspects of brain development for achievement: higher-order executive functions, such as planning, budgeting time, organizing, and thinking critically. A child's skill in this area in first grade can predict his or her achievement throughout academic life. This pathway is important for upper grades and college students, as the frontal lobe is still developing until around ages eighteen to twenty-five. This chapter discusses the role of the frontal lobe and how teachers can help students develop this part of the brain so critical to a quality life.

Education is a social activity, so it is critical that teachers understand the nature of the social brain, the topic of chapter 8. Some social activities can impair learning while others can contribute to it. This chapter explores the science of social status, social threat, and social interaction on learning, along with strategies for reducing social threat and enhancing learning through positive social experiences.

In the final chapter, we zoom out to look at the whole person and the big picture of curriculum. We look at how lifestyle and physiology affect learning and how schools can use scientific knowledge to create a school environment that enhances achievement, including performance on standardized tests. We examine what research is revealing about certain courses that are scientifically validated to enhance achievement but are being cut in many school systems. We look at where it all begins, early childhood, with an eye to getting children the kind of start that will have an impact on their learning throughout their lifetime. Finally, we look at the role of technology and how it may be changing brains. What is the role in a brain-compatible environment and how can you use it to strengthen, not hinder, learning?

In addition, every chapter contains some helpful features. The first is "Homework Options," which suggests many ways to diversify assignments relevant to that pathway. "Suggested Strategies" is a bulleted reference list of strategies explored in the chapter that are in alignment with the research. Finally, the "Suggested Reading" section lists books for further exploration of the topics covered in the chapter. Most of these are written for nonscientists and are entertaining as well as informative.

Readers who are interested in delving more into the science can consult the references provided for each chapter at the end of the book.

MULTIPLE WAYS OF USING THIS INFORMATION

You can use this book in multiple ways to serve your purpose at a given time. Some will want to read it completely through and then refer to the "Homework Menu" and "Suggested Strategies" sections when designing lessons. Others may want to skip right to the "Leaping into the Classroom" sections to jump-start their instruction and later return to "What Does the Research Say?" for an understanding of why the strategies work.

You can jump around in the chapters as a topic interests you. Since the brain is so complex and interactive, reading the chapters out of order should not pose a problem to understanding.

I hope all readers will use this book to inform their students about how their brain works and that they can change their brain. Chapter 1 should be sufficient for that purpose.

Education leaders may be particularly interested in the "What Does This Mean for Educators?" sections to inform their policy and curriculum decisions. The book is also designed to be used for teacher educators to train teachers in the science of learning. Although the questions in the "Reflect and Connect" section at the end of each chapter are useful for everyone to reflect and consolidate their learning, they can make excellent questions for assignments requiring teachers to increase their depth of understanding and apply what they have learned. This design is helpful for faculty book club reading and discussion as well.

● ● ●

The overriding purpose of the book is to inform you about the complexity of students' brains and, thus, the challenge and importance of teaching. Our daily choices as we orchestrate learning can make a significant impact on our students' brains and learning ability. The field of education is only going to get more exciting as we are at the beginning of this new frontier of inner space. I hope this book inspires and motivates you as you have me.

1

How the Brain Thinks and Learns

I just don't understand. For the last four weeks everything was ideal. I was really on top of my teaching game and the students were interested, engaged, answering questions in class, and turning in assignments. It couldn't have been better, I thought. Then I grade the exams and find that they didn't seem to have learned the material. What happened?

MAKING CONNECTIONS

What is learning? How does it differ from thinking? Could poor reading comprehension, math disability, or apparent lack of effort actually be something else? What is the purpose of homework?

Because our purpose as educators is to enhance and energize learning, we must understand the nature of learning in the brain to enhance, not hinder, the process. Even if you are not particularly interested in the neuroscience behind learning and are only looking for strategies, it is important to understand a few basic and essential processes and concepts in order to design more effective lessons. So let's wade into the technical information, just deep enough to understand the concepts. (For those interested in more information, I suggest additional readings at the end

Figure 1.1 Major Areas of the Brain

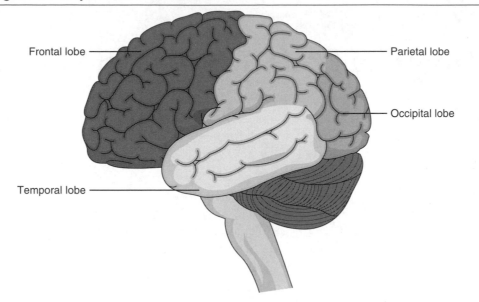

Frontal lobe

Parietal lobe

Occipital lobe

Temporal lobe

of the chapter.) Then we will examine the implications for the field of education before leaping into classroom strategies.

The brain is highly complex. As you work through this book, you will learn about many structures and functions as they relate to the topic of the chapters. In this chapter, we take a look at some of the major structures and functions.

Figure 1.1 shows the four major sections of the brain, called *lobes*. The word *cortex* refers to brain matter, so in discussing the frontal lobe, for example, we might refer to the frontal cortex, meaning the brain matter in the frontal lobe. Describing the functions of each lobe is not straightforward, as each lobe has many functions and also interacts extensively with other lobes. You will learn more about the lobes as you go along. For now, a quick overview is sufficient:

- *Frontal lobe:* involved extensively with many regions of the brain and regulates such things as emotion and attention. It is associated with executive functions, that is, higher-order thinking processes. It is also involved in movement, reasoning, and metacognition. Chapter 7 is devoted to this complex lobe.

- *Temporal lobe:* processes language, hearing, memory, comprehension, and emotion.
- *Parietal lobe:* integrates sensory information and is active in spatial processing and navigation, perception, arithmetic, and reading.
- *Occipital lobe:* processes vision.

The most important fact is that the lobes work together. For example, reading can activate all lobes but some specific regions are more activated than others.

PLASTICITY

If you are over forty years old, there is a good chance that what you learned in school about the brain is wrong. Until the last few decades, scientists believed that the brain could not change except during critical periods in early childhood. After the critical window, the consensus was that you were stuck with the brain that you had. Worse, if the brain was injured, there wasn't much that could be done to fix it. We now know that the brain is *plastic*—it changes as a result of experience. The implications are huge for teaching and learning. Let's explore the science of plasticity.

What Does the Research Say?

Beginning in the 1960s, pioneer neuroanatomist Marian Diamond and her colleagues were the first to show that experience or training changes the brain. In this landmark study, rats that had richer environments had greater changes in their brain anatomy, chemistry, and behavior (learning). The enriched environment consisted of the addition of toys into the cages where rats were kept in groups, as opposed to those kept alone and without any toys or just in groups. The addition of the toys with social interaction led to better brain development—better problem solving and learning. However, the environment was not as rich as it would have been had they lived in a normal environment outdoors. The enriched environment created better brains compared to a deprived environment. We have seen the effects of this in children who grow up with very little stimulation in their environment, such as orphans in some institutions. They did not perform as well on educational tasks as those who had the stimulation of activities along with language and touch from caretakers.

In the 1970s, the well-known scientist Michael Merzenich found that animals' brains remapped themselves as a result of changes to the nerve structure in the hand. What happened to the hand changed the brain. But would this happen in humans?

Rewiring

As time went on, experiments in plasticity proved that the human brain can indeed rewire itself as a result of experience. In persons born deaf and using sign language, the auditory cortex, which processes sounds, recognized visual sign language as language and processed it where hearing and language would normally be processed instead of the visual cortex even though the language was visual. Other studies have shown that engaging in specific movements changes the size of the area in the brain associated with that movement or experience. For example, researchers found that guitar players' thumb representation in the brain was larger compared to nonguitar players since guitar players use their thumb a great deal.

A series of landmark studies led by Eleanor Maguire at University College London looked at the brains of London taxi drivers using magnetic resonance imaging (MRI)

Figure 1.2 Hippocampus

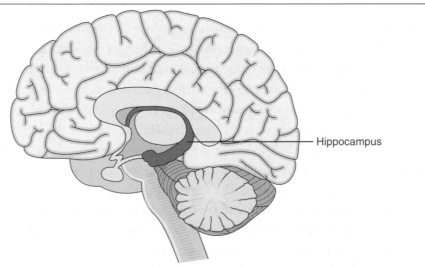

Hippocampus

and found that the part of the brain that processes spatial information (the rear part of the hippocampus; see figure 1.2) was much larger than normal—there was more gray matter (the neurons that hold information). Further investigations revealed that it was because they spent more time navigating (more experience) that the area grew. Interestingly, the front part of the hippocampus became smaller as a result. (This makes me wonder what the GPS is doing to our brain.)

Here is where it really gets exciting for teachers. In 2006 researchers led by Arne May studied the brains of medical students as they studied for exams. Brain scans using MRI were given three times during this process. In the first few months, students' brains increased in gray matter (figure 1.3) on both sides of their brain in the parietal lobe (see figure 1.1). The third scan was given three months after the exam during the semester break and found not much change at that time in parietal areas. However, another area, the rear part of the hippocampus (the same area that changed in the taxi drivers) increased in gray matter over time and actually grew more during the period *after* the exam. Researchers conclude that gray matter may change differentially in brain areas over time. Some kinds of learning may just take more time to process and change the brain.

Researchers conclude that gray matter may change differentially in brain areas over time. Some kinds of learning may just take more time to process and change the brain.

This plasticity is not limited to critical windows or to any age group. Although the brain is more easily changed early in life, it remains plastic throughout life. More evidence has corroborated plasticity to the point that now we are seeing amazing discoveries about just how much the brain can rewire itself.

What Does This Mean for Educators?

This discovery about plasticity means we are at the beginning of a new frontier in education. Not only do we have a deeper understanding of the importance of early childhood education, but for continuing education throughout life as well.

Figure 1.3 Gray and White Matter

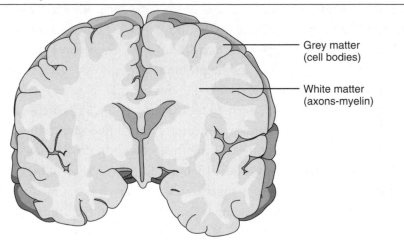

Grey matter
(cell bodies)

White matter
(axons-myelin)

Neuroscientists have recently begun looking at interventions as well as basic processes underlying learning, and we are starting to see implications for classroom practices. For example, neuroscientists and educators have worked together on studies researching whether the brains of children with dyslexia can be rewired to reroute anomalous reading circuits in the brain to traditional reading routes, leading to improved reading. For example, Michael Merzenich at the University of California, San Francisco, developed a program called FastForward. It uses digitized sound to help children with dyslexia hear the sound correctly so that they can learn to sound out words. Merzenich and colleagues report success in enabling students who work extensively with this computer program to improve their phonological performance. Sally Shaywitz, codirector of the Yale Center for Dyslexia and Creativity, has also worked with what she calls rewiring the reading pathways in poor readers. Other new software attempts rewiring to improve attention and working memory. As the field of educational neuroscience develops, we can expect to see more software targeting specific interventions.

Leaping into the Classroom

There is nothing more important to teachers than the concept of plasticity. Learning *is* rewiring. You will learn more about how the brain changes throughout this book. The important point to keep in mind now is that what we do changes our brain. And who orchestrates what our learners do? You! Such responsibility! For example, when you design lessons and homework, ask yourself what changes you hope to see as a result of this work. Because what students do changes the brain, think in terms of the changes you desire.

THE PROCESS OF LEARNING

Presenters about the brain say that "learning means growing dendrites." This section looks at what that means. What makes dendrites grow or not grow, and how is that *really* involved in learning? Let's learn a little more science.

What Does the Research Say?

Now that we know that the brain changes as a result of experience and learning is an important experience, the next questions are: How does it change as a result of learning? and How can we as educators affect that? Understanding this process requires learning some technical information that is important to a clear understanding of the elements involved in the thinking and learning process itself.

Let's explore thinking before learning, because they are not the same to the brain. I am going to oversimplify here. *Thinking* means the transmission of information among relevant neurons in the brain. *Neurons* are the gray matter that hold information that you have stored. How is this information held in your brain? Words? Pictures? No. This information is stored in the form of chemicals. In order to think, the neurons in the brain must communicate with each other through electrical impulses that allow the exchange of chemicals. Because these chemicals transmit information from neuron to neuron, they are called *neurotransmitters*. Two important neurotransmitters for learning are dopamine and norepinephrine (also known as noradrenalin).

In order for any system to communicate, it must have an input (we have an ear) and an output (we have a mouth). The neuron has an output called an *axon* and many inputs called *dendrites* (figure 1.4). An axon is a long, slender protrusion from the main cell body of the neuron that looks similar to a large branch on a tree. It has an axon terminal on the end that conducts the outgoing electrical impulses and neurotransmitter chemicals. The dendrite is the input structure on the neuron that conducts the electrical impulses into the neuron. Each neuron has many of these dendrite branches with receptors for the incoming information. The word *dendrite* comes from the Greek word for tree, and they look similar to the many branches of a tree. When the cells—the neurons—communicate and exchange chemicals, electrical impulses send the information down a long axon and *fire* the chemicals across a gap between the axon terminal of one neuron and the dendrite receptor of another neuron. This gap is called a *synapse*.

This firing of chemicals and communication between neurons enables thinking to take place. Thinking thus involves the communication of many neurons, with each neuron connecting to tens of thousands of dendrites on other neurons. But what is learning, and how does the brain process it differently from thinking?

Neuroscientists have a saying that "cells that fire together, wire together." This is called the Hebbian law, named after Nobel Prize winner Donald Hebb. In 1949 he proposed the concept of Hebbian learning, which is still the way we understand the general nature of learning in the brain. This concept means that when cells persistently fire together, the synapses strengthen and the dendrites get more stable. Referred to as *long-term potentiation*, this means that the more a network of neurons fires together, the more likely they are to fire together again over the long term. You already have an expression for that: Practice makes perfect. (I should amend that to "practice makes permanent," because wrong information can also be strengthened if it is continually reactivated.) The more a network fires, the stronger the network becomes, thus improving the ability of that network to fire again. Swiss neuroscientist Dominique Muller found that some synapses even double during learning. This ability to reactivate the network in the future is learning.

Think of the roots of a delicate young plant. If you don't strengthen them through watering and sunlight, they quickly wither and die. However, the roots of an oak

Multiple Pathways to the Student Brain

Figure 1.4 Neurons, Axons, Dendrites, and Synapses

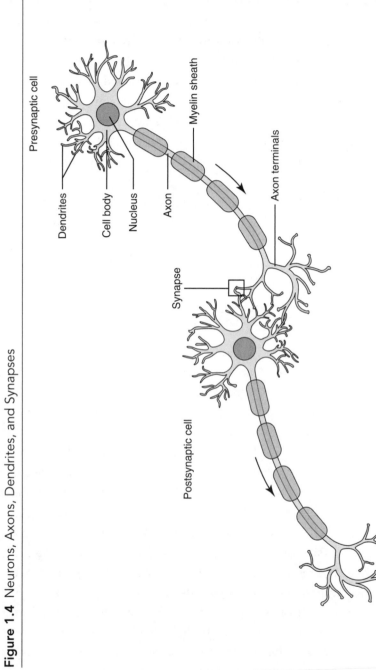

tree that have been strengthened over time can take a great deal of neglect without damage. When you first learned to drive, you had very weak connections and had to do a great deal of conscious thinking about the process. Now that you have an "oak tree" network for driving, you do not forget how to drive no matter how long you might go without activating the network by driving. Furthermore, you no longer have to think as consciously about it, since the network is wired, which means you have brain resources left over to daydream, plan, and carry on conversations. You may ask why texting is so dangerous then. Texting is not automatic like driving; it requires thinking and uses a great deal of cognitive resources, such that not enough are left to respond well to driving conditions. (You will learn more about this cognitive load in chapter 7.)

Learning literally strengthens and increases the connections between neurons and dendrites. As you learn, you grow more dendrites and synapses and increase your network of information.

What Does This Mean for Educators?

Experience is critical to learning. Learning changes the brain, and since educators orchestrate learning, they need to understand the importance of the activities we provide. The classroom must provide stimulating activities that create the desired activation in the brain, leading to desired change. This applies to early childhood through adult education.

The nature of learning and the Hebbian law cause us to rethink how we rush through curriculum. The goal has become to cover a certain amount of content and then test the students for memory of that content. In fact, this flies in the face of what we know about real learning: that depth may be better than breadth. We have to not only fire the network; we have to wire it. That means working with material over a period of time and in a recursive nature rather than rushing through in a linear fashion. For example, math courses revisit previously covered material and continue to strengthen the network, resulting in knowledge that lasts and isn't forgotten over the summer. Repetition, repeated firing of networks, is a critical component of most learning.

As we move from the brain in general to the individual learner, we realize that the learner must make a connection from his or her existing neural network (background knowledge) to the new material. Cell biologist James Zull, in his wonderful book

The Art of Changing the Brain, asserts that the single most important factor in learning is the learner's existing neural network; we should determine that and then proceed accordingly.

Educators already have terms for this existing neural network concept: *schema, background*, or *prior knowledge*. Neuroscience is supporting what educators have professed: that prior knowledge is critical. If a student has no prior knowledge on the topic, then not much is firing and not much can wire. It is not that a student is not good at, for example, math, but rather he or she has gaps in the existing network that need to be filled. This is a very different approach. We therefore should refer students to math or reading labs to "work on your network" without labeling these children as deficient or disabled.

However, we do not always provide for this prior knowledge in our curriculum or materials. We attempt to when we require prerequisites before taking a course, implying that certain prior knowledge is essential. Many times we introduce material without taking into account that achievement may be greatly affected by some students' prior experience as contrasted with those with different experiences. We have seen this bias in the past on standardized testing, and attempts have been made to rectify cultural and experiential gaps in knowledge. We still have more to do in this regard, which should be an important concern for administrators and curriculum specialists, as well as classroom teachers.

Culturally relevant materials can help students learn to read better because they contain relevant prior knowledge of these students. It is hard to have good reading comprehension when much of the material is unknown to such a degree that there is not sufficient context for vocabulary learning or comprehension. For example, in my work with teachers in Hawaii, I was told that when a teacher had requested culturally relevant reading materials, she was sent stories about Mexican children, with the assumption being that was "close enough" or somehow served the purpose. Obviously it did not. As our classrooms get more and more diverse, how we address students' cultural, experiential, and personal differences is an important topic.

Leaping into the Classroom

When students have learned material, they are able to *fire up* the network that connects that information in the brain and thus recall the information. However, the key point to keep in mind is that the network must be fired repeatedly and strongly enough that it is likely or able to be fired again. That is the difference between thinking and learning. It is not enough to fire it; you must wire it for learning to occur. Now let's think about the classroom. Let's say that you are doing your very best teaching and the students are doing their very best responding. Everything seems perfect, so the next day you move on, and then the next day, and so on. But when the test comes, the results show that the students don't know the material. The difficulty is that you *fired* it but you didn't *wire* it. You had great thinking, but for many, not great learning.

For learning to occur, the network must be wired. *Networks must be created and information moved into long-term memory.*

For learning to occur, the network must be *wired*. Networks must be created and information moved into long-term memory. Let's think about your learning process as you have just encountered this new information. Did you find any of the material exciting? If so, that is the easiest way to learn—through *arousal*. The body feels something and tells the brain to pay attention because this may be important. However, if you didn't find it exciting, then you have to learn it the hard way: fire it until you wire it. Think about it, talk about it, read about it, or use it. If you don't and the material is not reactivated, the brain can decide that it wasn't important and reabsorb the fragile new dendrites to be used for something that is important. Use it or lose it! Most students must activate the material (network) again and again for long-term memory or learning to occur.

If students have to fire it until they wire it, am I suggesting drill and kill? No. You are going to learn about multiple pathways that create more activation in each lesson. You may have heard that the more modalities by which you encode information, the easier it is to retrieve. Teachers may use visual, auditory, and kinesthetic methods (see it, say it, write it) to increase that activation. In this book, you will go beyond those pathways into *other* powerful pathways that can enhance and energize teaching and learning.

You might ask, "How much time does it take to wire it?" And the answer is, "As long as it takes." The length of time varies from individual to individual depending on many factors within the individual. The more the network is fired, the stronger the network becomes. Yet another factor may create the most impact: the importance of the information to the learner, according to James Zull. If the information is very important, such as a new friend's phone number, information may immediately be stored. However, if a student's brain does not see the incoming information as important, it will take more frequency or time, or both. You will learn more about the power of importance in the reward pathway in chapter 4.

Learning is effortful. Growing those new dendrites requires the synthesis of new proteins. It may require sustained attention and focus, which can be exhausting for the brain. If it were easy, then learners would just be firing what is already wired. That doesn't mean it can't be fun or engaging. The goal is to create new networks that fire together, a process that can take energy, time, and effort. K–12 English as a Second Language instructor Karen Solis concurs that learning can be challenging, but points out that when students are motivated and with a community of learners who are "in it to win it," it is no longer about learning on their own, but learning and being a resource for others who get stuck. When I have to share what I've learned, I am building more dendrites and making more connections as I explain to someone else.

Students need to know this important foundation. They need to know that they will often feel overwhelmed at the beginning of the learning cycle because their frontal lobe is working very hard and it is exhausting (for more on the frontal lobe, see chapter 7). Engagement with students is critical. The beginning of a learning cycle is often overwhelming, tiring, frustrating, discouraging, and threatening. This is normal. Educator Rita Smilkstein, author of *We're Born to Learn*, talks about what she calls the natural human learning process in which the early stages are discouraging while later stages lead to success and pleasure. That is the good news: learning activates the reward (pleasure) pathway as well (explored in chapter 4).

If I ask you to take a moment and point to your mibgus, you won't be able to comply because you do not have a neural network on the word *mibgus* because there is no such word. The point here is that you can't wire it if you can't even fire it. So this is like when you are in a class and you are saying particle, participle, integer, mibgus, mibgus, mibgus. Nothing is firing in the student's brain. Now you know what you must do before introducing new material.

It is critical that students have some prior knowledge, however general, in order to make sense of the new material. Students (and even teachers) often mistake a lack of prior knowledge for a lack of ability, however. For example, students may say, "I can't do math," and perhaps they did poorly in previous classes or seem at a loss at the beginning of the semester in your class. It is very helpful for teachers to point out to students that it is not a matter of can't but a matter of haven't: they have not created the necessary prior network to which the new information must connect. Often teachers assume a reading comprehension issue or a learning difference when it may be lack of prior knowledge. Direct students to a math lab, reading lab, tutoring center, or additional materials to learn the missing material and get up to speed. "You need to work on your neural network" is more motivating than, "Don't you know that? You had it last semester!" or for the student to think, "I am just not good at math." Intelligence is not who you *are* but what you *do*.

You must help the student make a connection to the new material, a critical step often overlooked. Once you understand that making these connections is how the brain actually learns, you can realize the critical nature of this step prior to introducing new information. The next sections look at how you can facilitate making connections.

Administer a Pretest

Now you realize the full implications of giving a pretest: it helps determine the extent of students' existing networks and, more important, helps them to see where they may have gaps in the information necessary to succeed in the coming material. This is based on two assumptions. First, the pretest should include questions on the previous material as well as the coming material and should be designed to determine if the student is bringing prior knowledge that is necessary for connecting the coming information. For example, math pretest questions should include basic problems from earlier instruction that are an essential part of the foundation for the new instruction. Students who can't do the first part of the pretest need help in the math lab or some supplemental review material before the new material is even introduced. This is presented to the student as "strengthening your neural networks for success."

The second assumption is that the student actually tries or cares about the pretest. It is not a valid measure if the student doesn't try. If students understand how the brain learns, they will understand the importance of evaluating their existing network before trying to add to it. However, we all know that we do not teach in an ideal world. I am sure you have experienced giving a pretest that the students quickly rush through with an "I don't know and I don't care" attitude because it "doesn't count toward the grade." When this is the case, the pretest is pretty much pointless.

You can change that. If you can create a pretest that is a dichotomy, such as a true/false, positive/negative, English/Spanish, or yes/no format, then you can use many pathways and motivate students while giving the pretest. Begin by telling students that one side of the room is true (or one of the dichotomies such as Spanish or English, positive or negative) and the other side is false. Students are to vote with their feet: they will get up and move to the side of the room indicating their answer as you read out the questions or put them on the board or screen. You will notice that students even discuss this as they move toward one side and maybe even change their minds. This is a good thing. Students enjoy seeing who is on their side and who disagrees. This is face-saving and nonthreatening because by the time you tell them the answers during the coming lessons, they will remember where *they* stood on every question but won't remember exactly what their classmates did.

When will you tell them the answers? They will hunt for them as you teach the material over the next class, week, or unit. This initial exercise sets intention and curiosity in the brain. They want to know if they were on the "right side" and will listen with intention and purpose to discover the answer as the lesson goes on. Without even understanding the pathways we will learn about in this book, you can already see that this activity activates multiple pathways. The students are moving (sensory motor), listening (auditory and language), evaluating (frontal lobe), paying attention (attention), thinking about it until they take a stand (working memory), enjoying the activity (emotion), engaging in social interaction (social), and realizing success (reward).

Facilitate Making Connections

Although it is helpful to determine prior knowledge, even a pretest is not totally sufficient. You must actively help students make connections. One way to help students do this is to start a new lesson with a "making connections" activity, which may be paper and pencil, pair-share, or class discussion. Provide a series of easy questions about information that should be part of their prior knowledge that relates to the new material.

For example, if you are teaching how to interpret an author's tone when reading, you can begin with what they already know about interpreting tone. Ask them, "When you send an e-mail, how do you let your reader know that you are joking—that your *tone* is a joking one?" They respond that they use acronyms such as LOL or emoticons such as the smiley face. Ask them what other emoticons or acronyms they use and what those say about their tone. Now students are becoming familiar with tone in an accessible way instead of tackling a difficult reading while at the same time trying to understand tone. You can also ask them if their parents have a special tone of voice when they are angry. What does that mean? Find something in their life that in some simple way relates to the new material and starts to bridge the gap. This may be related to new vocabulary, new concepts, or new facts.

Scaffold

If you are teaching a subject such as history, geography, science, or any other course that requires learning a great deal of factual information, you need to take some additional steps. You can scaffold the learner into the difficult language and concepts of the textbook by providing some preliminary steps.

Start with a video that provides some information about the locale, history, anatomy, or whatever is going to be introduced. This provides students with some visuals that will help them recall the information they will soon learn in their textbook. It also provides repetitions of key vocabulary in many cases. Students need to hear the new vocabulary and not just see it in textbooks, so a video with some of the upcoming vocabulary is very helpful. This is only a first step, similar to laying the foundation of a house. You can see where the rooms are going to be and start visualizing it, even though important details are still missing.

Next, as psychologist Daniel Willingham suggests in his book *Why Don't Students Like School?*, provide students with reading material on the upcoming topic that is two to four grade levels below their current (assumed) reading level. We are not dumbing down. This scaffolding helps the students get the big picture and creates a network to which they can add the details that will be provided in their actual textbook. Many times these materials have helpful visuals as well. Students may get some introduction to the vocabulary, and, also important, they add to the foundation that they are building. To continue our metaphor, now they are adding walls, and it becomes clearer what rooms are going to be where and how extensive the layout might be. At this time, provide any additional visuals that you may have and do a preview of the upcoming material, pointing out headings, subheadings, and illustrations. You might have begun a semester by teaching students to preview and by providing them with a format to use throughout the semester. For students who have this experience, assign a preview, ideally with some questions that they can answer with the preview.

The students now have a framework to which they can add this more difficult material. Now it is time to add important details to the network that has been created. Provide your lecture or your chapter assignment as you normally would have.

Pose a Question or Problem

Many instructors have turned to problem-based learning, in which the material is taught in response to a problem that is posed. This is similar to the discovery method often used in science courses and is common in health courses. This format of engaging students by posing a problem can be used in almost any course. For example, a history lesson can be framed as a problem that the people of that time had to solve. Ask the students to think of ways to solve the problem and then turn to the history book to see how that culture and time solved the problem. In math, before teaching a formula, pose a real-life problem that someone had to solve at home or on the job. For example, a sales representative is selling shelving on which to store heavy boxes of paper records. The sales representative doesn't want to be sued if she designs a large shelving system that might be too heavy for the floor load. What does she need to find out in order to make sure her system will be safe? She needs an algebra formula.

Posing a problem takes time. However, if it results in more effective learning and in students reading and understanding your textbook, it is time well spent. Much of this can be done as assignments outside class.

Provide for Reflection

Now that you know more about learning, you realize that the reflection component is a key component in real learning. I say that teaching is like medicine—an art and a science. Good teachers often have an instinct for what enhances learning, and neuroscience supports many early educational practices. In this case, educators have understood the importance of reflection prior to our understanding of how the brain learns. For example, educator Linda Flower in 1994 emphasized that reflection needed to be seen as a "genuine activity that merits class time and attention." Too often, we rush through content in the interest of time and believe we don't have time for reflective pauses. As educational theorist Jerome Bruner says, "The enemy of reflection is the breakneck pace." Adopting a motto of "reflect and connect" emphasizes that students must pause and make connections.

Adopting a motto of "reflect and connect" emphasizes that students must pause and make connections.

The ability to reflect develops into adulthood and is an effortful task with a high cognitive load. Therefore, we are probably going to have to require this process rather than expecting that students will naturally do this on their own. In early grades, you may just pause and ask students to verbally reflect on the material. When you ask a question of the students of any age, tell them that you will not accept any answers for the first thirty seconds (or time of your choice). This gives the slower (and maybe deeper) thinkers time and encourages reflection. In order for this to be effective, it should be a consistent policy. Maybe you count to twenty or some other method and make sure to pause for reflection time.

Another method that encourages reflection is a quiet moment with no upcoming response. You can ask the students to draw or even doodle. One interesting study divided students into two groups after giving them some content to learn. One group studied the material for an additional period of time, while the second group was told to doodle. Which group do you think did better on the following test? The doodlers. Not only did they get to rest their frontal lobe (see chapter 7), they had some time to consolidate the learning, make connections, and assimilate the information. With older students, you can require written reflections in a journal, in an e-mail to you after they read the assignment, or in writing as part of a homework assignment. However, even when it is required as an assignment to be done outside class, building reflection pauses into in-class lessons is important and time well spent.

Finally, keep in mind that the nature of the learning experience overall is a major component of whether connections are strengthened or even made. Giving students information to memorize is not as likely to make strong connections (at least not without a great deal of work) as giving them an experience. For example, if you do a demonstration in class, you are creating a widely distributed network in the brain. Students are activating visual, auditory, perhaps kinesthetic if they participate, emotional, social—probably every pathway addressed in this book. Obviously that is going to create a stronger and more lasting network (long-term potentiation) than reading a passage in a textbook. Emotional engagement creates more activation. As you go through this book, you will learn how to add multiple pathways to your lesson in order to develop instructional activities that are more likely to create stronger, longer-lasting networks.

SETTING THE STAGE FOR ACHIEVEMENT

Do students need to learn the science of how their brain learns? Would that make a difference in achievement?

What Does the Research Say?

Stanford University psychologist Carol Dweck and colleagues described two mind-sets, or ways of thinking, that affect achievement. Students who believed that intelligence is malleable and can be changed had higher achievement than students who believed that intelligence was fixed and couldn't be changed. In 2007, Dweck, along with colleagues Lisa Blackwell and Kali Trzesniewski, published an article that demonstrated an intervention that raised achievement in students, even previously low-performing students. They did two studies of twelve-year-olds. In the first study, they took a group of students who believed that intelligence was malleable and a group who believed that it was fixed. Those who believed that they could change their intelligence outperformed the other group over a two-year period. In the second study, the researchers taught one group of students how intelligence can change, while the other group did not receive that information; both groups received identical instruction in study skills. The group that learned about the nature of intelligence reversed its previously declining achievement and outscored the other group, whose scores continued to decline. Study skill instruction alone was not enough; learning that the brain changes was the significant variable.

Study skill instruction alone was not enough; learning that the brain changes was the significant variable.

What Does This Mean for Educators?

When students understand how the brain learns, that intelligence is malleable, and that they can take control of their learning, achievement rises, even in previously low-performing students. This one simple lesson can make a significant difference.

I believe this material should be required in school systems in a formal way, such as in English class in certain grades. English class is a logical choice because you can read and write about that information and all students have to take it. It could be taught in science class or taught schoolwide in every class on a given day at the beginning of a semester with materials provided to each teacher. In other words, it can't be left to chance, hoping that some teachers will cover it. In college, perhaps all instructors have to teach it unless the college requires a preliminary course in learning and the brain prior to freshman courses.

The information must be taught in a credible way. The information about how the brain learns can be taught at age-appropriate levels. It is not necessary for students (or teachers, for that matter) to memorize the names of brain regions. This lesson should be meaningful and interesting and not another instance of taking information and pulling out items to memorize so that a teacher can create a test. This will be learning for its own sake. The important information is that the brain changes as a result of experience and individuals have a choice to control and change their brains.

Research studies also reveal that when students learn this information, their effort, motivation, and attitude improve. When students know that their teachers understand how the brain learns, they are more likely to accept the strategies the teacher provides about how to best learn the course content. They would also have a more positive attitude about their abilities to perform in class. Of course, if the teacher explicitly explains why a strategy works based on what we know about learning, then it would be even more powerful in shaping students' attitude toward their class and encourage lifelong learning.

Leaping into the Classroom

Start the semester by teaching your students what you have learned about the brain and learning. It won't take much time if you keep it simple and to the point. Many materials are available for all age levels about how the brain learns. Two of the best sources are dana.org and Brainfacts.org, which contain instructional materials for all ages and are among the most credible. Throughout this book you will learn strategies to help students learn, and you can teach those to your students along with the explanation of why they work. When students realize that you know that they can change their brain throughout the semester, they may feel more empowered and not labeled. Throughout the semester, emphasize some basic principles to your students:

1. Check your existing neural network—your gaps in understanding. Do you need to strengthen it first?

2. Make sure you fire it until you wire it.

3. Learning is effortful. Persist!

4. Intelligence is not what you *are*; it is what you *do*. What are your strategies?

HOMEWORK OPTIONS

As we explore each pathway throughout this book, we will think about how to apply this information to our own teaching practice and to the students' brain-changing experiences. In future chapters, this section contains homework options you can put on a homework menu from which students select according to their strengths and interests. You will tweak and expand these items to fit your content. By including as many as possible from each chapter in this book, you will be able to come up with a menu of one or two dozen items from which the students can select homework assignments or group activities in class.

THE PURPOSE OF HOMEWORK

In this opening chapter, you may want to consider the purpose of homework. Do teachers assign homework because they need a number of graded assignments or because the textbook has questions or problems at the end? Let's look at homework from the perspective of the desired brain changes that you want:

- ***Strengthening or completing the existing network to prepare for new information.*** Address gaps in the student's existing neural network—prior knowledge—to make sure that the network is solid enough to process the new information. This would include background videos or readings or maybe a pretest with potential trips to the reading, math, or tutoring labs.

- **_Increasing the neural network._** Add to an existing network through reading or activities that build on it. This is often done initially through an assignment to read a chapter, through a lecture, or an experiential activity.

- **_Wiring it._** Once we have ascertained that a student will be able to think about and understand the new material (fire it), we want to make sure they wire it. This is the most common kind of homework assignment: activities, problems, questions, or writing assignments that give students practice or experience with the new material. However, busy educators often forget the underlying purpose of homework and create an assignment without thinking about what underlying processes and activations the assignment will engage. Keeping in mind that the purpose is to fire what you want to wire, create reinforcement, and strengthen the new learning, you can design more effective assignments.

- **_Providing for differentiation._** A fourth purpose of homework that is often overlooked is to give students with learning differences a chance outside the classroom to work with the material in an alternative way. This is not always easily provided for in the classroom. When teachers just assign the questions at the end of the chapter as homework, it is not provided for outside the classroom either. One way to design effective homework assignments that achieve the desired purpose of increasing real learning and address these learning differences is with a homework menu rather than a homework assignment. Near the end of each of the following chapters is the "Homework Menu" section, which lists many alternatives for having students interact with the material. Students select the option that they want. So that students do not always select the same type of option, such as creating a web page or a PowerPoint every time, you can require them to do more than one assignment from the menu or tell them that they can't select the same option more than once or twice in a semester. Students with learning differences will self-select based on their strengths. As you learn about the many invisible processes behind learning, you will see that we cannot credibly identify and label a student. We can observe some visible strengths and weaknesses. By providing multiple options for homework, those who learn differently have an opportunity to select what works best for them. This is far better than labeling students as a certain type of learner and assigning them tasks accordingly.

SUGGESTED STRATEGIES

Each of the following chapters concludes with some general strategies. It is far beyond the scope of this book to address specific strategies for teaching all subjects, and many worthwhile and brain-compatible theories, models, and strategies in education are not covered here. The "Leaping into the Classroom" and "Suggested Strategies" sections provide a few selected strategies as examples based on the research covered in that chapter.

The purpose of these sections is to think about our art from a new perspective—to understand the complexity of learners and see research through the eyes of a teacher. Although the strategies seldom have a direct link to the neuroscience research, they are derived from adding that new information to our existing knowledge of education theories and practices and seeing where there may be some common ground—seeing what practices align with the research findings. The research stimulates our thinking and leads us to select tools from our pedagogical toolbox that would appear to support what we have learned from the research. For example, in this chapter, we have seen research from psychology that indicates that when students learn that intelligence is not fixed, achievement rises. Therefore, this chapter suggests a strategy of teaching students about how the brain learns. This would indicate to the student that intelligence is malleable and is in line with the research. Other strategies may not be as direct. Keep in mind that the strategies come from multiple pathways of research: neuroscience, psychology, and education.

Here are some strategies based on what you have learned so far:

- Teach students about their brain and that they can change it.

- Begin lessons with opportunities to make connections with their prior knowledge.

- Address gaps in neural networks (i.e., prior knowledge).

- Provide opportunities for reflection.

- Consider the purpose of each homework assignment with regard to desired change.

REFLECT AND CONNECT

Based on what you learned in this chapter, how will you change your approach to a lesson?

Examine your homework assignments from a unit you have already taught. How would you change them based on what you have learned in this chapter?

SUGGESTED READING

Austen, J. (2000). *Mansfield Park*. London: Bloomsbury.

Blakemore, S. J., & Frith, U. (2005). *The learning brain: Lessons for education*. Malden, MA: Blackwell.

Bruner, J. (1996). *The culture of education*. Cambridge, MA: Harvard University Press.

Bruner, J. S. (1973). *Beyond the information given: Studies in the psychology of knowing*. New York: Norton.

Davis, R. D., & Braun, E. M. (2003). *The gift of learning*. New York, NY: Berkley Books.

Diamond, M., & Hopson, J. (1999). *The magic trees of the mind: How to nurture your child's intelligence, creativity, and healthy emotions from birth through adolescence.* New York: Plume.

Doidge, N. (2007). *The brain that changes itself: Stories of personal triumph from the frontiers of brain science.* New York: Penguin.

Dweck, C. (2006). *Mindset: The new psychology of success.* New York, NY: Random House.

Fischer, K. W., & Immordino-Yang, M. H. (Eds.), (2007). *The Jossey-Bass reader on the brain and learning.* San Francisco, CA: Jossey-Bass.

Flower, L. (1994). *The construction of negotiated meaning: A social cognitive theory of writing.* Carbondale: Southern Illinois University Press.

Frith, U., & Blakemore, S. J. (2005). *The learning brain: Lessons for education.* Oxford: Blackwell.

Gopnik, A., Meltzoff, A. N., & Kuhl, P. K. (1999). *The scientist in the crib: What early learning tells us about the mind.* New York, NY: HarperCollins.

Hebb, D. O. (1949). *The organization of behavior.* New York, NY: Wiley.

Leamnson, R. N. (1999). *Thinking about teaching and learning: Developing habits of learning with first year college and university students.* Sterling, VA: Stylus.

LeDoux, J. E. (2003). *Synaptic self: How our brains become who we are.* New York, NY: Penguin.

Posner, M. I., & Rothbart, M. K. (2007). *Educating the human brain.* Washington, DC: American Psychological Association.

Smilkstein, R. (1997). *Tools for writing: Using the natural human learning process.* Orlando, FL: Harcourt Brace.

Smilkstein, R. (2011). *We're born to learn: Using the brain's natural learning process to create today's curriculum.* Thousand Oaks, CA: Corwin Press.

Willingham, D. (2009). *Why don't students like school?* Hoboken, NJ: Wiley.

Zull, J. E. (2002). *The art of changing the brain: Enriching teaching by exploring the biology of learning.* Sterling, VA: Stylus.

Zull, J. E. (2011). *From brain to mind: Using neuroscience to guide change in education.* Sterling, VA: Stylus.

2

The Sensory Motor Pathway

When I call on Claudia, she often tells me that she knows it but can't say it. According to an Internet test I gave her, she is an auditory learner. I told her to tape information and play it back to study, and she does, but it doesn't seem to help. Her handwriting is terrible but regardless of how many times I take off points, she doesn't do any better. She doesn't even copy notes off the board correctly. It seems she doesn't care. I am at a loss as to how to help this student. Advice, please!

MAKING CONNECTIONS

Are some students visual learners and others auditory or kinesthetic? Should teachers diagnose and label learning styles? What is the best way to address learning preferences? When students say, "I know it, but I can't say it," is that true? How can an instructor incorporate the visual pathway without making the material juvenile? What are some ways to incorporate multiple pathways in one lesson?

So far you have thought about what happens prior to the initial exposure to content. Now you are ready to introduce new material to your class. This new information is presented to students' brains through their senses—sensory input—such as seeing, hearing, and touching. The student responds with sensory output—speaking, writing, or moving. Hidden weaknesses in the brain's sensory processing can underlie more visible processes, such as reading and language learning. Although you think someone is hearing and seeing what you hear and see, that may not actually be the case.

Even if the student has appropriate prior knowledge, the sensory information in the lesson may not get processed appropriately prior to the learning. For example, in order for a student to sound out a word, the brain must be able to accurately hear the sound. Auditory processing deficits may interfere and thus hinder the learning at this stage.

In addition, the reception of this new material is affected by the physiological state of the student in that moment. For example, a student whose arousal level is too low (she looks sleepy or is slouching in her chair, for example) will not receive as much sensory information as someone with appropriate arousal. Students who are ready to learn take in more information.

All students learn differently. You know there are several modes of instruction and you try to diversify your instruction by including visual, auditory, and kinesthetic (VAK) modes. The VAK model is really just one pathway—the sensory motor—with subsets of visual, auditory, speech, and motor. You will learn about additional pathways later in this book, but we start with the most commonly discussed pathways: visual, auditory, and kinesthetic. We'll explore each pathway in depth, beginning with some background in the science.

VISUAL

We see with our what? No, not our eyes. We see with our brain. We see what our brain tells us to see. Let's take a look at some of the research with an eye to its impact on education.

What Does the Research Say?

The eyes are the conduit for visual information sent to the thalamus, the relay station (figure 2.1). The thalamus evaluates the information. If it is recognized as visual stimuli, it is sent to the visual cortex in the back of the brain for further processing (figure 2.2). Many other pathways are then involved in associating this

Figure 2.1 The Thalamus

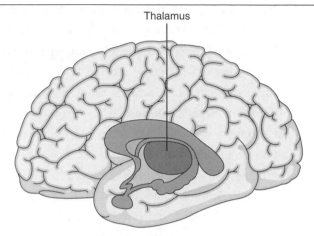

Thalamus

Figure 2.2 Important Sensory Motor Regions

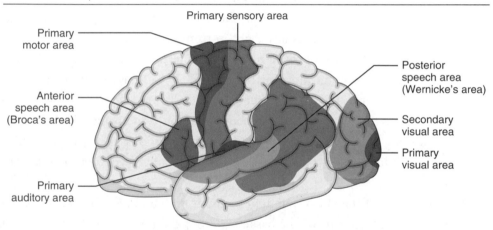

Primary sensory area

Primary
motor area

Posterior
speech area
(Wernicke's area)

Anterior
speech area
(Broca's area)

Secondary
visual area

Primary
visual area

Primary
auditory area

visual information with other existing information in the brain. For example, if this incoming visual information is recognized as a word, it may be processed by the visual word form area (VWFA) in the fusiform gyrus (not shown). The emotion centers of the brain are going to activate along with the visual cortex when seeing a picture that is emotionally arousing (see chapter 3).

The brain doesn't always see what the eyes see. If there are gaps or some confusion, the brain fills in those gaps with what it believes is there. In some surprising research that contradicts earlier beliefs that the visual cortex was "value neutral" (objective), neuroscientists Marshall Shuler and Mark Bear at MIT found that the visual cortex changed its response as a result of expected reward. It seems that expectations can affect what an individual sees. Another example of seeing what is not there occurs in optical illusions. Some people can't see the the alternative view in the optical illusion. Alternatively, sometimes people don't see what is there. Back up two sentences and reread the sentence that begins with "some people." Did you notice the word *the* was repeated twice? Most people don't notice. We often see what we expect to see. This explains why you can proofread and still miss typos.

Our experience affects what we see as well. Swiss radiologists Sven Haller and Ernst Radue compared the brains of radiologists to nonradiologists as they looked at an X-ray. The nonradiologists primarily activated the visual cortex; they had no idea what they were looking at, so they had little in the way of thought processes about it. The radiologists also showed frontal activation, indicating that they were actively thinking about the material as well as looking at it.

Sometimes attentional mechanisms in the frontal lobe help us see part of what is there and not see other things also right in front of our eyes. One example you may know about is the famous gorilla study by Daniel Simon's lab at the University of Illinois, known for studies in visual cognition. If you haven't seen the video, go to YouTube, search for "gorilla video basketball," and watch it now. While viewing, count the number of times someone wearing white passes the ball. Then continue reading here. *Spoiler alert!* If you are going to look at it, you must do it before you read further, or you will not get the effect and it will be ruined for you thereafter.

When viewers of the video were told to count the number of basketball passes among a group of teens throwing a basketball, they did not see a large gorilla walk right through the middle of the screen view. (Chapter 5 has more about this study and implications for attention.)

People from different cultures can even see the same pictures differently. For example, in a study led by neuroscientist John Gabrieli, Americans and East Asians were shown some pictures. Brain scans seemed to indicate that Americans were focusing more on the object in the foreground while the Asian participants focused more on the scenery in the background. They were looking at the same picture but had different perceptions of it. Visual input is clearly complex. As with other brain pathways, the system doesn't always work as expected, and it varies from individual to individual.

Psychologist Stephen Kosslyn at Harvard studies how mental images are strongly linked to vision. He says the same parts of the brain that are activated when we actually see something—the visual cortex—also activate when we imagine the same thing. Another study reported that if an emotion accompanied the mental imagery, the visual cortex activated even more strongly.

What Does This Mean for Educators?

The current paradigm that only some students are visual learners is erroneous and prevents us from tapping into a powerful circuit that can enhance learning. An understanding of the importance of visuals to the brain can help us design and orchestrate learning more effectively.

Pictorial Superiority Effect

In the brain, images are preferable to words. In fact, scientists have a term for the power of visuals: the *pictorial superiority effect*, which means that we remember pictures more easily than words. Visual circuits are very efficient, having evolved before language did in human development. Including visuals therefore is critical to effective teaching and learning. This is true for all learners. Some may need support from other sensory pathways, but all seeing individuals are highly visually inclined. As neuroscientist John Medina says, "Vision trumps all other senses."*

Including visuals is critical to effective teaching and learning.

If pictures are presented with words rather than words alone, the recall is more than six times better. Most interesting is that psychologist Kevin Durkin's lab found that this effect increases with age, which has implications for adult education.

---

* Medina, J. (2008). *Brain rules: Twelve principles for surviving and thriving at work, home and school.* Seattle, WA: Pear Press. p. 240.

Individual Differences

You can't take for granted that every student sees things the same way, and not just metaphorically but literally. Understanding how vision works can help us understand our students better and why they are sometimes not on the same page. Some students may consciously focus on one aspect of a visual and not another, thus not seeing the same details as others. Educators need training in cultural awareness and diversity to recognize differences in perception. Our experience, worldviews, biases, emotions, and other individual characteristics affect what we see. If you are doing a demonstration, learners with more understanding may notice more aspects of the demonstration than those without. Textbook diagrams, grids, maps, and charts may convey more information to those who understand how to read charts and graphs or who have more prior knowledge than those who don't.

Some students are more visually skilled than others and may become graphic designers, interior designers, engineers, architects, or web designers. They may benefit more than others from working visually on their homework assignments or projects. Others may be visually impaired, not in the sense of actual vision itself but in the sense of processing visual information. One hypothesized subtype of dyslexia is impairment in the visual processing system. Readers may have trouble processing fast-moving visual information: reading a *b* for a *d* may indicate trouble processing letters that are similar visually. However, many people with dyslexia are highly skilled at other visual tasks.

As educators we need to work with these weaknesses and strengths just as we do with the myriad others discussed in this book. Since we can't diagnose, we don't label a student as a "visual learner"; instead, we provide opportunities for the use of visual skills as a way of understanding and representing information. Be aware that not all students see the same things as others, coordinate the brain pathways and activations in the same way, or have the same visual processing skills.

Leaping into the Classroom

Early childhood educators have recognized the impact of visuals on learning. Textbook writers often include graphics to help learners visualize the information. But generally, we have overlooked the power of visuals and the many ways we can use them.

Pictorial Superiority Effect

By emphasizing visual explanations of content, teachers can design lessons that tap into this powerful, efficient circuit. Indeed, from a neurological perspective, a picture is worth a thousand words. All students who are not impaired in their eyesight learn better with visuals. This information becomes even more valuable in high school and college where the use of visuals tends to taper off.

We need to get over the idea that pictures are juvenile. Providing pictures with text or oral information results in over six times better recall than when presented in oral or textual form alone. However, unrelated clip art is a waste of brain resources. Although illustrations have been shown to increase comprehension in younger children, this applied only to relevant pictures that make material meaningful or enhance and explain the material. When we include relevant pictures in our materials, we can increase student retention of the material.

Individual Differences

When an explanatory picture is provided concurrent with written or spoken language, the student engages multiple pathways in a single lesson. This also allows students who are not highly language proficient, such as those with dyslexia or second-language issues, to capture and recall information. Visuals are not heavily reliant on language and are easier to hold in memory than words are. Having pictures to support learning reduces the effort required by the brain, thus freeing up resources for the task at hand. Students with dyslexia often are highly visual, and using pictures helps them compensate for reading challenges by using strengths. Since some students have visual skill as a strength, we should provide for the use of visual output as a valid means of working with material and demonstrating competence. The "Homework Menu" section at the end of the chapter provides suggestions for assignments allowing students to accomplish learning outcomes using visual strengths.

Using Visuals

New material should always be introduced with visuals. Ideally the images might be presented first, followed by the verbal information, a process that helps memory and comprehension of the material. This doesn't mean you must provide visuals for the students. It is more effective if the students find the visual material themselves and thus advance one step in your making-connections process.

Is the dictionary definition actually helpful in understanding vocabulary when unfamiliar content is being addressed? For example, if you look up the word *trestle* in the *Collins English Dictionary*, you find the following:

trestle [' trɛsəl]
    n

1. (Miscellaneous Technologies/Building) a framework in the form of a horizontal member supported at each end by a pair of splayed legs, used to carry scaffold boards, a table top, etc.
2. (Engineering/Civil Engineering)
   a. a braced structural tower-like framework of timber, metal, or reinforced concrete that is used to support a bridge or ropeway
   b. a bridge constructed of such frameworks

[from Old French *trestel*, ultimately from Latin *trānstrum* transom]

Really, was that helpful? How many of those words would your students know? If you had never seen a trestle, would you have a vivid picture, and would that help your understanding of the reading material to come?

Now consider Google Images. I like to have students look up three pictures for each word. A single picture might not be clear about what part is the trestle, but in three pictures, students learn the meaning in the way the brain likes to learn—through patterning. Students see a common element and understand. We are not dumbing down. We are using a better tool. Of course there are times we need a dictionary and a thesaurus. The point is to take advantage of this new tool to provide the visual input helpful to learning and memory.

Another strategy for using imagery is to provide videos. These are especially helpful prior to explanations of new information to enable students to create a neural network that can make connections to the unfamiliar material. YouTube has an educational component with wonderful resources for this purpose (http://www.youtube .com/t/education). If you provide your lecture to students, a video would be better than a recording. Demonstrations by you or your students allow the pictorial superiority effect to influence cognition.

Gesture is important to language comprehension and to learning; thus, physical expressiveness is one aspect of visual-centered teaching. Keep in mind that you are not likely to gesture if you are seated, so being up and moving around the room can lead to more gesturing on your part. The same principle applies to students.

You also have visuals in your textbook materials. But students often skip these, and content instructors often leave it to the reading instructors to teach reading strategies that take advantage of the visuals. I suggest that all content teachers should direct students' attention to the visuals prior to the assignment of the chapter. For example, an assignment could ask students to find three more visuals and e-mail them to you, print and turn them in, or post them on their classroom Pinterest page or web page.

An important way to use images in the classroom is to have students create the visuals. To reduce cognitive load and help students organize course work, ask them to draw or design content-related visuals. This is why mind maps, especially those with drawings in addition to words, can be helpful. Creating a mind map shows the relationships using key words and reduces the amount of language needed to explain the relationships. This is a highly productive way to use visuals in the students' learning process because they fire and wire. We can also use them in our assessment process in this same manner. It is as valid for a student to illustrate a concept as to describe it in words (unless you are teaching writing). If the point is to work with the material or demonstrate competence, there is no need to privilege one skill set over another. Visual products are acceptable alternatives, although the quality, effort, and thoroughness should meet the rubric or standards of the course.

In spite of the increasing amount of research supporting the value of drawing as part of the learning process, we seldom see this as students move into high school and college. An excellent neuroanatomy textbook used with medical and neuroscience students is *Neuroanatomy: Draw It to Know It* (Fisch, 2012). As the students learn about each feature in the brain, they draw increasingly complex illustrations as they work through the book. This is an ideal teaching strategy that can be applied to any academic level.

When I had my developmental community college students draw, they groaned because requiring the brain to create a visual can take a great deal of effort and temporarily increases the cognitive load. However, once the drawing was finished, the students were amazed at how well they could recall the material. I would ask them to outline a brief reading using only pictures. Do not grade the artistic quality of the drawing itself, only the concept. We are not talking about *art*. Stick figures and simple shapes are not only acceptable, they are more useful since they don't require a great deal of thinking that might take away from the learning process. In some cases, such as the sciences and trade courses, the drawing may need to be more representative and realistic. Be sure to set your expectations according to the purpose of the drawing.

A combination of pictures and words is most useful typically. If you have students search for a term on Google Images, have them draw it as the final step. Playing a version of *Pictionary* or *Draw Something* can be great for learning new vocabulary. Finally, give the students a test without letting them use the drawings. They will be amazed at how much they remember.

Imagined images can also be superior to words. In fact, the brain can't distinguish between mental and visual images. Certainly we know the difference between real and imagined, but the effect in the brain is the same. Have students imagine processes or imagine them doing a process. Visualization during reading is important for comprehension, and this should be taught and modeled. Instructors can speak aloud about what they are "seeing" or picturing during a reading passage. Ask students how they imagine a person looks or describe the scene as they see it.

Visualization can be used in all content areas. For example, in paramedic training, ask future emergency medical technicians to visualize the scene and how they would respond. Students can picture processes, as in science and health classes. Visualization not only helps comprehension; it is a powerful memory tool and should be in every teacher's toolbox.

AUDITORY

Some recent cutting-edge research is showing a significant relationship between reading or language learning and the auditory system in the brain. Let's take a look at how sounds and language are processed in the brain.

What Does the Research Say?

Auditory sensory input (sounds, language) goes from the ears to the thalamus, just as other sensory information does (figure 2.1). In this case, the thalamus determines that the incoming information is sound and the sensory information is relayed to the auditory cortex for processing (figure 2.2), which determines what kind of sound is being processed. If it is language, it is sent to Wernicke's area, a region involved in language comprehension (figure 2.2). If it is a frightening sound, such as a loud bang, the center for emotional processing is activated (this is discussed in chapter 3). The frontal lobe may become involved too in determining the meaning of the sounds, such as when you hear a banging in the middle of the night and you figure out that the wind is causing the tree branches to hit the window (chapter 7).

The auditory cortex develops in response to sensory input, as do other parts of the brain. If that auditory cortex doesn't develop well, it can have an impact on learning. Researcher George Hollich, a specialist at Purdue University in how infants learn first and second languages, found that noisy homes were associated with poorer vocabulary skills. Subsequent research at Johns Hopkins found that even moderate noise affects language learning in children. If infants can't clearly hear speech, they may not acquire some of the finer phonetic distinctions essential to language and reading. For example, an important study done in 2013 by Nina Kraus's lab at Northwestern University's Department of Neurobiology found a positive relationship between how consistently someone encoded sound and how well he or she could read. This suggests that at least one type of reading deficit is related to the brain's inability to accurately hear the sound and thus make the sound or phoneme correspondence.

Many students have poor spelling. Poor spelling is not associated with lower intelligence; however, it is associated with some developmental disorders, such as dyslexia. The brain may not be hearing the sounds well enough to match the sounds to the letters.

Some research indicates that the structure of the auditory cortex can affect processes involved in learning. The primary auditory cortex in the brain is Heschl's gyrus (figure 2.2). A recent study led by Narly Golestani at the Brain and Language Lab at the University of Geneva found that more white matter (enabling communication) in Heschl's gyrus was associated with being better at learning a new language. It does not mean someone with a difference in Heschl's gyrus has a language learning advantage, but it may predispose him or her. This learning advantage can be positively or negatively mediated by other factors such as quality of instruction, life experiences, and other environmental differences.

Interestingly, the auditory cortex can change to accommodate visual input. An example of the amazing plasticity of the auditory cortex comes from studies of people who are deaf and learned sign language early. Most people might suspect that sign language is being processed in the visual cortex because it must be seen. In fact, researchers have found that the brain recognized the sign language as language; therefore, the auditory cortex used to process sound rewired itself for visual language.

What Does This Mean for Educators?

Sometimes the brain has limitations that can't be seen but affect learning.

Sometimes the brain has limitations that can't be seen but affect learning. Kraus's important research demonstrates how neuroscience and education can work together to improve student learning. Her lab found that with extensive digitized training on specific sounds, the brain's ability to hear them could be improved due to the plasticity of the brain. This may lead to early testing and targeted interventions that could help young readers.

A caution is in order. To make significant changes that rewire deficits in the brain requires specialized and intensive experience that at this time is not able to be done in the classroom in most cases, although some software exists that can be used in the educational environment. FastForWord is a software program that helps some learners with dyslexia hear sounds more clearly and improve their phonological ability, which improves their reading. This can be effective in children with the phonological subtype of dyslexia. Designing targeted interventions is an exciting new development in educational neuroscience. If neuroscientific interventions become policy, great strides can be made in reading and other proficiencies for large populations of students.

Another study in Kraus's lab found that musicians have a greater ability to differentiate speech sounds. Similarly, neuroscientist Dana Strait presented her research at the 2009 meeting of the Society for Neuroscience showing that musical training strengthens hearing-specific cognitive abilities. This line of research could have implications for early childhood and bilingual education and potential interventions down the road for language disorders as educational neuroscientists bridge lab research with classroom research (see chapter 9).

The neuroscientific research on auditory processing doesn't support the concept that some learners are either auditory or visual learners, because we use both senses to learn unless we have no visual or auditory stimulation, such as being blind or deaf. However, on certain tasks, some learners may benefit from adding auditory input, such as listening to the material on a recording. Rather than tell a student that he or she is an auditory learner because of some preferences for auditory material, it can be more helpful to simply provide all students with supplemental auditory material and let them self-select. The "Homework Menu" section at the end of the chapter has suggestions.

Leaping into the Classroom

If you are not yet able to provide intensive rewiring in the classroom, what can you do? Since the brain changes as a result of experience, you are still providing experiences that enable children to grow and learn. Again, the goal is not to diagnose but rather to provide for all diverse and struggling learners. Here are some ways to do that.

Hearing and Reading

It's clear that if the brain cannot hear the sound, it may not be able to read the sound either. We can refer students for further testing if we believe that is the problem. Students who may have trouble processing the fast sounds of language benefit from seeing material, especially students who can't sound out words on their own. Phonological deficits that impair the ability to sound out words have an enormous impact on reading comprehension. If a word is important enough to be in your lesson, perhaps a key vocabulary word, then it is important enough to show and say to the student. We can also provide Internet sites where students can go to hear words pronounced for them.

Along these lines, you should read the board or slides verbatim, word for word, when presenting words to the students visually. Yes, we all have been told not to do that because boring slides can lead to death by PowerPoint. However, students in a class may have invisible impediments. If you are saying one thing and they are seeing another, this can be a hurdle for those with processing deficits. You may complain that students can't seem to copy from the board, but perhaps they are experiencing interference from what you are saying when it doesn't match what they are seeing.

Auditory and visual stimuli are processed in two different pathways, and some learners may have an impediment in coordinating the two. For students with sensory coordination challenges and those with dyslexia, attention deficits, or second-language learners, it is advisable to see and hear the information at the same time. First, read it aloud as it is written. Then paraphrase and explain.

Audio Input

Why would we privilege one sense over the other as the input mechanism? As teachers, we want to provide the optimal learning experience. Sometimes we require students to use their weakest modality because we are providing them with experiences to strengthen it. However, many times we just require a verbal format because that is how we have always done it or because we believe reading is more academic than listening. Is it fair to require a student to work with material and demonstrate competence in every subject almost every time using the weakest modality? I don't think so. If you want students to learn a process or content, you must help them learn it most effectively. Therefore, providing the material in audio format is one more way to help diverse and struggling learners, while at the same time benefiting intermediate and high-performing students. It is not dumbing down. Actually, listening is quite effortful. Augusto Buchweitz, a researcher at the Center for Cognitive Brain Imaging in Brazil, found that the brain activated more areas in listening than in reading, indicating that it requires more effort.

Some instructors are now going to a flipped classroom format in which what was typically provided in class, such as lectures, is now provided outside class and homework-type or lab-type activities are now done in class. This has many advantages, especially for those with auditory processing deficits or for English language learners. If you provide lectures in video format in which students can also see you, they can replay the material. You will learn more about working memory in chapter 5, but suffice it to say for now that some students can't hold enough material "online" in working memory to comprehend a long sentence or a concept spread out over a long paragraph. Being able to replay information assists those students as well.

You can also provide additional lessons in audio format for homework or in a lab. You can create these lessons, or other students can create these video or audio lessons as one of their homework options. Keep in mind the important principle that we want to provide students with ways of using their strengths to compensate for weaknesses and provide opportunities to strengthen weaknesses. The homework menu at the end of the chapter provides for both.

SPEAKING, WRITING, AND MOVEMENT: AN INTRODUCTION

Speaking and writing are expressive pathways, whereas listening and seeing are receptive. Too often we focus only on the receptive aspects of learning, when the expressive pathways may lead to better learning. Speaking, writing, and moving are primarily mediated by the sensory motor area of the brain. Let's look at some research to understand why we as educators need to know more about motor aspects in the brain.

What Does the Research Say?

The sensory motor strip, involved in bodily movement, is part of the frontal lobe and has three subsections (figure 2.2). Simple movements activate the primary motor cortex, while more complex movements activate the premotor and somatic sensory (supplementary) motor cortex areas. These two regions are involved when one intends to execute a goal-directed activity and in the carrying out of complex movements, such as picking up an object or sinking a basketball into a hoop. The motor strip is involved in body movement, so of course it is engaged in speaking and writing. The cerebellum (located near the lower rear of the brain and part of what has been called the reptilian brain) is also involved in movement (figure 2.2).

As with the auditory and visual processes, the motor cortex receives input from the relay station—the thalamus (figure 2.1). It also receives input from the basal ganglia (initiating and regulating movement) (not shown) and the cerebellum (regulating the sequence and duration of movements) (figure 2.2). As with other pathways, many other regions are active in processes that work with the motor cortex: information about goals and strategies, memories of past strategies, and body awareness. Although I have given a highly simplified version here, we are looking at a complex process from input to desired output. The more educators understand about the processes in the brain, the more awe inspiring it is that so much actually goes well.

SPEAKING

Speaking is an important part of the learning process—perhaps more than we have realized. A look into the brain may clarify why sometimes students know something but can't say it.

What Does the Research Say?

How is speaking processed in the brain? Broca's area, a location for speech and language production, is activated and sends information to the motor cortex (figure 2.2). The motor cortex then produces the information that enables the mouth to make the correct movements to produce speech. Speaking also requires frontal lobe activation in planning the content of what to say, along with information in other parts of the brain related to syntax and meaning. According to Jubin Abutalebi, an Italian research specialist in bilingualism, language comprehension is much more passive than language production. Speaking requires assembling the information from multiple locations in the brain: we must gather our thoughts, activate the motor cortex, and formulate the words. Once again, something we take for granted, such as speaking in class, calls on many brain processes that must work together.

What Does This Mean for Educators?

The importance of having students speak cannot be overstated. In order to produce speech, the expressive output pathway must be fired and wired. It isn't enough to have students listen over and over and then expect them to be able to express their thoughts in words. When students have trouble remembering how to pronounce a word, they have not fired the output pathway sufficiently. Sometimes it is not that students do not know the word that you want them to say, but they are having trouble with the motor skills of formulating and pronouncing the word. This important skill is often overlooked in classrooms in favor of an emphasis on reading and listening. We do not want to spend most of the practice time presenting information to students through their receptive pathway—eyes and ears: we want to spend it having students express the information through speech and writing.

> *The importance of having students speak cannot be overstated.*

Leaping into the Classroom

We have all experienced students who say they know something but can't say it. Although you will learn more about memory in chapter 5, one important fact about memory is related to this output issue: memory must be reassembled because it is stored in distributed regions in the brain. The student has fired and wired the receptive pathway (heard and seen it repeatedly). When is the first time we ask the student to reassemble the memory? It is usually on the test—which is also the first time the student realizes he or she can't reassemble the pieces. The expressive pathway must be fired and wired as well.

Think back to a time you read something really interesting and later tried to explain it to a friend. Was your explanation perfectly coherent? Probably not. You understood the information earlier, but you had never reassembled or practiced explaining it. In other words, you knew it well enough to understand but not to express it. That is why students stumble and try to explain that they really did understand it; they just can't say it.

Too often we overlook speaking and then wonder why students can't express themselves well in class. Students must speak more in the classroom to learn vocabulary or pronunciation, help them think better, and retain information by having them reassemble their memory and put it together in a meaningful way. This also helps students discover whether they actually can do this before they get to the test. Research results suggest that when students speak during the learning process, they learn faster with more transfer.

One strategy that should be used about every twenty minutes is called "stand up and explain." All students stand and get in pairs. You say that one of them (distinguishing them by, say, most jewelry, most buttons, brightest colors, biggest feet) explains (defines, summarizes) what was just presented to the other student. This gets half of the class speaking at the same time because many times it is the practice or experience for the student more than you hearing their answer that matters. Another way to get more speaking into the classroom is to put students in groups enabling more of them to speak at a given time. Many teachers have found a whisper phone to be effective. This is a curved device in which sound is transmitted from the mouth to the ear so students can clearly hear their own speech and yet it does not disturb the class. These can be purchased or made from PVC pipe. Teach students about the importance of speaking aloud as they study at home and perhaps provide these devices so that they can speak aloud in class.

Another way to get students speaking is through singing. Many materials are available online that put content information to music. This may sound juvenile, but it is not. I have seen YouTube videos teaching pharmacology and microbiology through songs. Ideally, the students should prepare this material as a homework option. Very few will select it, but if they do, I think you will find it is of a high caliber. I suggest not requiring students to perform; it is an option.

WRITING

Written work involves two aspects: the handwriting and the content. While handwriting is a motor skill function, the content of written work relies more on executive functions mediated by the frontal lobe (see chapter 7).

What Does the Research Say?

The process of writing involves many brain areas working together smoothly and with excellent timing. Whether print or cursive, handwriting involves fine motor skills. You may have noticed many students with other learning differences also have poor handwriting skills. Many learning differences are called developmental disorders: because the brain developed atypically, and these developmental differences sometimes include weaknesses in the development of fine motor skills.

Handwriting is unilateral (it uses one side of the body) and keyboarding is bilateral (it uses both hands). Most aspects of language are in the left hemisphere. About 70 percent of people write with their right hand. The left side of the brain controls the right side of the body—a direct route for right-handed people. However, some left-handed people have language in the left hemisphere and have to make an extra connection in their brain as signals are sent over to the right hemisphere to control movement on the left side of the body. In using a keyboard, one is using both the left and right hands simultaneously in order to compose. This uses the brain differently. The implications of this are still to be determined.

Some new research indicates handwriting is an important skill for the brain in several ways. Virginia Berninger, a University of Washington specialist in the nature-versus-nurture aspects of learning to read and write, says that handwriting involves sequential strokes for each letter as opposed to keyboarding with one stroke per letter. Brain scans show that sequential finger movements activate a larger area in the brain in regions involved in thinking, language, and working memory. She also found that students wrote better essays by hand than when they used keyboards.

Learning to write and practicing it can help children learn their letters, help develop fine motor skills, and may also help them express themselves. Neuropsychologist Karin Harman Jones at Indiana University concludes there is something about writing and drawing that is helpful for learning.

What Does This Mean for Educators?

Sadly, many schools are devoting less time to handwriting skill, so parents may need to encourage handwriting at home. Teachers need to understand why we do not penalize for poor handwriting.

Leaping into the Classroom

Encourage students to write out important information as part of their learning process. This may be especially helpful when students are learning a language, according to researchers studying that method with Chinese language learners. Writing increases the sensory input for the information, helps them visualize the vocabulary, and provides repetition. Writing is part of the expressive pathway and helps students reassemble and articulate information.

Penalizing students for poor handwriting is not appropriate. Poor handwriting may not be a matter of not practicing, sloppiness, or indifference but brain processing. As with other processes, it needs to be fired and wired; however, in some cases, poor handwriting may be a lifelong issue because of differences in the individual brain. While we can all become better at making our handwriting attractive and clear, handwriting is not totally under the control of our frontal lobe conscious efforts. Keep this in mind in later grades and decide if it is worth your efforts to address. You can remind a student to try to be neater, but if that fails, then you have another learning difference that must be accounted for in your practices. Instead, compensate. Perhaps older students can use keyboard input if you can't read their reports.

I recall a student in development composition in a community college who wrote effective essays but continued to fail the exit exam. The exit exam was graded by a team of teachers, and I believe the student was failed on the unconscious bias toward his poor handwriting. While these teachers were wonderful professors, unconsciously they couldn't see past the very poor handwriting. When he retested and used the computer to type his answers, he passed with flying colors.

Just as we do not hold other developmental disorders, such as dyslexia, against students, we must be just as tolerant of handwriting issues. Of course I am not talking about the early grades when students are being taught handwriting, although even then, teachers need to exercise caution and determine whether they are dealing with a potentially persistent fine motor disability or just a learning curve.

MOVEMENT

Movement begins in the brain, although the processing is so fast that we don't realize we have thought about reaching for something. The body affects learning. Some kinds of movement, such as gesturing, seem to be closely related to language and may enhance learning.

What Does the Research Say?

The motor circuits drawn on in speech and sensory information are involved in bodily movement along with the cerebellum (figure 2.2). We have known that the cerebellum is important in such motor skills as balance, posture, and coordination. However, recent evidence indicates the cerebellum is also interactive with many other parts of the brain related to learning. Researcher Peter Strick, a neurobiologist at the University of Pittsburgh who specializes in the neural basis of cognition, found that the cerebellum interacts with brain regions involved in memory and attention. Leading neuroscientist Adele Diamond describes how the cerebellum interacts with the dorsolateral prefrontal cortex, which is important in working memory, an important academic skill (chapter 5). She believes motor development is related to cognitive development. A growing body of research on exercise supports cognitive benefits related to achievement (see chapter 9 for more on exercise).

The brain requires a steady supply of fuel. An important component of the brain's energy supply is oxygen, and movement provides more oxygen. Blood flow increases oxygenation, and movement increases blood flow to the brain, providing more fuel. It stands to reason that sitting all day is not advantageous for brain health, as well as not good for learning.

One kind of movement generated by the motor cortex is gesture. Some researchers believe that gesture may have been the first language, and results from research increasingly indicate that gesture is an important function in language communication and in thinking. San Francisco State University psychologists Patricia Miller and Gina O'Neill in the first study of this kind investigated preschool children and found that those who gestured more performed better on problem-solving tasks. Psycholinguist Uta Sassenberg and colleagues at the Berlin School of Mind and Brain in Germany found that gesturing may contribute to brain development. In their study of high school students, they found that those with higher fluid intelligence (the ability to reason quickly and think abstractly) gestured more than the others. In fact, just watching students' hands enabled these researchers to differentiate the more intelligent students. They surmise that gesturing reflects a simulation in the brain as part of their reasoning. In addition, through neuroimaging, she found thicker cortical tissue in several areas in the brains of the gesturing students.

Another aspect of the motor cortex is the learning of motor movements, such as when you learn to do a surgical procedure, execute a golf swing, take blood from a patient, knit, or perform cardiopulmonary resuscitation. For example, how does the phlebotomist hold the syringe that is in the patient with one hand while changing the tubes that capture the blood with the other? Part of this is motor learning and motor memory. Emily Cross, a neuroscientist at Dartmouth College, found that people can acquire these motor skills through seeing (passive learning) as well as through doing. She found similar brain activity whether the movements were actively or passively experienced.

What Does This Mean for Educators?

As experts in education, we should have basic knowledge about the physiology of learning and implement that knowledge in the classroom. Administrators should know the importance of fuel to the brain. Since activity provides more oxygen (fuel) to the brain, classrooms need to be designed with stand-up desks available to students who want them. Students should be allowed to stand up and listen when the need arises rather than asking them to quit fidgeting, kicking, or squirming. (See chapter 9 regarding exercise and learning.)

Leaping into the Classroom

We have long understood that we think better on our feet (i.e., when standing). During debates, for example, the speakers stand. In fact, a few generations ago teachers required students to stand up to recite in class. I think teaching is as much art as science, and it seems good teachers realized the importance of getting students up and out of their seats. Leaders of some church congregations understand this fundamental physical connection to being alert and ask people to stand up periodically throughout the service. Some students have more trouble sitting for long periods than others, so be sure to provide opportunities for them to get up and move.

It isn't hard to come up with solutions in the early grades to get students on their feet, but what about grades 5 and up through college? Let's look at some purposeful ways to get students moving.

Earlier you learned about the stand up and explain strategy to use when students are doing a pair-share. Have them stand while doing it, and look at their hands: you will observe lots of gestures. This also reveals who is on task. Disengaged students usually have their hands down at their side, while those who are truly trying to explain will be gesturing. Try to do this approximately every twenty minutes in a class, but at least once an hour. It takes only a minute, and the results are important. (You can also use the "take a stand" activity explained in chapter 1.)

Students who are asked to gesture as part of their learning process learn better. Gesturing helps children learn new math concepts, for example. It is more likely a person will engage in gesture when standing rather than sitting. If we had more standing during communication in the classroom, we would be able to address both oxygen and gesture at the same time in a productive manner.

Students who are asked to gesture as part of their learning process learn better.

In addition, demonstrate with your hands too. Cindy Seiger, an early education and English as a Second Language teacher, has her students get into groups and plan how to present vocabulary words with hand signals for the other students to guess. Incorporate gestures into problem-solving tasks. Make gestures part of math discussion, and allow students to use their fingers when counting. When people mentally count, the finger representation area in the brain is activated, so this connection may be helpful in the classroom. Using your fingers is naturally activated in the brain when counting. It is not juvenile.

Allow students to stand in the back of the room if they wish. This can be very helpful for students who get fidgety or adults who find it uncomfortable to sit for long periods. Ideally, you could have standing-height tables in the back for these students.

When students get up to form groups, they are moving around a bit. They are as well when they come to the board or to the front of the room to get materials rather than your passing them out. On the Internet you can find ways to engage students in activities involving movement, but make sure it is really a learning experience at the same time.

HOMEWORK MENU

The options that follow are not specific directions for an assignment, but ideas for generating an assignment by tailoring the directions to an individual lesson or unit. Try to keep all assignments parallel in strength, time, and expertise through your instructions and rubric. For more difficult assignments, you may wish to mark them as acceptable for a group of a specified number of people. Briefer, less complex assignments may be marked as individual only. Because this chapter discusses three subpathways (visual, auditory, and motor), the items are divided into the individual pathways. Include items from each subpathway.

Visual

- Create a timeline of events or steps with illustrations.
- Illustrate a character or all the characters, whether from a story or a historical figure.
- Illustrate the lesson through a series of pictures, as in a graphic novel.
- Create a poster.
- Create a web page.
- Create a Pinterest page.
- Create a PowerPoint.
- Design an illustrated handout.
- Create a mind map showing the relationships.
- Represent information in graphs or charts.
- Create a cartoon that illustrates the concept.
- Find three pictures for every vocabulary word (or ten unfamiliar words in the assignment).

Auditory

- Listen to an auditory version, and answer questions.
- Watch a supplemental video, and answer questions.

Motor

- Give a speech to the class or on video for the teacher explaining the lesson or concept.
- Act out the material with others.
- Create a game of charades based on the vocabulary (specify the number of clues).
- Teach another student the lesson in a study session or using Skype. Then video it.
- Create an audio or video lesson. This includes an agreement allowing the video to be used in future classes for other learners.
- Write a written report.

- Create a model.
- Do a demonstration.

SUGGESTED STRATEGIES

- Use pictures to help the students make connections to new concepts or vocabulary.
- Use a video that demonstrates a process or provides background information.
- Have students draw as part of their learning process.
- Provide visual options as part of the homework or assessment process.
- Remind students to stop reading from time to time and visualize what they are reading.
- Direct students' attention to the visuals in the textbook.
- Ask test questions about textbook visuals to make using them part of students' reading habits.
- Create a narrated PowerPoint teaching the lesson for viewing outside class.
- Use demonstrations and modeling.
- Create a video that teaches the lesson so students can review it outside class.
- Show and say the words for students when introducing vocabulary.
- Avoid saying one thing while presenting something different on the board or screen.
- Provide options for listening to lectures in a recorded format.
- Provide options for listening to texts in addition to reading the texts.
- Provide many opportunities for speaking.
- Get students briefly on their feet every twenty minutes, but make the reason purposeful.
- Allow students the option of standing in the back of the room when listening.
- Allow students to work out problems "aloud" or speak to themselves by moving lips, speaking quietly or using whisper phones.
- Stand up, be visible, and use gestures when presenting information.

REFLECT AND CONNECT

How have you addressed visual and auditory pathways in the past?

What would you do differently as a result of reading this chapter?

How much do you have students speak, and how can you get more speaking?

Describe the extent to which you have incorporated movement in the classroom.

Choose one movement strategy, and discuss how you can incorporate it.

What is one strategy from each subpathway in the sensory motor system that you will add to your practice on a routine basis?

SUGGESTED READING

Dunn, P. A. (2001). *Talking, sketching, moving: Multiple literacies in the teaching of writing.* Portsmouth, NH: Heinemann.

Farah, M. J. (2000). *The cognitive neuroscience of vision.* Malden, MA: Blackwell.

Fisch, A. (2012). *Neuroanatomy: Draw it to know it.* New York: Oxford University Press.

Forsten, C. (2010). *Step-by-step model drawing: Solving word problems the Singapore way.* Peterborough, NH: Crystal Springs Books.

Medina, J. (2008). *Brain rules: 12 principles for surviving and thriving at work, home and school.* Seattle, WA: Pear Press.

Roam, D. (2009). *The back of the napkin: Solving problems and selling ideas with pictures.* New York, NY: Penguin.

Roam, D. (2011). *Blah blah blah: What to do when words don't work.* New York, NY: Penguin.

Sobanski, J. (2002). *Visual math: See how math makes sense.* New York, NY: LearningExpress.

3

The Emotion Pathway

I don't know why Kevin seems so angry. I have asked him if there is anything about the class that upsets him or if he is mad, and he shrugs and says no, nothing is wrong. But he is clearly withdrawn, unresponsive, and seemingly hostile. His expressions vary between boredom and anger. The other students and I all treat him well, but his attitude is getting to me. What else can I do? Why is he acting so angry in my class?

MAKING CONNECTIONS

How does emotion affect thinking and learning? Could creating stress in the classroom ever be good? Is it true you should start out stern and then ease up? Could you unconsciously create hidden triggers for stress? What makes students feel threatened (unsafe)? What is the effect of *your* stress on students' learning?

The first chapter reviewed how the brain learns and how to set the stage prior to instruction. In the second chapter, you learned about sensory input and output and the relationship to learning. Both of these pathways affect emotion, and emotion affects those pathways, as well as all of the other pathways we explore in this book. Understanding the effects of anxiety, high stress, trauma, and positive emotion will enable you to enhance and energize instruction. Let's look at the science of emotion and see how we can use it.

EMOTION, ANXIETY, AND LEARNING

We all know students with anxiety about tests, speaking in class, or reading or math. This anxiety diminishes their ability to think and learn. We can reduce the effects with targeted strategies.

What Does the Research Say?

By studying patients whose thinking and life skills were impaired through damage to the emotional area of the brain, scientists have learned about the connection between emotion and learning. Patients with damage to emotional areas could no longer make decisions. When asked what day they could come back for the next appointment, they never could decide because no emotion was attached to any of the days. Their thinking and life skills were impaired. Scientists realized that the long-held belief in the duality of mind and body was not true: emotion and learning cannot be separated.

We have since learned how emotions can affect thinking, attention, memory, and therefore learning. Until the last couple of decades, no scientist dared to study emotion, which was considered outside the realm of science. Fortunately, some important pioneers such as Antonio Damasio, Joseph LeDoux, Bruce McEwen, and Daniel Goleman ventured into this area and have given us insights that can dramatically affect teaching and learning. Originally most of the research on emotion was on negative emotions, such as stress and fear. Recently a new field of inquiry has emerged, *positive psychology*, that investigates the role of positive emotions, such as gratitude, compassion, and joy, which affect thinking and learning as well.

Regions of Interest

The emotion pathway interacts with multiple pathways in the brain. However, the location of emotion is typically associated with the limbic system, a group of structures deep in the brain involved in emotion and memory. These include the thalamus, hypothalamus, cingulate gyrus, amygdala, hippocampus (figure 3.1), and basal ganglia (not shown). The amygdala and the hippocampus are the major players.

The amygdala, the region most often mentioned with regard to emotion in the classroom, consists of two almond-shaped structures (hence the name, which is

Figure 3.1 Regions Involved in Emotions

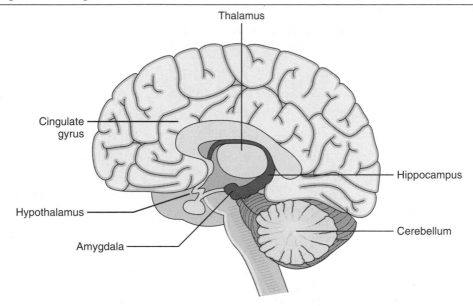

Greek for almond)—one in each hemisphere. It receives input from all of the senses, enabling us to tune in quickly to threat. It processes emotions and is active in our storing of memories. Amygdala activation is typically discussed in terms of threat or stress, a condition impairing learning. However, it is also involved in the recognition of emotion in faces and in music, which is pleasurable.

The hippocampus, often associated with memory, is greatly affected by high stress as well. Prolonged high stress can actually shrink the hippocampus.

In addition to the limbic system, the frontal lobe (see chapter 7) is involved, particularly in the control of emotion. The frontal lobe in healthy individuals is able to regulate emotion and evaluate a potential threat and dismiss it if it proves to be benign. However, strong emotions or a weak frontal lobe can lead to the emotional centers' taking over the frontal lobe's higher-order thinking functions and reducing its effectiveness. Neuroscientist Joseph LeDoux calls this bypassing, or taking over the frontal lobe, "the low road" that goes straight to the amygdala with little or no thinking—without brakes or alternative responses. However, a healthy emotional response would be processed more reasonably through the "high road" of frontal lobe reasoning. Some individuals, such as those engaged in road rage, feel anger and immediately respond emotionally, while healthier brains would process this emotion in the frontal lobe and think, *Do I really want to go to jail just to get even with this person?* and put the brakes on the emotional response.

Overall Effects

Emotion can have positive or negative effects on learning. The effect we most often think about in regard to learning is that strong negative emotions impair thinking and, therefore, learning in general. As resources are diverted to the limbic system, they are less available to the higher-order thinking processes mediated by the frontal lobe, and the effect on learning is significant.

Emotion has a great impact on memory. We remember emotional events more than neutral events, both positive and negative ones. Research indicates it is the arousal more than the meaning of the event that makes the memory last. If an event doesn't affect someone very much physiologically (heart rate, breathing), then the person may not remember it. For example, one person sees a spider and forgets about it, while another person remembers the event of seeing the spider and the associated fear because the arousal (fear) of the spider solidified the memory.

Emotion also has an effect on another pathway, attention, which we examine in chapter 5. Attention is diminished during high emotion because the emotion is diverting resources.

Anxiety

Anxiety—test anxiety, math anxiety, reading anxiety, social anxiety, or general anxiety—is a problem for many learners. Researchers at the University of Western Ontario's Brain and Mind Institute found that people who often suffer from anxiety had poor working memory performance (the ability to hold information "online" in the mind to work with it). Researchers in England found that pretest anxiety improved performance in those with good working memory capacity, but impaired performance in those with low working memory capacity. The degree of anxiety and reaction to anxiety can also be factors.

As with other brain processes, both activation and inhibition are important. In order to think well and perform well in school, students may need to inhibit their anxious thoughts in order to focus. Inhibition is an important task of an area in the frontal cortex (ventrolateral prefrontal), which enables us to focus on the task at hand (see chapter 5). Inhibition uses the brain's resources just as activation does, so suppressing anxieties can be mentally exhausting. Psychologist Trey Hedden at Harvard in the Center of Biomedical Imaging and cognitive neuroscientist John D. E. Gabrieli at MIT found that anxious students may be more inwardly aware. They are focusing on fearful thoughts or negative symptoms in the body and paying less attention to external stimuli, such as the learning environment and material being presented. This inward awareness takes more resources and attention, further reducing learning and performance.

The brain has a feedforward/feedbackward system that plays into this. The breathing of a person who is stressed is shallow and fast and is associated in the brain with danger. Slow, deep breathing is associated with safety and relaxation—freedom from threat. Fortunately, information can feed backward—from the body to the brain—as well as forward—from the brain to the body. Deliberately slow and deep breathing sends a message to the brain that the danger is gone.

Much of the research on anxiety and learning has been done on math anxiety. Psychologists Ian Lyons and Sian Bellock at the University of Chicago found that the anxiety aroused by the anticipation (anxiety) of doing math triggered areas in the brain associated with actual physical pain, although actually doing the math did not.

Anxiety aroused by the anticipation (anxiety) of doing math triggered areas in the brain associated with actual physical pain.

A study that raises serious concerns about the negative effects of anxiety was done by Mark Ashcraft at the University of Nevada. He discovered that in children as young as seven years old, math anxiety diminished their working memory capacity. Working memory is often at the root of math disability, so this could be a vicious circle brought on by the anxiety. Furthermore, he found that this anxiety also diminished attention and frontal lobe functions. Again, we have a vicious circle of anxiety creating poor performance as it affects other processes and poor performance creating additional anxiety. The implications for all educational anxiety and performance are important.

Another kind of anxiety is threat, in which situations make a person feel unsafe. All kinds of things can be a threat, and this can vary from person to person. Threat of any kind also has a negative impact on learning. The brain of someone who feels unsafe is unconsciously scanning the environment for danger, which means that this person has fewer resources available for higher-order thinking and learning. Neuroscience research indicates that persistent early exposure to fearful or threatening events in early childhood can alter the brain's structural development and affect learning. Early trauma can permanently alter the brain's emotional responses as well.

What Does This Mean for Educators?

As orchestrators of learning, we must address stress and anxiety in education. Estimates of the number of students with test anxiety are as high as 40 percent. Add to that the percentage of students who have other kinds of anxiety and those who have stress from trauma, and easily half the class could be unable to perform to their capability.

Research studies reveal that what is mistakenly assumed to be math or reading disability is often actually related to working memory capacity. This capacity may be affected by anxiety issues over math or reading performance. If we address poor reading or math performance on high-stakes tests and put more pressure on students to perform, we may actually make math or reading performance worse if anxiety is the underlying cause.

If students feel unsafe psychologically or physically, the result might be high stress or a low level of threat that is reducing the ability to learn. One significant form of stress is bullying. Not only is bullying a danger to students physically and psychologically, it has a negative impact on achievement. An overt policy on bullying must be in place in every educational environment, but that is not sufficient. A proactive educational program must be in place as well to teach students about emotional intelligence, that is, a person's ability to recognize emotions, understand the importance of them, regulate his or her emotions, and engage in emotional growth.

High-stakes testing can create high anxiety in students or even in entire schools that may have been labeled as low performing. Ironically, this anxiety, if high, does not help students perform better; it in fact reduces performance and achievement. A deep understanding of the nature of anxiety and how to reduce it is required. Pep rallies and other high-energy social events designed to reduce anxiety prior to high-stakes testing don't adequately address the anxiety.

Leaping into the Classroom

The research clearly shows that emotions can have a negative impact on our students' performance at every age level. How can we address these individual differences while addressing all of the other individual learning differences in the classroom? The good news is what is good for traumatized or anxious students is generally good for all students. We can add some simple strategies to our classroom that create the most desirable learning environment.

Anxiety

Taking a test, reading aloud, going into math class, or standing in front of a class are just some of the behaviors in school that can create anxiety. Anxiety has a negative impact on thinking and higher-order executive functions, such as planning, budgeting time, organization, critical thinking, and metacognition. We must take measures to reduce anxiety.

Certainly we want to address anxiety before a test. One way is to have students take a few deep breaths immediately prior to testing. Before I learned about the science, I thought that was silly advice, just something to say to people. Then I learned about the brain's feedforward/feedbackward system. If we deliberately make our breathing slow and deep, as we do when we are safe and calm, a message goes backward from the body to the brain saying, "All is well. No danger!" The stress chemicals stop, or if they are caught prior to release, they don't even flood the body. As soon as students come in the room on test day, do a few slow, deep breaths with them. Then do it again right before the test. Of course, teach them the science behind this so they understand the importance and the effectiveness of this simple procedure. They will also get more oxygen to the brain and think better.

Another way to reduce test anxiety is to give students some control on the test, as a sense of control can reduce stress. Assume you typically write twenty questions on a test. Include five additional questions in such a way that you can group the questions and direct the student to "answer four of these five." When students know ahead of time that is how you test, their anxiety falls and the reward increases. They think if they are not able to memorize everything in the chapter or they mistakenly overlook some information, they still have a shot at doing well. And this is more like real life. In real life we are not always 100 percent on target. Our memories are not perfect. Students will be motivated to study harder believing a test is something they can succeed at because they feel that they have more control over the outcome. Of course, there will still be some required core questions on the test you want every student to answer.

Often final exams or standardized tests are given in a different room from the classroom, which is problematic with regard to text anxiety. You may have heard that the brain likes novelty, but not all novelty is good. Novel environments, in fact, create some anxiety because anxiety is also a protective survival mechanism. Unknown environments could have danger, so some of our brain's resources are used to unconsciously scan for threat, consuming resources that could be used for concentration and higher-order thinking instead. Fortunately, we can work around this in two ways. Optimally, take the students to the room where the test will be administered ahead of time, for even the briefest of visits or, if necessary, tell college students to stop by and check out the room. Ideally, have students review material in that room prior to the test. Learning is state dependent, meaning we recall information better when we are in the same state as when we learned it. That can be an emotional state or an environment.

Classroom management procedures are always threatening to students. If rules are unclear or inconsistently enforced, students might worry that they will inadvertently break them, which may lead to feelings of threat. When consequences are unpredictable, threat also rises. If sarcasm, humiliation, or threats are used to control their behavior, the sense of fear and threat increases, further hindering learning. Procedures and consequences should be distributed listing the rules you expect students to follow. For example, a typical rule sheet states, "Cheating will not be tolerated." A less threatening approach would be to say, "In this class we do our own work, and we do not copy from other people or sources." Then the specific consequence is stated. Whenever possible, state the behavior positively. Even better, create the list on the first day of school with the students. Instructor Maxine Anchondo, a teacher of English as a Second Language, suggests having students brainstorm what they think their behaviors in the classroom should be on the left side of a chart and what they think the teacher's behaviors should be on the right side. She does this for hallway rules, reading rules, and group rules.

We can create a positive atmosphere in the classroom and enforce rules without getting angry or threatening. You can say when someone has violated a rule, "As you can see from the Procedures and Consequences chart, there are consequences for this. I am afraid I must [send you to the principal or whatever else is the consequence] but I will be glad to see you when you return." In short, deal with the behavior, not the student. When the rules are predictable, threat is lessened and consequences can be taken less personally.

One way to reduce students' tendency toward performance anxiety is to teach them about mind-sets. Author Carol Dweck describes in her book *Mindset* how students who believe that performance is based on experience and effort do better than those who believe that performance is related to talent. Students who believe that they are "just not good at" something have anxiety. Teach them a mind-set that they can change their performance and improve it through effort and experience, which can help reduce anxiety and improve achievement.

Engagement also reduces anxiety. Of course we always have the goal of engaging students, but understanding this relationship makes us increase our efforts, especially in populations where many of the students have been traumatized, such as by school violence or natural disaster. The "flipped classroom" is very helpful under these conditions: classroom time is used for interactive applications and repetitions of the information, while the basic information is presented outside class through teacher-made videos or other materials. (Engagement is discussed in more detail in the next chapter.)

Hidden Triggers for Threat

You could be engaging in practices that increase stress or anxiety in the students without being aware of this effect. When students are taking a test that you are proctoring or administering, do you smile kindly, walk around the room, and stand behind students and look over their shoulder to show you care? If you do, stop! You are looming! The brain reacts with threatened feelings when a shadow (literally or figuratively) is being cast on the person from someone coming up behind them. This taps into survival threat: the looming shadow might be a predator or adversary, which can unconsciously raise anxiety in students. Simply approach from the front and don't hover over them.

Another potential practice is inadvertently priming the student's brain unconsciously with your word choices. Priming is early information that makes some responses more likely than others. If I were talking about food and then asked you to name a word, any word, beginning with *a*, you might say *apple* or *avocado* rather than *ant* or *attitude* because your brain was primed by earlier words referring to food. When you say, "Don't *worry*; study *hard*," you might well be increasing anxiety with those words. Instead say something like, "Do your *best*; study *well*." In fact, watch how you use words overall. Researchers in Japan, for example, found that sarcasm activated the amygdala—the center of fear and anger. We don't want that!

Another important factor in reducing threat is the predictability factor. Unpredictability increases threat. You can see how this relates to the survival pathway: anything uncertain or unpredictable could be life threatening. The brain reacts unconsciously so this can come into play in the classroom where, of course, nothing should be life threatening, but the student's emotional response could make it seem that way. As teachers, we need to balance predictability with novelty to keep the classroom interesting yet also predictable and, therefore, safe. Using pop quizzes may or may not improve homework completion, but it does increase an overall sense of threat and uncertainty. Anything that might induce feelings of fear should be as predictable as possible while novelty should be introduced in lessons to stimulate attention.

When something new comes into the environment (such as you on the first day of school), it is unconsciously scanned to see if it may be a threat or a reward. Starting off the first day of the year on the right foot is essential. We do not want to be seen as a threat, so starting off stern and then easing up may not be the best approach. This does not mean we will be perceived as easy or lax. Being clear, firm, and friendly can set the tone that we are there to teach and support the students. Our frowns and threatening remarks are not as helpful as clear directions as to the type of behavior we want from them. Positive statements of desired actions, such as "one person speaking at a time" are better than "don't talk while I am speaking." It is not always a matter of what is said as how it is said.

HIGH STRESS OR TRAUMA AND LEARNING

It is a neuromyth that stress is bad. What is bad is high stress and one's attitude toward stress. Negative effects can come from temporary, existing, or past high stress. A better understanding of the nature of stress can help us recognize and respond more effectively.

What Does the Research Say?

Much of the research on emotion has focused on stress, which David Diamond, a leading researcher of posttraumatic stress disorder, defines as something arousing. Of course, many things, such as riding a roller coaster, are arousing, but not everyone perceives them as stress. He says it must also be aversive (one would avoid it if possible). Therefore, he emphasizes that the stress comes not from what happened but how the person perceives what happened. A feeling of control and predictability can reduce stress; the lack of that feeling can greatly increase stress.

Stress comes not from what happened but how the person perceives what happened.

Freeze, Flight, or Fight

The brain and body system has three basic responses to high stress—freeze, flight, or fight—and they are our natural response to threat. Early in human history, this response served a role in survival. It was better to hide, fight, or outrun the tiger than to outthink it. Now, however, we usually have to think our way out of stressful situations. Ironically, this system actually makes thinking worse because resources are diverted to body strength and ability to fight or run rather than to think.

When a threat is perceived and we feel in danger, the body prepares us to react quickly and without having to think about it. For survival, the system wants to deactivate the higher-order thinking processes because by the time we have thought about the best way to respond, the tiger presumably will have already eaten us. The brain then engages multiple resources. The hypothalamus activates the sympathetic nervous system, the system that speeds up the heart rate, strengthens muscles, and makes us alert, enabling us to run if possible or at least fight off the danger. Digestion shuts down, pupils take in more light as they dilate, the immune system turns off, blood pressure rises, and we have trouble focusing on small tasks. This process also releases several stress hormones into our system. While you may have heard about adrenaline (epinephrine) and noradrenaline (norepinephrine) and cortisol, about thirty stress hormones flood the body so that we can react in the best way for survival.

At first, someone in a stressful situation may briefly have heightened cognition—thinking quickly how to get out of the situation. But soon the negative effects of these hormones begin to set in. If this system is activated frequently, you can imagine what would happen to your health with frequent rises in blood pressure and a weakened immune system. Unfortunately, we do activate it often, because it is not just life-or-death situations that activate it. Rather, we face all kinds of threats regularly that activate this response. Perhaps your boss says he wants to have a talk with you at the end of the day after everyone else has left—and almost immediately in response, your heart pounds and blood pressure rises as the stress hormones flood your body. If you could take action by flight (running) or fighting, your body would use those chemicals before they could do long-term damage. However, since it is not a good idea to use those behaviors with your boss, you can't take physical action that would process the chemicals. We "stew in our own juices" as they say. Keep in mind that the purpose of emotion is to take action, and later in this chapter we look at some things we can do to help.

Neuroscience researchers Bo Li and Josh Huang recently found that certain types of neurons in a subdivision of the amygdala play a role in fear-related reactions. Their research supports the hypothesis that strengthening connections between neurons encodes fear memory. Because cells that fire together wire together, fear memories can get wired into us and persist. This is a factor in, for example, math anxiety and posttraumatic stress disorder (PTSD).

Addressing trauma and PTSD is beyond the scope of this book. However, since traumatized students make up a portion of the school population, I offer a brief introduction to this concept. PTSD is defined by a cluster of symptoms that may include flashbacks to the event, flashbulb memories, nightmares, a strong startle response, or some combination of these responses. PTSD in some people is associated with sleep disorders, depression, and substance abuse. It could be manifested in the classroom as impulsivity, hostility, distraction, hypervigilance, problems with attention and memory, or trouble with relationships.

Some nonpharmacological interventions are suitable for an education environment, such as instilling coping self-efficacy. Educator Albert Bandura's social cognitive theory explains the role of self-efficacy—the belief that one can handle a situation or overcome a challenge—from an educational perspective. Researchers

Charles Benight and Michelle Harper, who specialize in the effects of natural disaster, found that coping self-efficacy was a potential intervention for recovery from natural disasters. In addition, meditation, yoga, and exercise are widely supported in the scientific literature as interventions.

What Does This Mean for Educators?

We are seeing ever higher populations of traumatized individuals in our schools than in the past. We have returning soldiers suffering from PTSD. Immigrant, migrant, and Native American populations have PTSD incidence as high as 23 percent. Childhood neglect, child abuse, and domestic violence occur in many homes. Poverty and living in depressed urban areas increase the risk. Other risk factors for trauma as documented by research are exposure to fire, life-threatening situations, rape, threat with a weapon, violence, and breast cancer diagnosis, to name a few. In the case of school violence or natural disaster, the entire school population is at risk for PTSD. Educational institutions therefore have a responsibility to provide professional development about anxiety and trauma in order to appropriately address these learners. Classroom practices that reduce anxiety are particularly beneficial for this group, as well as all other learners.

Leaping into the Classroom

The impact of stress on student learning must be addressed at every grade level. Classroom teachers must be educated about the prevalence, causes, effects, and interventions for stress.

The Effects of Freeze, Flight, or Fight   Let's look at how freeze, flight, or fight can affect students' behavior. *Freezing* is the proverbial "deer in the headlights" reaction and is quite common in the classroom. Students can experience this when taking tests. Sometimes their mind goes blank and they freeze up. Some students freeze when the teacher calls on them unexpectedly in class. This reaction of freezing may help a rabbit not be noticed by the fox nearby, but it is not the response we want our students to experience. A strategy to offer wait time to students before they answer reduces that kind of stress.

The second response is *flight*. Students who feel fear and anxiety may respond by refusing to participate in some activities or do some assignments because they find them too threatening. But if they are not allowed to refuse, they may go into physical flight mode: their heart starts pounding, their palms sweat, their breathing is rapid, and their mind goes blank (because this process inhibits activation in frontal lobe and higher-order thinking). Consequently, their performance does not reflect their actual ability because they can't think clearly at this moment. Understanding that the body is taking over the brain and that it is not just that the student "won't calm down" supports the need for allowing some students to demonstrate achievement in alternative formats. Should a student with a phobia of speaking be required to give a speech in front of the entire class? Should you be required to handle a snake so you can get over that fear in case you ever have to do that in a future job? Food for thought.

The *fight* response may be observed in some students who respond to threat, fear, or anxiety with anger. Their instinct when they are threatened may be to attack verbally or even physically. Think about whether the student may actually be angry or whether this is a manifestation of fear. Questioning the student to get to a deeper understanding behind the anger may be a better response than responding to the outward manifestation of what may be an entirely different emotion.

Regardless of how the freeze, flight, or fight response manifests, it diminishes the thinking ability of the student and affects his or her performance. Reducing anxiety can prevent students from going into these modes.

High Stress and Posttraumatic Stress Disorder

Sometimes anxiety becomes especially problematic when students are under high stress or have experienced trauma. Here is a partial list of the events that have been documented by research as potentially causing PTSD:

- Combat
- Natural disaster
- Being in a fire or life-threatening situation
- Domestic or child abuse
- Sexual molestation
- Rape

- Being threatened with a weapon

- Victim of violent crime (58 percent get PTSD)

- Childhood neglect

- Exposure to violence

- Seeing someone hurt or killed

- Poverty

- Living in migrant, Native American reservations, depressed urban areas (23 percent)

- Living in a war zone

- Breast cancer diagnosis (and probably any other life-threatening illness)

Students who have been subjected to one or more of these events do not necessarily develop PTSD, but they could. (A discussion of teaching, learning, and trauma are beyond the scope of this book. You can find additional information on my web page, www.brainresearch.us, on the tab entitled Butterfly Project.) Everything discussed in this book to reduce anxiety and stress is applicable to these students. It's important to realize that some of our students are under a great deal of stress that is affecting their performance, and we can take steps to teach in a way that addresses their needs.

Students who are traumatized perceive more threats in their environment than those who are not traumatized. Researchers have found it is not that the person is more anxious, but that he or she pays attention to more potential or seemingly threatening events, noises, or situations in their environment. Students who are traumatized or highly stressed may exhibit behaviors that look like boredom or anger, for example. It is important not to take these bodily and facial manifestations at face value and to understand that other emotions, such as fear, anxiety, or trauma, may underlie these postures and expressions.

A growing body of research shows it is not so much the stress itself that poses a problem: the key factor is the person's sense of control over the stress. It is important for students to have a sense of control. This doesn't mean you should not have overall control, but it need not be an either-or situation. You can give students some control in certain areas. For example, you can teach them that they can take control of their learning (see chapter 1). In other words, they will have learned not that they "can't" learn but they "haven't" yet, and they need to build their neural network. They have a sense of control in that they have acquired a set of strategies they can access. Students need to learn they can control their effort as well. Remind them that learning is effortful, and they are in control of putting forth the amount of effort required by their brain. This knowledge can help students with content anxiety, such as reading anxiety or math anxiety.

However, if the classroom environment isn't providing a sense of control and instead is making them feel powerless, then it may undermine this sense that they can control their learning. You can provide a sense of control in the classroom without losing your control. Offer students some choice, which gives them control. Ask them if they want the quiz at the beginning or end of class and on Monday or Wednesday, for example. You are looking for ways in which students have some voice in things, some self-efficacy, in realistic ways supporting the requirements of the course.

You can provide a sense of control in the classroom without losing your control.

Providing choice with assessment is also important. To provide even more choice and to allow students to work with their strengths, you can give multiple options to them for showing proficiency or knowledge. You may not want to do this every time or allow students to select the same modality every time. They can choose to create a poster or write a paper, for example, but sometimes they may be required to take the objective test. That is something you determine based on the nature of your course.

Predictability also reduces the feeling of threat. Classroom procedures that could be stressful should be as predictable as possible. Make it explicit when homework is due and the consequences if it is turned in late.

Another way to reduce threat is to turn the challenge from competing against others to competing against their own previous performance. Once students have learned about creating neural networks, they understand why someone else may catch on faster or outperform them. Direct their attention toward how much progress they are making with their neural networks and their executive functions (see chapter 7), tying into the sense of progress that cell biologist James Zull says is huge in learning. We have seen the effectiveness of many video games in which one tries to best a previous score or get rewards in the form of coins, tokens, or additional resources.

Even at a preschool age, children have a sense of fairness. Fairness activates dopamine, which feels good. Whatever age group you teach, you can be certain everyone is expecting to be treated fairly. However, fairness is a perception and often can be misperceived. For example, some believe being treated equally is what constitutes fairness, but we all know different students have varying personalities, abilities, and tendencies that must be factored in. A perception of unfairness triggers students' negative emotions, activating the anterior (front portion) insula, a structure associated with disgust. Unfairness also activates the limbic system, where fear and anger are mediated. Not only must we be fair, we must be perceived to be fair. Be transparent with students. Explain why you have made a decision that might be perceived as unfair. Involve students in the decisions when possible.

One aspect of emotion that is important to learning is learned helplessness. Sometimes when people feel they have no control or struggle for a long time, they "learn" to be helpless. This belief needs to be turned around, and one way to do that is through learned coping self-efficacy. Once again, when we teach students they can change their brain, make new connections, and take control, they become empowered, which can abate learned helplessness. Couple this with a strategy-oriented approach.

Albert Bandura, a well-known educator, has written some scholarly articles on how greater self-efficacy can be created in our students. One example he gives is through modeling. How do we react? If technology fails, do we say, "Just my luck" or, "This always happens to me," thus modeling learned helplessness? Or do we say, "If I can't fix this, I bet I can find someone who can."

This section has looked at ways to lessen anxiety, reduce threat, and avoid creating more threat—reducing negative emotion. Now let's look at how we can introduce some positive emotion.

POSITIVE EMOTION

Because it was not considered appropriate to study positive emotion until recently, we do not have a great deal of science about positive emotion and learning. Recently the new field of positive psychology is giving us insight into positive emotion, and I hope that more research will bridge to education. However, we do know a good deal about the reward pathway (the topic of chapter 4), also known as the pleasure pathway, so most of the information about positive emotion is covered in the next chapter. In this chapter, we look more generally at positive emotion.

What Does the Research Say?

Unlike negative emotions, positive emotions, for example, interest, engagement, and curiosity, do not shut down the higher-order thinking in the frontal lobe. Quite the contrary—they engage it. Positive emotion increases arousal and attention and leads to better memory. We say something is engaging when it engages the emotion and attention of the person.

Scientists and educators are studying emotional intelligence and the impact on learning. Emotional intelligence is related to success in school and in the rest of life. Neuroscientist Aron Barbey at the University of Illinois found a correlation between general intelligence (IQ) and emotional intelligence in both brain and behavior. Many of the same brain regions are involved, including frontal and parietal lobes.

James Parker, a researcher at the University of South Carolina, and colleagues studied high school students in Huntsville, Alabama. They gave them tests of emotional intelligence and compared their scores with their academic achievement, finding that many aspects of emotional intelligence were associated with academic achievement. Robert Vela, an education researcher at Texas A&M, looked at emotional intelligence in over seven hundred first-year college students in Texas. He included such variables as SAT scores, gender, and ethnicity. Data analysis indicated a significant relationship between emotional intelligence scores and first-year achievement.

What Does This Mean for Educators?

Positive emotion drives learning. An important goal is to address and minimize emotions hindering learning and create and enhance emotions promoting learning. Evidence that emotional and general intelligence are linked also indicates we must teach students about emotions and how to manage them. School can be a stressful experience, but awareness and thoughtful actions can help students reduce stress and enhance learning outcomes.

Since emotional intelligence can be taught and it is associated with achievement, schools must include social and emotional intelligence in the curriculum.

Schools must include social and emotional intelligence in the curriculum.

Because emotion has an effect on learning, it is our responsibility to orchestrate the classroom environment to create positive emotions. This does not mean an anything-goes atmosphere: it means joyful, hopeful, and supportive.

Approach/Avoidance

Students always have emotion in class, whether we see it or not. At any given moment students are in either an approach state or an avoidance state. An approach state is similar to what it sounds like: the student is moving toward something emotionally. This would be seen in positive emotional states such as engagement, effective collaboration, sharing, laughing, fairness, status, creativity, some kinds of novelty, and figuring something out. An avoidance state is also as it sounds: the student is moving emotionally away from something. This would be seen in negative emotional states, such as fear, anxiety, some kinds of novelty, uncertainty, unfairness, embarrassment, lack of control, and threat.

An approach state is ideal for learning. When students feel safe, they can be more fully engaged. When students are in an avoidance state, it is hard for them to learn. If we stop and think about whether the class or individual students are in an approach or avoidant state, then we may find it necessary to redirect emotions first before learning can proceed. Let's create an approach state through the development of positive emotion.

On the first day of class, the students are assessing both you and the classroom environment and determining "friend or foe." This is survival behavior, essential to staying alive in early human history. First impressions are very important. The old adage of starting off tough (even scaring the students the first day) and then getting easier is not effective in terms of brain reaction. We want students to be in a positive state, an approach state, full of interest or at least curiosity—a state of openness. We definitely do not want them to perceive the class as threatening or us as foe. Unfortunately, that is often the case, especially if they have anxiety about reading, math, or learning in general.

Teachers need to consciously set a positive emotional tone in the class. We model appropriate and positive emotions for the students. Therefore, start your first day in a smiling, welcoming manner. Create positive emotion by laughing with your students, greeting them by name, and smiling at them. Through modeling, let them know that the classroom is a place of positive emotion. With younger students, we can create a happy atmosphere—one that is playful and cheerful. With older students, it is one of positive emotions such as welcoming, supportive, and "we are all in this together" attitudes.

Establish that you are there to help move students along in their journey and to support them. This does not mean that you are setting a loose or chaotic tone. I started the first day of class by telling my community college students, "It is more important to me that you are a good person than an A student." They are relieved and think, *Hmmm, I can do that*. I want them to know that, to me, they are a person, not a grade or a performance in class. Everyone is aware that some students will do better than others, so let everyone know from the beginning that performance has nothing to do with the person you are. Keep in mind that we are not grading them on that, just not judging them by their performance on tests. There is a difference. Not surprisingly, this feeling of safety motivates students to try harder.

Creating Positive Emotions

This section looks at some kinds of positive emotions shown to enhance learning. One aspect ties in with the topic of emotion covered in this chapter: stress. There has been a great deal of talk in brain-based circles that stress can have a negative impact on learning. However, that applies to high stress. Mild stress, positive stress, such as that which comes from being challenged, actually enhances learning. It would be stressful, for example, to be on a game show, but that kind of stress is usually perceived as a challenge and not a threat. Positive stress creates the kind of arousal that helps to focus attention. Being timed, cramming for a test, and competing are all stressors that perhaps not everyone sees as positive, but they are not negative. Therefore, you can include games and challenges in class that are engaging and exciting. Be sure not to have penalties associated with them to avoid the winner/losers competition mentality in favor of an atmosphere of individuals trying to better previous scores or all students trying to achieve. Of course, there is a role for team challenges in the classroom, but they should be handled with care.

Setting a time limit for an activity has no negative consequences. A challenge in the moment with no win/lose aspect can create arousal and positive emotion. For example, ask the class to see how many plural words they can list in two minutes. Who got five? Ten? Fifteen? More? Everyone gets to raise a hand at least once. Then starting with those who got only a few, ask them for their answers and put those on the board. Then call on those who got a few more and ask if they have any new words to add, until you get to the highest-performing students and ask them if they have any additional words to offer. In this way, students with all levels of ability and performance get attention and have their words on the board and those who are higher performing are reaching a higher level of challenge as more words are added. The time element is positive stress, and positive emotion accrues when all students get to contribute. This should not be done for assessment—only as a brief, engaging activity.

An activity that increases positive stress while teaching study strategies is one in which students learn other students' names on the first or second day of class. Tell the students they have approximately fifteen minutes to learn everyone's name in the class (I used half a minute per student to arrive at my total, adding a little more for lower grade levels). They can do it any way they want. This activity creates a great sense of urgency and arousal with low threat because there are no negative consequences. During this time, leave the room or sit in the back of the room doing something else so they see you are completely uninvolved and they are on their own. After the time is up, ask them to tell how they went about learning the names, and write their strategies on the board. It is wonderful to see how many learning strategies they already know. Classes have used association, saying they would go around and around having everyone say their name while they memorized the face (association and repetition). Some would write the names down as everyone said them and write them over and over (visual and repetition). Some classes would put all the names on the board as students said them. Tell them they can use these strategies that worked effectively here when they are learning material in your course.

Whether a situation is negatively stressful is based on the perception of the individual. For example, some people find a roller-coaster ride exciting, while for me, it would be negative stress. Talking to students about feeling the excitement and the "rush," rather than perceiving something as stressful, can help them reframe a negative into a positive emotion. Some cutting-edge research shows that even high stress from negative situations can be made harmless to the body and mind by thinking of the symptoms as your body is marshaling its resources to take care of you. The attitude toward the stress seems to negate the harmful effects.

Sometimes individuals deliberately, although perhaps unconsciously, create stress by waiting until a deadline to begin working. They feel this stress gives them the arousal and motivation to jump in, focus, and complete the tasks. Understanding that this type of stress exists and that it can be positive can help us understand students. We may realize that sometimes students (and perhaps you as well) wait until the last moment to create this stress that creates arousal and motivation. However, the student needs to understand and have some self-awareness as to whether this is what they are doing or whether they are simply procrastinating. The proof is in the outcome: those who unconsciously do this to get motivated and meet deadlines have an effective strategy. If they fail to meet deadlines, this is not a strategy but a problem that needs be addressed. For students who feel stressed but meet deadlines, help them see that this may be a positive stress that they use as motivation.

Drawing attention to students' awareness of arousal levels can help them modulate their arousal to a level more conducive to learning. The appropriate level can vary from individual to individual, so each student must find that feeling in which he or she is alert and focused in a relaxed way. When you see students very engaged and focused on a task, have them stop and tune in to their body. How do they feel when they are in that state? What is their mind doing? Their body? Point out that how their brain and body are performing in that moment is ideal for learning and ask them to think about trying to recreate that feeling when they are studying.

Positive emotion is more likely when students have a high level of emotional intelligence, which they acquire by observing others (learning implicitly) and by being explicitly taught. In homes where parents do not model good emotional intelligence, children do not learn emotional skills. As teachers we can work this into our lessons—not to be *in locus parentis*, but because we orchestrate learning, and this affects learning. Teach emotional skills by asking students questions about stories they read. Ask them to think about their emotions in class and how they affect their learning. Discuss bullying and how others may feel as a result of certain behaviors. Daniel Goleman's book *Emotional Intelligence* is an outstanding resource for learning more.

Music is a powerful tool (see chapter 9) that can change the emotional state quickly. Try playing music as students arrive at your classroom to put them into a positive emotional state. This music can have words and can be of a somewhat higher arousal level than concentration music. However, it should convey a positive message. We don't want to play some angry lyrics and active their amygdala and agitate them as they walk in. We are not playing the music necessarily because they like the particular piece but as a tool. Select something positive and upbeat. Some people like to use the same song every day to create a theme song that immediately makes the students feel a sense of belonging and familiarity. Others like to vary the music and even let students bring the music—signing up ahead of time and getting approval because we want positive music with the appropriate arousal level.

• • •

As you can see, emotion underlies learning to a great deal and interacts with a number of pathways. Teaching students about the role of emotion and learning can help them realize they can control their emotions in such a way as to make learning easier for themselves. In the next chapter, we look more at positive emotion—pleasure, engagement, and motivation—in another pathway in the brain, the reward pathway.

HOMEWORK MENU

Understanding that choice reduces anxiety and stress, you may want to take the time to look at this section at the end of most chapters when planning lessons to give students a choice in how to fire and wire material (i.e., do their homework). One word about homework and trauma: traumatized students are going to have trouble with homework. This high stress has a negative impact on frontal lobe executive functions required to complete homework, such as budgeting time, planning, organization, and self-monitoring. It may be helpful to have these students complete their homework in tutoring centers or math labs. Be sure to consider this as a homework option.

These two homework options tie into positive emotion:

- Create your own assignment. Submit the plan and get approval.
- Design a game based on the lesson. Include written rules for playing and scoring.

SUGGESTED STRATEGIES

- Teach students what happens to their brain and body when they are stressed.
- Build in stress reduction techniques, such as breathing, music, and humor.
- Prepare students for testing by familiarizing them with the testing environment.
- Offer alternative assessments for students with serious test anxiety.

- Have written procedures and consequences rather than disciplining on the fly.
- Give students warning before calling on them or giving quizzes.
- Give students choice as much as possible—on assignments, on tests, and on classroom decisions.
- Be predictable. Routine helps traumatized students as well as those with anxiety.
- Think in terms of challenge and progress rather than a sense of competition.
- Create a perception of fairness by being transparent.
- Introduce games, challenges, and timed activities (ungraded) to create positive stress.
- Model emotional intelligence and coping, that is, self-efficacy.
- Teach students emotional intelligence.

REFLECT AND CONNECT

Look back to the first day with your current students. What emotional climate did you create that day? How has that played out over the semester?

Have you consciously used strategies to address emotion? Describe what you have done.

What three things will you begin doing differently as a result of reading this chapter?

SUGGESTED READING

Damasio, A. R. (1994). *Descartes' error: Emotion, reason, and the human brain*. New York: Putnam.

Davidson, R. J. (1998). *Neuropsychological perspectives on affective and anxiety disorders*. New York, NY: Psychology Press.

Dweck, C. (2006). *Mindset: The new psychology of success*. New York, NY: Random House.

Goleman, D. (2006). *Emotional intelligence: Why it can matter more than IQ*. New York, NY: Random House.

Haidt, J. (2005). *The happiness hypothesis*. New York, NY: Basic Books.

LeDoux, J. (1998). *The emotional brain: The mysterious underpinnings of emotional life*. New York, NY: Simon & Schuster.

McEwen, B. S., & Lasley, E. (2002). *The end of stress as we know it*. New York, NY: Dana Press.

Siegel, D. J. (2007). *The mindful brain: Reflection and attunement in the cultivation of well-being*. New York, NY: Norton.

Williams, M., Teasdale, J. D., Segal, Z. V., & Kabat-Zinn, J. (2007). *The mindful way through depression: Freeing yourself from chronic unhappiness*. New York, NY: Guilford Press.

4

The Reward Pathway

No matter how easy I try to make the class, I can't seem to get students motivated. Achievement isn't where I would like it to be, either. I went all out last semester. For example, I distributed notes on the chapter with everything they needed to know for the test. How much easier could I make it to study? Yet they didn't do well on the test.

MAKING CONNECTIONS

How does rigor affect the brain and learning? What kinds of academic activities give students pleasure? How do students know when they are improving? How can you get students more motivated and engaged?

While chapter 4 on the emotion pathway primarily discussed negative emotions of stress and threat, this chapter focuses on the opposite: reward. Reward emotions include pleasure, happiness, motivation, and engagement.

Reward is a powerful pathway in the brain linked to survival, pleasure, and addiction. The structures shown in figure 4.1 comprise the reward pathway in the brain (although there is a great deal of interaction among many areas). When the sensory motor pathway (which we explored in chapter 2) senses incoming pleasurable stimuli, the brain sends a signal to the ventral tegmental area (VTA), which causes the chemical dopamine to be released into the amygdala (see chapter 3), the prefrontal cortex, and a small structure called the nucleus accumbens.

In the 1950s two psychologists from McGill University, James Olds and Peter Milner, found that rats would press a bar up to two thousand times an hour to get a pleasurable response from electrodes that had been placed in certain regions of their brain. They had discovered the pleasure center. Interestingly, in that same decade, Robert Heath, at Tulane University, in what would later become my office, used electrodes to stimulate sexual pleasure in humans and, yes, people would press the bar over and over to get the response.

Figure 4.1 The Brain Regions Most Active in Reward

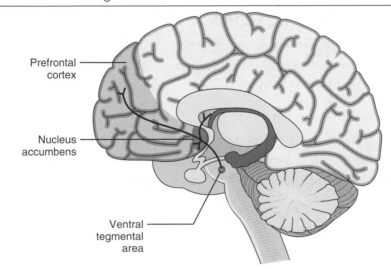

Prefrontal cortex

Nucleus accumbens

Ventral tegmental area

Activating Reward

Certain behaviors stimulate the release of pleasure chemicals. Researchers initially called dopamine the "pleasure chemical" and later found others, such as serotonin, oxytocin, and endorphins. This release of chemicals reinforces the behavior by giving us pleasure and causing us to pay more attention to those behaviors. This process is a survival mechanism, so eating and mating activate it (primary rewards). Other activities that activate this powerful system are money, music, and socializing (secondary rewards). Researcher Morton Kringelbach, a neuroscientist at the University of Oxford specializing in research on pleasure, recently reported that the brain regions involved in both type of rewards overlap.

This pathway is also called the addiction pathway, because drugs of abuse hijack it (figure 4.2). When people become addicted to something, they are addicted to the brain's response to it. Psychologist Elizabeth Dunn at the University of British Columbia and colleagues, using neuroimaging of the brain, found that giving money to others made the study participants happy; that is, the action stimulated the reward chemicals. Fortunately, this includes any kind of giving or doing for others, because reciprocal helping increases the odds of survival. Clinton Kilts is a neuropsychopharmacologist specializing in mechanisms of drug actions at Emory University. He conducted a study that used neuroimaging and found that cooperation activates the reward pathway, illustrating again that humans have had to cooperate in order to survive.

Seeing patterns and figuring things out also activate the reward pathway, along with the right frontal lobe (chapter 7), and release dopamine. The brain is a natural pattern seeker. In fact, we can't stop the brain from seeing patterns; it does so unconsciously because it has a strong need to make sense of the world for survival. Survival depended on seeing the camouflaged snake in the leaves or the wild animal in the bushes and patterns in the environment.

Seeing patterns and figuring things out also activate the reward pathway.

Discovering patterns is also our earliest form of learning: even prenatally, babies are hearing patterns in language (see chapter 6). Our brain is so finely tuned to see patterns (or especially deviation from a typical pattern) that no computer software

Figure 4.2 Drugs of Abuse Hijacking the Reward Pathway

Drugs of abuse increase dopamine

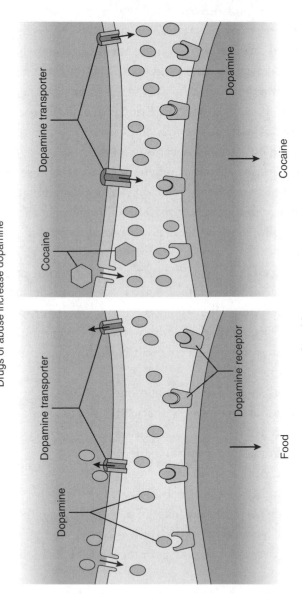

Source: Reprinted with permission of the National Institutes of Health.

can match our ability. Recognizing, repeating, or creating patterns enlists the basal ganglia (not shown in figure 4.1) which assist the mind in recognizing patterns and creating repetition. The more we repeat a pattern, the less attention we have to pay to it, thus freeing up the brain to focus on additional information.

Another activity that activates the reward pathway is feeling progress because it encourages persistence, which also is critical to survival. Video games capitalize on this, which is one reason they are highly engaging. Players are motivated to get to the next level or to get medallions or badges.

Metaphors, stories, and demonstrations are rewarding to the brain and tie into our natural way of learning. Metaphors, analogies, parables, and similes have persisted throughout human history. Metaphor taps into a large neural network. Researchers in Japan found metaphor-activated areas beyond the traditional language areas of the brain. When you think of a metaphor, it can call up visual, auditory, and other sensory information. Neurologist Krish Sathian at Emory University found that metaphors involving the sense of touch activated the same areas of the brain as if one actually felt the texture. Using a metaphor links new material to a strong, existing network and contributes to comprehension and recall.

Throughout human history, stories have been powerful. They activate the brain differently than straightforward textual information does, activating multisensory, emotion, and social pathways. Demonstrations are realistic and meaningful, thus rewarding. They also tap into multisensory and social pathways, activating our mirror neurons, which may be a mechanism by which we are naturally wired to learn from others.

Motivation

While the neurotransmitter dopamine has long been associated with pleasure, a recent study concludes that dopamine's effect is more likely the motivation to act. Neuroscientist Alison Adcock finds that it encourages us to act, either approaching or avoiding. Seeing patterns and figuring things out also activate the reward pathway. It is linked to persistence. Since this chemical varies from person to person, it might help explain why some people are more persistent or more motivated than others. Two psychologists at the University of Rochester, Edward Deci and Richard Ryan, find that motivation increases with control and autonomy.

Research studies are revealing that extrinsic rewards such as grades and treats are not as motivating as intrinsic rewards such as doing something for its own sake.

Psychologists Edward Deci and colleagues examined 128 studies on this topic and found that all external, tangible, or expected rewards undermined free-choice intrinsic motivation. They also found that positive feedback enhanced motivation and interest. Other research shows that unexpected rewards release dopamine, as when we get a treat for no reason.

Rigor

Recently scientist Kelly Lambert discovered what he believes is an additional part of the reward pathway activated by effort. Results that come too easily can actually have a negative emotional impact. Lambert hypothesizes that rigor is part of the reward pathway, resulting in a new model of the reward pathway called the *effort-driven-rewards circuit*: an accumbens-striatal-cortical network (not shown) connecting movement, emotion, and thinking. Throughout most of human history, survival was rigorous. Getting and preparing food, for example, required enormous effort. Therefore, a subsequent feeling of pleasure and gratification came from the results of this effort. Think about this in your life. We persist in hobbies and sports that are difficult to learn because the eventual achievement is rewarding.

Scientist Joe Tsien and colleagues found a surprising effect: sometimes dopamine can be released during negative experiences, such as doing or thinking about something scary. Perhaps this relates to the challenge aspect.

You can help your students get dopamine from the good experiences in school because dopamine is also released when learning is pleasurable—that is, rewarding. Real learning, a feeling of understanding and engagement, is rewarding. Unfortunately, much of the way we are required to learn is not so rewarding.

What Does This Mean for Educators?

The brain's reward system is what keeps people hooked on video games, Sudoku, and addictions, such as gambling or shopping. This reward pathway is a potentially powerful pathway for us to leverage for education. The wonderful news is that some academic activities have been found to activate this powerful pathway, and one of those is learning. In fact, the experience of learning is pleasurable for everyone. This effect makes sense: we couldn't survive if we didn't learn. When students have a sense that they have learned something, they feel great. Too many times, though, the learning process is so frustrating or so easy that they do not get to the reward at the end. An appropriate challenge level of about 80 percent success is rewarding: that is, a student is able to answer approximately 80 percent of the answers correctly, meaning it is not too easy or too hard.

Activating Reward

The need to make sense and see patterns increases reward and motivation, but often curricula and especially textbooks are not designed that way. We have tried so hard to make learning easy that we may have robbed it of reward and pleasure. Thinking and struggling with material for a bit is not a bad thing. All too often students are told to memorize the answer and move on. Rushing through curriculum, however, does not allow students time to process, struggle, achieve, and feel rewarded.

A sense of progress is highly motivating. Think about when you finish a project or large task and you have a sense that you have made progress. Currently our educational system is not built around individual progress, while the private marketplace has capitalized on this with technology. Online materials often provide a sense of progress through moving to another level—sounds or icons or bars that show progress, for example. Most curricula identify progress as moving to the next grade level, not the sort of progress that releases feel-good chemicals. However, many online courses give this sense of progress because a student moves ahead to more and more challenging material in progressing through the course at his or her own rate. Hopefully, more individualized, progress-at-your-own-rate software that makes student progress more visible will become available.

Motivation

Schools are typically places where students have very little control, even at the college level, and yet control increases motivation. (My motivation and learning really accelerated in my doctoral program because I had more freedom to choose topics along the lines of my individual interest.) Control and self-efficacy are important not only to increasing motivation but also to reducing stress (see chapter 3). However, since that isn't the way most of our educational system is designed, our current system often works against motivation.

Our current system often works against motivation.

While many people think of motivation as associated with tangible rewards, such as praise, money, and good grades, intrinsic reward—a job well done, satisfaction—is stronger and more durable than those extrinsic rewards. However, teachers (and parents too) find it difficult to affect the intrinsic and often rely instead on the extrinsic, external reward to motivate. This reliance has its dangers: it has been shown that once a student works for a reward, he or she begins to lose the enjoyment of the activity itself. For example, a student may love coloring or journaling and do it for hours, but according to research, once we pay them to do it, they spend less time on it and report less enjoyment. This can apply to learning and school work in general: a student who is working for an external reward such as a grade could lose interest in the process. Psychologist Elizabeth Gunderson at Temple University found that toddlers who heard praise directed at *effort* rather than results were more likely to pick more challenging tasks and to believe that they could improve with effort. She calls it "process praise" ("you are improving") as opposed to "person praise" ("you are so smart"), which results in decreased performance and less persistence.

We have to think about how we use rewards in the educational system. Grades may not be the best way to motivate students and do not always represent students' abilities, but experiments with other methods have not led to an overhaul of this system. If we can't change that system, let's increase the reward in other ways.

We need to recognize the importance of rigor. Rewarding everyone for participating is not as rewarding as acknowledging rigorous achievement. I am not arguing for more competitive environments but for environments where we expect much from our students. Enhancing learning through brain-friendly strategies may be more fun, but it is not less rigorous. Homework menus do not mean that assignments are frivolous or that students can pick something "easy." Rigorous standards should apply throughout a school as a matter of pride and because rigor is rewarding. Rigor is motivating. and motivation leads to achievement.

Leaping into the Classroom

Students are not motivated when their reward pathway is not engaged. It is hard for a student to be motivated about behaviors that are not rewarding when he or she could engage instead in so many rewarding alternatives, such as video games, eating, and socializing. The good news is that many classroom activities are rewarding, as is

Multiple Pathways to the Student Brain

learning. Many behaviors that activate the reward pathway can be adapted easily for lessons, activities, assignments, and classroom environment. We can increase motivation by integrating these behaviors and conditions.

Activating Reward

We know that metaphors are rewarding. Since they can tie into existing networks and this connection is important to learning, we need to put metaphors into our teaching. Children are very metaphorical and the love of metaphors seems to persist, so we see implications for early childhood through adulthood.

Before presenting a lesson, try to come up with a metaphor, parable, or analogy to make an initial connection to the material. You are not always the one who needs to come up with a metaphor to explain what you are teaching. The students can do it. Add to your homework menu an option to explain a concept that was taught in terms of a metaphor. If students select this option, you have teaching material for the next semester.

In this book, I use the metaphor of an orchestra—that is, we teachers orchestrate the lesson. Most, maybe all, readers have a strong neural network on orchestra. You know what it is and a few facts about it, and you may have seen an orchestra. You can picture it. Attaching what you learn about the brain to this existing network not only helps you remember the new material but helps you make more sense of it. When I say that the frontal lobe is the conductor of the brain, you learn something about the frontal lobe before I even start explaining based on what you already know about a conductor. This is powerful.

Good teachers tells stories. Stories put information into a more emotional and meaningful context, and everyone loves them. Do not hesitate to tell your stories to your students. Better yet, perhaps you can turn the lesson into a story. Start with a question—a problem to solve. Then talk about how the problem was solved. You can tell a fascinating story about the author, the historical figure, or the scientist behind what you are learning. Tap into this powerful genre, and you tap into the reward pathway.

The trend now is toward more nonfiction in school readings, but we must not forget the importance of stories, this ancient human genre. Presenting nonfiction such as history in story form can be a powerful form of teaching.

Although there is a great deal of talk in education circles about hands-on learning, most schools are not including demonstrations to the degree that they could.

Demonstrations can be effective in many content areas, not just ones associated with hands-on learning. They can be done in many ways and not just by you. With technology, demonstrations are easier than ever before. Find an expert on YouTube to demonstrate something that you are teaching. Again, think about the homework menu. For example, determine what a student could demonstrate to classmates based on a lesson and make that an option. You do not have to use class time for this; students can make a video, for example, out of school. (Because of the social nature of demonstrations, I explore this topic in more detail in chapter 8.)

If helping someone else and working together cooperatively are shown to increase pleasure and motivation, we want to build that into classroom practices. Certainly an attitude of cooperation rather than competition should be fostered in the classroom, and group work is the most common way to increase cooperation (this is explored extensively in chapter 8). One of the best study techniques is teaching material to another, an activity that increases reward, retention, and comprehension of material. We can offer that as a homework option in which students sign into a lab and tutor others or videotape themselves tutoring a student for a grade.

Using Pattern Detection

When we make sense of something, figure something out, solve a puzzle, or see a pattern, we get an aha! moment. The brain rewards us by making us feel good for figuring something out so that we will continue to try to make sense of our world. That is why people who are very busy still take time to work jigsaw or crossword puzzles or Sudoku, or play the electronic game Words With Friends, Candy Crush, and other games. Finding that missing piece or the right number or word provides a chemical reward to our brain, thus making the puzzle an enjoyable pastime.

The brain gets pleasure from working hard to figure something out or make sense of something, but here's the kicker: when teachers create a handout for the class outlining everything students need to know for the unit so they can memorize the information, we have robbed students of the joy of learning. The joy of learning comes from figuring something out. If we want learning to be engaging, then we can capitalize on this pathway—one of the most important pathways in the brain—by requiring students to figure things out rather than memorizing answers. Memorizing some material is important for educated citizens; however, in many cases memorization is not always essential in a given instance based on future goals. Memorizing formulas or rules does not give the brain pleasure. However, looking at many examples of a rule or formula and figuring out the formula does. And this is the kind of memory that lasts beyond the test. Think of lessons in terms of

Think of lessons in terms of patterns and puzzles.

patterns and puzzles. Create puzzles or something for learners to figure out as they work with the material in a unit. Many teachers use graphic organizers. These visual resources are very helpful, but maybe not as much as they could be if we hand them out to the students already completed. "Here, students, is what you need to know for this chapter. Go memorize it," is how one professor of mine approached the textbook content with his graphic organizers and notes. My task was to memorize, and it was not rewarding. You can use graphic organizers, but have the students create them or make incomplete ones for them to search and complete. Have them look for patterns (such as three causes, or two steps, or three examples). They will listen better if their brain is searching for answers rather than following along on notes handed out before the lecture or slide handouts.

As you create a lesson, put this powerful pathway in the forefront of your mind. Ask yourself, *What part of the lesson can students figure out themselves?* For example, in teaching math, we typically ask students to memorize a formula and then apply it. Instead, illustrate the area of a rectangle with multiple drawings. Eventually students can figure out that the answer comes from simply multiplying one side by the other side—length times width. They see it, they work with it, they determine the meaning, and they understand it. Then the formula is easy for them to recall.

Giving students multiple examples and having them come up with the formula is exciting and rewarding to them. They can also test their hypothesis about the rule governing all the examples. Put their ideas on the board, generate more examples, and test the hypothesis. You can also put students in groups to brainstorm further. Once they figure it out for themselves, there is no need to memorize, and the application is easily accomplished.

All students engage in the quest to discover the key that unlocks learning. It may take them some time and scaffolding is helpful with this. Figuring things out is high cognitive load (chapter 7), so guiding them and providing help along the way is important.

This method can also be used when teaching grammar rules or other overriding principles in other subjects. For example, in an English class, ask, "Class, what is the pattern in this list?"

Boy runs, boys run

Girl walks, girls walk

Cow grazes, cows graze

They may not understand plural/singular or subject/object yet, but that is not the point. They are looking for a pattern. Eventually a student realizes that every pair contains an *s*. We formulate a rule that every pair must have an *s*. Next have students list on the board as many examples as they can and test this hypothesis. Eventually someone will list an exception, such as *mouse/mice*. Explain that rules often have exceptions, and for now you are going to put those words on another board or somewhere less prominent. Continue listing and adding exceptions to the exception list. Students will soon see there are more examples following the rule than there are exceptions. By the time you have a significant list, everyone should understand the rule and be able to generate an example.

Then tell the students to check their latest writing assignment: they are to examine similar types of word pairs and look for an *s*. Then they will figure out that the placement of the *s* depends on how many are involved. The next step is for them to discuss the number: the difference between the first and second set. Now introduce the concept of singular and plural. Finally, use this same example to have them discover the concept of subject and object. After generating numerous examples, the students should begin to see some pattern between the first and second word in each pair of words. Later you can use this strategy to help them figure out subject and object.

Humans learn language by seeing patterns is a powerful and natural way of learning. Alison Gopnik's book *The Scientist in the Crib* describes how infants derive the principles of language sounds and phonemes from hearing many, many examples and formulating the rules implicitly. We learn a great deal in this manner, such as how to tell the difference between a dog and a cat. It isn't from the definition but by formulating a concept implicitly from many examples.

I call this *backward teaching*, or inductive teaching, because it is the reverse of the way most textbooks teach. James Zull, the cell biologist at Case Western University who wrote *The Art of Changing the Brain: Enriching Teaching by Exploring the Biology of Learning*, suggests teaching from experience first and then information. Textbooks traditionally start with a definition or concept, then an explanation; then they give examples and ask students to do problems or answer questions. Effective teaching reverses this process.

In the traditional method, the word and definition presented initially are basically meaningless. If students do not immediately grasp the material (and I think often when they do, it is because they have figured it out themselves already and have a neural network in place formed from prior experience), it is meaningless. The examples often remain meaningless too because learners do not fully understand the examples. Then we wonder why they can't answer the simple questions in the book because, we think, we just taught it to them. Because learning means making meaning and meaning comes from making connections, connect the examples to real experience first, and then give formal definitions after the students figure out the principle.

This can apply to teaching essay writing. Give the students a handout with questions such as, "What is the main idea?" and "What are the details?" before you teach the main idea or details. Give them a chance to see if they can recognize, guess, and figure out the difference between main idea and detail. If one person sees the pattern, that becomes the explicit lesson.

Provide examples from the first lesson of what a passing essay would look like. There may be objections that this approach would stifle students' creativity, and it is correct that this approach would not work with creative writing, but for most purposes it will. My college instructors graded our final essays on a strict rubric; if that is the case in your class, show the students the rubric and essays matching it. This is how they will learn—through patterning and modeling. Show them the goal first. This is experience and creating prior knowledge because *we* have had experience reading and writing essays but they may have never seen an essay or the ones they have seen are far above their skill at this point. College professor Vicki Moulson suggests giving students the rubric and having them grade sample essays and make comments as if they were the instructor. If you test with essay questions, show them appropriate answers for an essay question, albeit on a different topic from what you are testing.

One of my most memorable teaching moments was a developmental composition class with only seven students at night. It was the hardest class I ever taught. Why? The students had been out of school a long time and were very afraid. In addition, they had no idea what an *essay* was and assumed it must be some high-falutin' college thing far beyond their ability. The requirement was for them to write an essay with a main idea and details in order to pass the required exit exam. No matter how much I tried to get them to start simple with a brief main idea and some details, they would go along with me and then when it came to writing the "essay," they would revert back to writing random meaningless sentences with no coherence that they thought sounded like an essay. There was no logic, organization, or purpose to the piece.

One night I brought in an article from *Time* magazine debating whether boxing should be made illegal due to blood flow and blood-borne disease and asked them to discuss it. They were so engaged that at one point, a very tall woman and a small man were standing nose to nose and arguing. I intervened and said, "No one can hear another's viewpoint, so I will make you a deal. You write down your argument and I will read it and everyone will have to listen." They wrote feverishly and enthusiastically. Then I read their essays—their argumentative essays. They were very good, and when I said to them, "Now these are essays!" the most argumentative man said, "You mean that is what writing is—putting your ideas on paper? I can do that." And so he did, and he passed the course. This is the power of making an experience realistic and meaningful.

Sensing Progress

You can capitalize on another behavior that increases reward: a sense of progress. Getting a better grade on a test than the one before does not really accomplish a sense of progress. It needs to be more immediate and yet ongoing. One way to encourage students to have a sense of progress is to have them talk about their performance, for example, how they have improved. Rather than looking for competition with other students, encourage students to compete against their own previous performance, stopping from time to time to become aware of their progress.

Often we do not notice our own progress; we think only of the current effort or frustration. I often have more on my to-do list than I can possibly do and the list just keeps accumulating, so I eventually feel I am getting nowhere (no doubt this happens to you too!). One day I started keeping a progress notebook: every evening I wrote down what I had accomplished (as opposed to only facing the never-ending to-do list). I was amazed at my progress. My motivation increased, and every day I felt rewarded as I realized I was actually moving forward.

Having students take a moment to write about how their skills have progressed in the course so far can be helpful. If your students keep a journal, once a week they can write a few sentences about the progress they made that week. Maybe their grades weren't better this time, but they completed three of the assignments instead of only one as they had previously. Maybe their attendance was better. Any kind of progress counts. Everyone should be able to find at least one thing that signifies progress.

Increasing Motivation

Motivation is important to learning. When activated, the reward pathway releases dopamine, a chemical involved in motivation. Therefore, using strategies that are rewarding and release dopamine are likely to increase motivation.

One way to increase motivation is to make the information connect to real life—relevant and meaningful. You can imagine why the brain would respond more positively and release pleasurable chemicals to something meaningful: it might be important for survival. We need to do a better job of this. The current division between school and community is part of this problem. Getting students out into the community in project-based or service-based learning can tap into this pathway. Projects involving creating web pages, working on a student newspaper, doing art projects for the school, or making a project for the science fair can be relevant and meaningful. Students know when they are being taught to the test, and this approach reduces the relevance and meaningfulness that drives powerful long-term memory.

Psychologist Christopher Hulleman at the University of Maryland discovered a way to create motivation through journal writing that was especially helpful for students who had low expectations of success. He had half the students write a summary of material and the other half write about how the material related to their lives. He did this throughout the entire semester. The students who made connections between real life and the material outperformed those who reviewed the material through summary writing.

The students who made connections between real life and the material outperformed those who reviewed the material through summary writing.

We can have students make this connection in various ways throughout the semester—for example, with group discussion, journal entries, or a bonus two-point essay question. I suspect it is more effective when the students find the connection themselves rather than an instructor telling them the material is meaningful to real life, although we need to do that too. Ideally this would be when the material in that moment actually is relevant to real life, such as realistic activities and projects. For example, if the lesson is to calculate the area of a rectangle, have the students measure their bedroom and determine how much carpet they would need to buy.

Sometimes material is not meaningful because we are teaching outside a meaningful context. We are teaching details, not the big picture, but the brain sees the big picture and the details. As instructors, we need to provide both parts, but sometimes we fail to connect the details to the big picture. This mistake can be as simple as teaching a math formula without ever explaining why it would be helpful in real life or when it would be applied to real situations. Word problems are often used to make meaning, but they are often meaningless to students, such as if you were on a train going 50 miles an hour in one direction and your friend was—you get the picture. When would they need that? If they need to know how to calculate trains moving in different directions, under what circumstances would that be? Or is it the underlying calculation that is important. If so, when?

Showing a movie putting a historical period in context prior to teaching the details of a war or the culture or art history makes the learning more meaningful. Ask yourself, *What is this information part of? How does it fit into a bigger context or meaning? What problem (survival) did this solve for a group of people?* Tying new material into a bigger picture also leads to a more developed and stronger neural network of connections, thus making it easier for students to understand and retrieve information.

Feeling that we are empowered, have some control, and can handle what comes up (self-efficacy) creates motivation. One of the ways to give students a sense of control and self-efficacy is to provide a sense of choice in the classroom. This can be done by offering a homework menu. Another option is letting students select whether they want to work the odd- or even-numbered problems (when we typically assign either odd or even ourselves). Ask them to pick which chapter or section of a chapter they are going to be the miniexpert on. Let them decide whether they want to create a mind map or an outline. Once you put the concept of offering a choice in the forefront of your mind when you are planning lessons, you will find many ways to increase motivation through this option.

Promoting Rigor

Scientists have postulated that rigor is part of the reward pathway: when we achieve something effortful, dopamine is released, and we feel pleasure. This makes sense for survival because our brain rewards us when we work hard to accomplish something. We therefore need to put more emphasis on rigor in the classroom. Think about why you would choose a five-hundred-piece jigsaw puzzle over a ten-piece one you could put together without much effort. It is the effort that is part of the reward. There really is no reward for doing something so easy. The harder we work for something, the bigger the payoff is emotionally when we achieve it. Discuss rigor and effort with students in your class. Talk about not giving up easily, about resilience and bouncing back, and knowing when to abandon one strategy and try another one.

When I discuss diversifying strategies or providing options to reach diverse and struggling learners, I am not talking about lowering standards. Rigor is essential. High standards in the class imply that students are capable of high achievement. Teachers shouldn't reward or praise routine work. Instead we reward and praise improvement and progress or exceptional quality. Every student encounters success and challenge. Material that is graduated in terms of difficulty can be rewarding to students when they understand they might not get all the way to the end, but it would be exciting if they could! This also keeps more successful students challenged while others are working with more difficulty on the first questions.

Empower students by teaching them that they can change their brain with effort. This is what to reinforce in school: effort and the attempts to change the brain, not the fixed result on an activity or test at one point in time. Since progress is highly reward-ing to the brain, direct the praise toward effort and progress rather than results. I am not saying that every child gets a trophy for effort, because that waters down the reward. Praise given after a special effort or step forward is more helpful than generic praise overused. Indeed, one of the faults I find with our current system is the overuse of praise and the meaningless distribution of awards and trophies so no one feels left out. I suspect the person receiving the "everyone gets something" trophy does not get the feel-good chemical result that comes from knowing he or she surpassed expec-tations and rose to a challenge. We may be robbing students of real reward. For a reward to be real, it must release feel-good chemicals in the brain.

Students need to know that learning is effortful. Otherwise they are just firing what is already wired. I think that we have tried so hard to make learning easier that we have removed the challenge and the rigor that provide the intrinsic reward of achievement. The reward creates lifelong learners.

• • •

These first four chapters have focused on preparing students mentally, experientially, and emotionally in order to make the most of the learning you will orchestrate. Chapter 5 looks at two invisible processes that underlie and greatly affect achievement: attention and memory.

HOMEWORK MENU

- Create a service project related to the lesson. Explain the process and outcome of your project, and present it to the instructor for approval.

- Create a web page useful to others in studying this material. Provide links to explanatory sources, visuals, and definitions.

- Find three YouTube videos that teach this material. Write a summary of the videos, and then critique them. Find one new fact in each video.

- Pick one chapter or topic in the syllabus that you are going to be the expert on. Begin researching it now, and prepare to present the information to the class in the format that you choose: oral report, video, PowerPoint, web page, Pinterest page, or something else.

- Volunteer to help another student in the class prepare for the test. Plan to spend two hours with them. Turn in a description of how you will work with the student.

- Find three ways this unit is applicable outside school, and present those examples however you wish.

- Find a metaphor that explains the lesson and present it in one of these:
  — Essay
  — Video
  — Poster

- Turn the lesson into a story. Present this story in one of these:
  — Written format
  — A play on a video

- Do a demonstration on video or in class as per instructor.

SUGGESTED STRATEGIES

- Praise effort, not outcome.
- Praise the performance, not the person.
- Provide a sense of progress.
- Use graphic organizers that students complete.
- Let students attempt to figure out problems before you teach formulas or rules.
- Turn lessons into puzzles.
- Provide experience first, then the vocabulary or details.
- Focus on the pattern or the relationships in the lesson.
- Make the connection to real life.
- Provide choices in assignments and assessments.
- Tell a story.
- Do a demonstration.
- Provide a metaphor.

REFLECT AND CONNECT

What strategies have you used to increase motivation and engagement?

In light of what you have learned in this chapter, how would you adapt or change those strategies?

How have you used metaphors, stories, or demonstrations?

List one example of each that you can incorporate into an upcoming lesson.

Can you think of a specific lesson you have taught that would benefit from teaching backward, that is, requiring the student to figure out the concept? Describe how you taught the lesson previously and how you would do it differently now.

SUGGESTED READING

Gilbert, D. T. (2006). *Stumbling on happiness.* New York: Knopf.

Gopnik, A., Meltzoff, A. N., & Kuhl, P. K. (2001). *The scientist in the crib: What early learning tells us about the mind.* New York, NY: HarperCollins.

Hanson, R. (2009). *Buddha's brain: The practical neuroscience of happiness, love, and wisdom.* Oakland, CA: New Harbinger.

Kohn, A. (1999). *Punished by rewards: The trouble with gold stars, incentive plans, A's, praise, and other bribes.* Boston, MA: Houghton Mifflin.

Mellin, L. (2010). *Wired for joy: A revolutionary method for creating happiness from within.* Carlsbad, CA: Hay House.

Tamblyn, D. (2003). *Laugh and learn: 95 ways to use humor for more effective teaching and training.* New York, NY: AMACOM.

Wallenstein, G. (2009). *The pleasure instinct: Why we crave adventure, chocolate, pheromones, and music.* Hoboken, NJ: Wiley.

Zull, J. E. (2002). *The art of changing the brain: Enriching teaching by exploring the biology of learning.* Sterling, VA: Stylus.

The Attention and Memory Pathways

There is some kind of disconnect between what I ask students to do and what happens. Let me give an example. Yesterday I gave the following instructions: "For homework, go to page 169 at the end of chapter 4. Answer the even-numbered questions for section A and the odd-numbered questions for section B. Then select one of the five problems in the third section. This is due Wednesday." Right away, hands go up. "What did you say?" Then others don't turn in homework because they didn't understand the assignment. Others do the wrong questions. What is the problem? Are they not listening? Do some have attention deficit? Are these excuses?

MAKING CONNECTIONS

What does it really mean to pay attention? Is there more than one kind of attention? What can you do to help students pay attention? What is the difference between short-term memory, working memory, and long-term memory? How does a memory become long term? Are you creating working memory problems for your students?

Attention and working memory may be two of the most critical brain processes with regard to learning. Recent research reveals that these processes underlie many learning difficulties misperceived as reading or math deficits.

In the 1500s Juan Luis Vives, often referred to as the "father of modern psychology" for his integration of medicine, emotion, memory, and learning, found that the more someone paid attention to stimuli, the better he or she would remember the stimuli. He thus discovered the link between attention and memory. Over time, psychology, cognitive psychology, and eventually neuroscience developed our understanding of this complex attention and working memory mechanism. Researchers Adam Gazzaley, a neuroscientist at the University of California, and Anna Nobre, a psychology researcher at the University of Oxford, found that attention and working memory—information held temporarily in order to work with it—are overlapping pathways in which sensory cortex, prefrontal, and parietal regions all work together. Interestingly, they believe that one of the reasons older adults have trouble with working memory is due to their impaired selective attention processing, particularly with regard to ignoring distractions. Paying attention is critical to holding something in working memory, which is necessary before it can be moved to long-term memory. Nobel Prize–winning neuroscientist Eric Kandel argues that one of the most important neuroscience issues is discovering how attention affects memory.

You read in chapter 1 that learning means creating networks in the brain. These networks develop as a result of behavior—what you do, think, study, practice, and especially pay attention to. Of course, the sensory motor system (chapter 2) affects what we pay attention to, as does emotion (chapter 3). We pay attention to rewarding behaviors as well (chapter 4). These pathways all work together and underlie students' behaviors in an invisible way. Attention and memory are highly complex and have been categorized in inconsistent ways. We are going to look at some of the more common terms and basic processes in this chapter.

ATTENTION

What Does the Research Say?

Attention is the act of selectively attending to some stimuli rather than other stimuli. It may surprise you to know it does not mean taking in more information: it means taking in less. We could be paying attention to thousands of things from the sensory motor input (everything we see, hear, feel, taste, smell, and touch) or from all our memories and emotions. Attention is the mechanism by which the brain conserves

its resources and focuses on specific information. This affects what we actually see and hear.

Attention is an important factor in changing
the brain as a result of learning or practice. We
say that experience changes the brain, but it is
often only the part of experience we are paying
attention to that changes the brain.

It is often only the part of experience we are paying attention to that changes the brain.

Attention Networks

According to renowned attention researcher Michael Posner, there are three attention networks in the brain—the alerting network, the orienting network, and the
executive attention network—and they are neurochemically different.

First, attention is captured by the *alerting network*. This attention network, also
often called *captured attention*, occurs when something happens that alerts us to pay
attention. This is also called *bottom-up processing, stimulus-driven attention*, or *exogenous attention* because the attention pathway is engaged by specific external stimuli.
Then the chemical norepinephrine, a transmitter of arousal, is secreted. You ask, for
example, "What was that loud bang? Are we in danger? Was it a car backfire or a
gunshot?" If you are studying in a construction zone, loud bangs and crashes may
not activate the alerting network, but if you are in a quiet spot in your home and you
hear glass breaking, you are going to lose focus and the alerting network will take
over—as it should. This alerting network actually diminishes the activation of the
selective attention network critical to academic success.

This second network, the *orienting network*, is important to academics because
it is where we consciously decide to focus on something to the exclusion of other
things. As you might expect, orienting involves visual and auditory regions, as well
as the parietal cortex (figure 6.4) and superior colliculus (not shown). It is controlled
by the person, not the external environment. This happens when you are searching
for a friend's face in a crowd. You don't notice the other faces or what is going on
around you because you have narrowed your focus to look for specific stimuli—for
example, your brown-haired tall female friend.

The third type is the *executive attention network*. Once we have oriented to
the desired object, we engage our attention pathway to focus on this. This is also
called *top-down processing*, since the conscious mind itself is engaging the attention

Figure 5.1 Some Areas of Function Associated with Attention and Memory

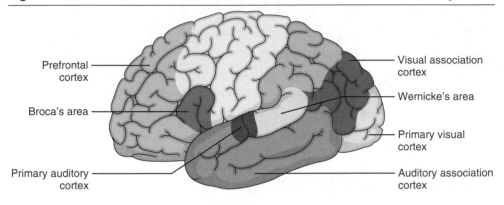

Prefrontal cortex

Broca's area

Primary auditory cortex

Visual association cortex

Wernicke's area

Primary visual cortex

Auditory association cortex

pathway. It is also called *goal-driven attention, endogenous attention*, and *executive attention*. This is the opposite of being distracted. This attention network is driven by dopamine, a transmitter involved in interest and pleasure. Since this is also called the executive network, you can guess it is mediated primarily by the frontal lobe, particularly the prefrontal cortex (figure 5.1). This is the type of attention most associated with working memory and the encoding of long-term memory. For example, researchers Do-Joon Yi and Marvin Chun, researchers in the Yale Visual Cognitive Neuroscience Laboratory, showed people overlapping scenes and faces. It turns out that their subjects could remember only what they were paying attention to—the faces *or* the scenes. Even repetition didn't help if they were not consciously paying attention to the specific thing.

This network is impaired in attention-deficit hyperactivity disorder, autism, and anxiety and has been associated with lower socioeconomic status. An interesting study by Imran Dhamani, a speech, language, and linguistics researcher at Macquarie University in Australia, of children who had trouble listening in a noisy classroom were found to have nothing at all wrong with their hearing. They had trouble switching attention when there were multiple talkers—problems with their top-down executive functioning.

Focused Versus Divided Attention

Another way researchers categorize attention is focused versus divided attention. Focused attention is optimal when we find we have lost ourselves in something, losing track of time because we are so focused. We see examples of this when someone is watching sports or playing video games and you call and call his or her name and get no response. David Simon's lab, widely known for research on selective attention, has shown the impact of selective attention in the famous gorilla basketball video discussed in chapter 2. The extreme form of focused attention is that of experienced meditators. In focused attention, you determine what does and does not get your resources—your attention—and you are able to screen the unimportant information out. This ability is critical to academic achievement.

On the other end of the spectrum is extensive multitasking, in which attention may be divided among two, three, four, or even more objects, such as studying while the TV, instant messaging, e-mail, and other social media all compete for attention in the moment. When you choose to multitask, you are choosing to divide up your attention. Students claim they are experts at it, but the research says something quite different. Psychologist David Sanbonmatsu at the University of Utah claims that those who multitask the most are actually the worst at it. Ironically, the ones who were the best at multitasking did it the least! Why would they do it the least? Because they are better at focusing attention, they do not want to be distracted. Those who multitask may actually be worse at focusing attention, which is why they multitask.

Those who multitask the most are actually the worst at it.

What Does This Mean for Educators?

Chapter 1 discussed the importance of neurons firing together in order to wire learning. As it turns out, attention is key to this. If the person is attending to the stimulus, the firing will be stronger than if the person is simply aware of the stimulus. We talk about paying attention, but most of us do not teach faculty and students about the nature of attention and how it strengthens learning. We complain about students who have trouble with attention, but most of us do not include attention training in our curriculum although it benefits all learners.

It is possible to direct children's attention beginning in infancy. In early childhood, we must help children develop effortful control in which they are able to sustain their attention for longer periods because this skill is critical to academic achievement.

Performing tasks that require sustained attention improves attention. Music training and meditation have been scientifically shown to improve attention, and attention is critical to achievement, yet most schools do not offer these. Sports, yoga, martial arts, and tai chi require sustained and selective attention, thus improving attention. All students, especially students with attention difficulty, should be directed to these activities to strengthen their attention.

Leaping into the Classroom

What you pay attention to gets a stronger chemical reaction with stronger firing in the brain. This has many implications for the classroom. We must direct students' attention. At the beginning of the semester, we must teach students how attention works and that they control it with their mind. They direct attention as a way of using their brain's resources. Tell them during a lesson what specifically it is in that lesson they should be paying attention to. Early Childhood and English as a Second Language teacher Cindy Seiger suggests that actively involving students in the process of learning about attention can pique their interest in the topic. As the students become secure at learning about attention, you could engage them in activities to lengthen the time they are using their attention in a variety of ways.

Alerting

Classrooms often have many distractions that can activate the alerting network. Some students with attention problems are easily distracted. Scientists would say they are stimulus driven, meaning they react to incoming stimuli, such as noises and movement and other distractions, rather than controlling their attention and staying focused. When someone walks into the room while students are taking a timed test, for example, test takers will stop and look up even though time is of the essence. This is a survival mechanism that is hard to override. People coming and going may be distracting to some people; others acclimate and can work in a busy atmosphere such as a coffee shop. Distraction is more about the unexpectedness of the stimulus than the actual stimulus. Prepare your students for this response, especially when standardized testing is coming up, by giving them practice in ignoring distractions.

Students need an appropriate state of arousal (alertness, wakefulness) for optimal attention. If they have too little arousal, they may not alert to incoming stimuli. Before orienting students' attention, you may want to tell them to sit up and at least act as if they are interested (said with a smile) and then the feed-backward system may give them more arousal. Attention problems can be caused by too much arousal as well, as with anxiety (chapter 3).

Orienting

The orienting network is important in the classroom because this is the stage at which students consciously direct their attention toward the task at hand. It makes sense to explicitly tell students what to focus on. Many students with attention issues have difficulty because they are taking in too much, not too little. You can help them by directing their attention and suggesting they control it in a certain fashion. Pointing to the material on the board or having younger students put their finger on the graph they are looking at in the book, and saying, "Now listen carefully to my next sentence," are all ways of helping students to orient their attention.

Many students with attention issues have difficulty because they are taking in too much, not too little.

Selectively Attending

The third pathway is the most critical for academic tasks: selective attention, that is, ignoring distractions. The key here is focus. The student must focus intently long enough for changes to take place in the brain. It may be that problems in attention underlie what appear to be problems in math, reading, or other textbook comprehension. Clearly, improving attention in our students is critical to their ability to learn. The good news is that the ability to selectively focus can be improved with practice. Explicit instruction in attention may be as important as content. Repeated attention to the learning process is essential. Draw attention to students' strategies, a metacognitive assessment (see chapter 7) of their performance, and specific aspects of content.

Divided Attention: Multitasking

Multitasking reduces the amount of attention that an individual can pay to a task. In one study, scientist Harold Pashler found that multitasking with just two competing tasks caused IQ in adults to drop to that of an eight-year-old. (Imagine if you divided your attention among several tasks!) Do an Internet search for Stroop task (an entertaining and informative activity that creates divided attention) and take the test to experience the effects of divided attention. Have your students take this test too, either online or using a handout you print from the site, so they can experience the negative effects of multitasking. You and they will find the task is slow, effortful, and full of errors because their attention was divided.

Students commonly assert that they are great multitaskers, but the research does not support this claim. Teachers are quite familiar with students' assertions that they study better when listening to music. But music with words creates a Stroop effect with a verbal task that interferes with another verbal task and uses some of the brain's resources and attention that are then not available for the task at hand.

Teach students about the negative effects of multitasking by using a metaphor of comparing attention to money in their pocket. If you spend some of it on small, inexpensive items, you may not have enough money left to purchase a costly item you really wanted. Ask them, "How are you spending your attention in the moment? If your attention was represented by $100 in your pocket while you are studying, where is the money being spent?" Estimate that $20 was spent in the background with your auditory system taking in music. Then interruptions of instant messaging, very distracting and engaging, were taking about $30. Another $20 is taken up with environmental stimuli in the background, such as the coffee shop or public area where you may be studying. If your cell phone is on, another $10 might be devoted to text messages coming across. Finally, "you've got mail" pings take another $15. You now have only $5 left for studying! "In other words," tell your students, "only 5 percent of your attention may be on the material. Therefore, think about what distractions you can remove. As you remove items, add up the percentages now available to you. You might still have environmental noise, but much can be removed, leaving you a greater percentage of attention for your task."

The effect of this divided attention is to decrease performance, not just waste time. Remind students to ask themselves the purpose of the primary task they are doing. Is it to remember something for a test, get accurate answers to math problems, or comprehend difficult material, for example. Then ask them if accuracy and quality of performance are important? If the answer is yes, then turn off everything else. Yes, they will argue that they study better with music on. And sometimes it may be true, as when they are using one distractor, such as music, to block out something which would be even more distracting, such as conversation in a coffee shop, for example.

Advise them to make intelligent choices. They will see that different circumstances warrant alternative behaviors, and so they should stop and evaluate whether the multitasking could be a distraction.

We can address students' beliefs that they can multitask well by pointing out perhaps it is the inability to control their attention that is occurring rather than high cognitive skill that allows them to multitask. Explain the research and engage them in the Stroop task that shows them what happens when they divide their attention.

There are times when divided attention or multitasking is okay. When we are performing a fluent, effortless task, such as washing dishes, very little attention needs to be paid to the task at hand, freeing up brain resources for thinking about other things. If you are watching a TV show, you may also have enough mental energy to check e-mail. But if you need to provide a thoughtful response, an activity requiring good mental resources, then the TV show may interfere, depending on how much of your attention it takes. Listening to music without words doesn't create much interference on a verbal task. There is a balancing act here of stimuli versus resources.

Divided attention that comes from always being available to e-mail and instant messages creates another impediment: stress. As you read in chapter 3, high stress or chronic stress can have a negative impact on learning. The brain is on alert, especially in individuals with anxiety or posttraumatic stress disorder. Staying on alert with media can have a further impact on the overall load of stress (this is called *allostatic load*), especially when e-mails may be work related and create anxiety or a feeling of being overwhelmed.

Finally, the overall effect of multitasking is mental fatigue. The brain gets tired, and this also has an impact on performance and how long one can work effectively. It can have effects throughout the day as well. If your primary goal is intense thinking, such as writing a grant or a document, or intense learning, then you need to allocate your resources and your mental energy just as you would your physical energy. If you knew you had to be on your feet all evening teaching a course, then you might want to think about how much you were on your feet all day, especially if you had foot pain. Allocate your mental resources as well.

Improving Attention

Selective or executive attention allows students to sustain attention and ignore distractions, a critical skill in academic achievement. When students were required to memorize long poems in school, an excellent memory and attention training activity, the mind had to stay focused. Engaging students in activities requiring focused attention strengthens that network over time. We can teach our students strategies to improve their attention over time and make a difference during a class period as well. Here are a few attention-improving strategies that will work in a classroom:

- Meditation has been scientifically documented to improve attention in as little as fifteen minutes a day over two weeks. Although it is not feasible to devote that amount of class time, a couple of meditation strategies are quick and effective for classroom use and can make a difference during the class period:

  — *Focused attention.* Ask students to look at a designated object in the room. Pick something simple, not a clock or something with words to read. Then ask them to see if they can focus on that object without thinking any thoughts. Start with ten seconds and work them up to a minute as the semester goes on. You can also use sounds instead of an object. If the clock has a loud tick or you can hear birds, ask them to focus on that and clear their mind of thoughts. When thoughts intervene, bring the attention back to the sound.

  — *Mindfulness.* Ask students to try to clear their mind of all thoughts and then be mindful about how their body feels and notice whether thoughts come through. When thoughts do arise, ask them not to react but just to dismiss the thought and clear their mind again by focusing on their senses: feeling the temperature, hearing the sounds, noticing smells and sensations. Tell them to try to focus only on what is coming in through their senses, not through their thoughts. Start with ten seconds and work up to a minute as the semester goes on.

- A few deep breaths can focus attention by reducing arousal. Using a form of breath meditation is quite effective. Have students sit quietly and focus only on breath awareness. Have them mentally follow their breath in and out. Start with ten seconds and work up to a minute.

- Visualization can focus the brain. Ask students to imagine a room in their home. Then imagine a wild monkey comes into the room and begins wreaking monkey havoc. Have them spend about twenty seconds thinking of the damage the monkey could do. Then tell them to stare into the monkey's eyes until it calms down and then imagine the room instantly back to normal. Finally, remind them that their brain can be like a wild monkey.

- Sometimes thoughts of stressful issues interfere with students' ability to pay attention and create stress arousal. When students come into class and you are taking roll or handing out papers, ask students to write down any interfering thoughts in their journal. These may consist of things they have to do later, a worry or concern, or anything else on their mind. Tell them to "leave it on the page" until they leave the classroom and then they can deal with these concerns. It is a kind of clearing of the mind.

Just as with other processes you have learned about so far, attentional control is something that develops over time and varies from individual to individual. It is also affected by the pathways that we have explored in previous chapters and will in the ones that follow in this book.

MEMORY

Working memory is what we are attending to in the moment—holding something in our memory in order to work with it to solve a problem or carry out a task. *Long-term memory* is the stored memory we can access later.

What Does the Research Say?

The brain's capacity at any given time is limited. Yes, we can learn an unlimited amount of information, but we can hold only so much in our mind at one time. Attention is the mechanism that allocates this resource. If attention is divided when memory is being encoded, the

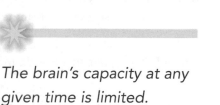

The brain's capacity at any given time is limited.

memory will not be as strong as if it had focused attention. Everything you learned previously in this chapter will have an impact on what you are now going to learn about memory.

The memory process is not well understood. In addition, the terminology has not stabilized, so there is overlap and discrepancy in the categories used to describe types of memories. The discussion in this book results from an examination of proposed memory systems seen in education, psychology, and neuroscience. The goal of this synthesis of the literature on memory is to establish a model that will be helpful to teachers and students by using categories that are meaningful to the learning process and including aspects of memory applicable to teaching and learning.

I will keep it simple. Basically there are three kinds of memory: *episodic* (what we did in the past), *procedural* (how to drive a car or tie your shoes), and *declarative*, sometimes called semantic (facts). We will look primarily at declarative memory since that is the type of memory people use when studying for tests.

Memory begins with sensory input that is strongly affected by attention. The hippocampus (figure 5.2) orchestrates sensory working memory: visual, auditory, and spatial (the location of objects in space) memory. Spatial memory helps us navigate, recall a place, and know where we put our glasses and is typically involved in episodic and procedural memory. Episodic and procedural memory involves the neostriatum (not shown in the figure).

Memory is not a place or a thing, but a process and a distributed network. It involves neurons that are part of many memory networks that overlap and interconnect. Recalling a memory actually involves reconstructing the bits and pieces of a memory from many areas in the brain; therefore, it is often faulty.

The work of Joaquin Furster, a researcher at the Semel Institute for Neuroscience and Human Behavior at the University of California, Los Angeles, supports new models of memory in which memory is a distributed network involving prefrontal and posterior (rear) association areas (figure 5.1). Neuroscientists Arne Ekstrom and his colleagues at the Center for Neuroscience, University of California, Davis, have recently demonstrated that remembering involves simultaneous activity across

Figure 5.2 Regions Involved in Memory

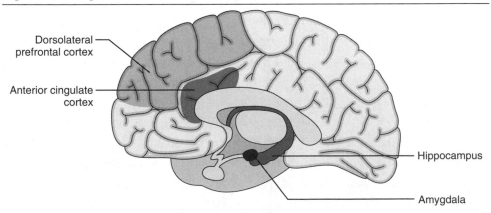

Dorsolateral prefrontal cortex

Anterior cingulate cortex

Hippocampus

Amygdala

multiple brain regions rather than a series of activations following on each other. Furthermore, they found that the medial temporal lobe (near the middle of the temporal lobe) is centrally involved in the network, which substantiated earlier studies. Interestingly, memories of where and when operate at the same time but at different frequencies in the brain. What this means is that memory is more complex than we thought; in fact, students can be affected in many ways.

Kinds of Memory

It is well established that there are two overall kinds of memory: short term and long term. The current terminology for short-term memory, and the one used here, is *working memory*. As the name implies, it is the type of memory held "online" as we actively work with information. Long-term memory is the memory we have stored and can access when needed. These two types of memories use different brain processes. Working memory activates the dorsolateral prefrontal cortex (DLPC) part of the frontal lobe (figure 5.2), along with sensory regions. Long-term memory is stored in various areas, depending on the type of memory. For example, memory that causes fear conditioning (long-term fears) is stored in the amygdala (figure 5.2). It was believed the hippocampus stored fear memories; however, psychologist Ilene Bernstein and colleagues' research indicates the hippocampus processes and transmits the information to the amygdala or the frontal lobe, depending on the type of memory. According to Christine Smith and Larry Squire, researchers in the Memory Research Laboratory at the University of California, San Diego, the age of the memory affects where it is stored.

You read in chapter 1 that thinking and learning are different to the brain. Working memory is like the thinking process in that the neurons are modified temporarily. Long-term memory and learning involve lasting changes and require the creation of new proteins. It is believed these proteins strengthen existing connections and aid in the growth of new connections formed during learning. We will call working memory *firing* and long-term memory *wiring*.

Working Memory

Individuals vary in how much they can hold momentarily in their thoughts while they work with it (i.e., hold in working memory). Working memory seems to increase

Figure 5.3 Changes in Working Memory over the Life Span

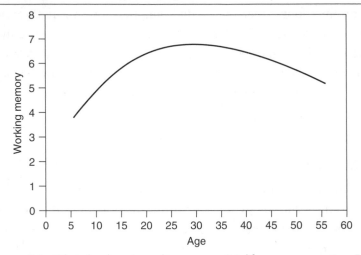

Source: Swanson, H.L., What develops in working memory? A life span perspective. *Developmental Psychology*, 35(4), 986–1000, 1999, American Psychological Association, reprinted with permission

from around ages seven to twenty-two according to psychiatrist Hower Kwon at Stanford, while education researcher Lee Swanson indicates it peaks around age thirty (figure 5.3). Some students have learning differences that can have a negative impact on their working memory capacity, and anxiety in any student can interfere with working memory. Other research has found that students with less working memory capacity had a harder time focusing their attention and keeping it focused than did those with a larger working memory capacity. Capacity, however, can be improved. In addition, we can resort to quick fixes to help us hold more in working memory.

One of those quick fixes is a technique called *chunking*. In his landmark study in 1956, George Miller, a leader in the field of psychlinguistics and cognitive psychology, found that we can hold a maximum of seven items in short-term memory, depending on our working memory capacity. However, a new study by Australian researcher Gordon Parker reanalyzed the data and concluded that the number of items is more like four. One scientist, Brian McElree, even argues we can realistically work only with one chunk online in selective attention at a time. Since many items are much longer than that, we chunk the information into groups. For telephone numbers, for example, the area code is one chunk, the three-digit prefix is another, and the last four digits of a phone number are a third chunk.

The amount we can hold online at a given time depends on the complexity of the material as well: the more complex something is, the fewer items we can successfully hold online. How familiar we are with the material also affects our capacity. For example, if we are accessing our mental grocery list while in the store, we can hold onto more items than if we were trying to recall it in another location.

Researchers Adrian Owen and Adam Hampshire at the Brain and Mind Institute at the University of Western Ontario found that IQ does not explain everything about achievement; rather, working memory has a strong contribution to performance on IQ tests. Susan Gathercole, a cognitive psychology researcher at York University, noted that students who had a small working memory capacity (approximately 15 percent of all children) had trouble remembering their teacher's instructions as well as their own plan for carrying out the instructions. Neuroscientists Iroise Dumontheil and Torkel Klingberg in Sweden gave brain scans to students and found activation in the area of visual-spatial working memory (required for math), which predicted future math performance.

LONG-TERM MEMORY

The scientific term for learning is *long-term potentiation* (LTP), meaning that the more a group of neurons fires together, the more likely they are to fire together again. Long-term memory must be encoded—that is, manipulated in some way that makes connections and neural networks in the brain stronger. As we say, fire it until you wire it.

What Does This Mean for Educators?

Understanding the role of working memory is critical for education since it is an invisible pathway underlying achievement. This is valuable to education in that early diagnosis could lead to faster and more targeted interventions. We are concerned about standardized test scores and try to strengthen our math and reading instruction when an underlying issue could actually be working memory. Yet we do not hear underlying issues of working memory discussed in education circles.

What we do more of gets more territory in the brain. We therefore need to strengthen the cognitive skill of working memory in our students by progressively including more working memory tasks. Although some claims about improved cognition through software are not yet substantiated, other new software is demonstrating an ability to improve working memory. It is well documented that meditation improves working memory, a skill critical to achievement, and yet we do not offer this in school. Music training has been shown to increase working memory capacity, and yet it is one of the first areas to get cut when budgets are tight. We need to focus on some of these invisible underlying pathways as much as we do the visible measures of content knowledge. If we want to "raise IQ" or raise achievement and improve learning, we need to address the mental ability of working memory.

Leaping into the Classroom

We can't have learning without memory. Understanding the nature of memory can help us design activities to enhance the movement of memories into long-term storage.

Working Memory

Working memory is either visual-spatial (the mind's eye—we can picture it) or auditory (we can hear it, as when we mentally repeat a phone number until we can get to the phone to dial it). As it turns out, the visual-spatial pathway is the stronger, so that is something we can emphasize to students. Visuals have been known to help with working memory capacity, as in the memory strategy of assigning items to a place in a room or picturing a visual with a person's name to help remember it. Capitalize on visual-spatial working memory by asking students to create a visual, whether a drawing or a diagram, to make it easier to hold the memory "online." They don't have to draw a picture. It might be picturing your face as you explained it or visual recall of which student may have been talking about it in group. (Chapter 2 offers additional ideas.)

The card game Concentration, where players have to remember where the cards are placed, is excellent training for working memory. You could make a classroom game in which students match questions and answers or words and definitions or Spanish/English translation or any number of facts that must be learned. While they are learning, they are improving their working memory at the same time; like other mental and physical skills, the more we exercise it, the stronger it gets.

If your students can't seem to follow instructions, consider looking at the instructions. Perhaps they are too long for working memory—for example, your instructions to "turn to the questions on page 62 and answer the even numbers in section A and the odd numbers in section B, and then select one of the questions in section C, and turn this in online by next Wednesday." We must watch out for exceeding the constraints of working memory in verbal instructions; test instructions, questions, and multiple choice answers; and printed materials created for the students, such as handouts or e-mails.

Moving Information into Long-Term Memory

Many times we do not need to move information from working memory to long-term memory because we need to remember it just long enough to complete an action and then we are done with it. This is a wonderful design by the brain to keep our minds clear. However, in school and other areas, we do need to move the information into long-term storage. We must do something with the information to make sure it gets stored. In other words, we must fire it but also wire it.

As you read in chapter 1, learning involves creating neural networks. When we teach students numerous facts in a chapter or lecture, students (and sometimes teachers) expect this may be sufficient to "learn" or remember the material. In fact, this goes against what we know about how the brain learns. Networks must be created by working with the material in such a way that it goes from working memory (hearing the lecture or reading the chapter) and into long-term memory (recalling the information). There is no way around this. According to Nobel Prize–winner Carl Wieman, a physicist, "This is basic biology." Learning is a process.

Figure 5.4 shows my educational working model of the memory process. This model is a simplified version geared toward classroom application (see also table 5.1). You can see there are two common ways to hold material online in working memory: (1) rehearsal and repetition and (2) chunking. Six methods encode information into long-term storage. These are ways to work with the material to actively encode it. The next phase lists aspects that make information more likely to stay in long-term memory. For example, we know that paying attention creates stronger memories. We can create lessons that create this likelihood.

Students must have a model—a network of related ideas about the material—not just isolated facts. They must think deeply and extensively about the material. This process involves connecting the new material to prior knowledge. Then the material

Figure 5.4 Zadina Model of Academic Memory

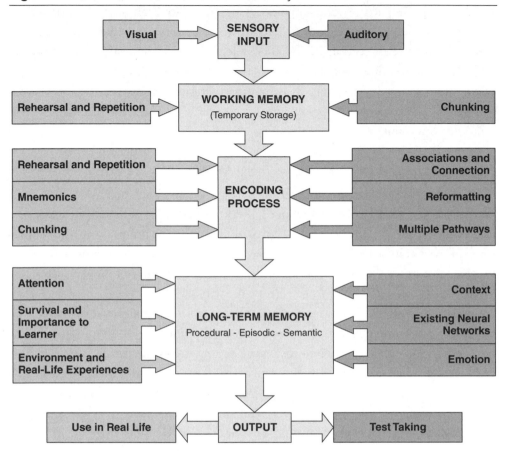

must be fired and wired—worked with in multiple ways to create a strong neural network and encode the material into long-term memory.

People are more likely to remember new information when they reformat it into categories or networks of related information.

Strategies

People are more likely to remember new information when they reformat it into categories or networks of related information. Using a strategy of category construction as part of the learning process is an effective

Table 5.1 Some Memory Processes

Working memory

Rehearsal, repetition, reassembling	Reviewing material, repeating material, recalling the image, reassembling the memory such as practice testing
Chunking	Grouping information into categories or chunks, such as separating a phone number into three groups: 727–732–0000

Encoding process

Rehearsal and repetition	Reviewing material, repeating material, recalling the image
Mnemonics	Using a formula, pattern, or rhyme to remember material, such as using **P**lease **E**xcuse **M**y **D**ear **A**unt **S**ally to remember order of operations: parenthesis, exponents, multiply, divide, add, subtract
Chunking	Grouping information into categories or chunks, such as separating a phone number into three groups: 727–732–0000
Associations and connections	Associating or connecting new information with something already known, such as associating the name John Carpenter with an image of him hammering a nail or connecting how the brain is like an orchestra to remember facts about the brain
Reformatting	Putting information into a format that is easier or more familiar, such as turning a paragraph into a list or writing a long sentence into several shorter ones
Multiple pathways	Using as many senses as possible, such as saying something while writing it

Long-term memory

Attention	Focusing attention on something
Survival and importance to learner	Thinking of a way this information would be helpful; the more important, the easier to remember
Environment and real-life experience	Using information or thinking of how it affects the world around you or how you could use it in life
Context	Thinking of the context—the situation or information surrounding the material to be learned; putting information into a bigger picture
Existing neural networks	Attaching new information to something you already know; familiarity with the topic
Emotion	Attaching positive emotion to information

method. We know this for many reasons, including the nature of learning itself. It has been noted that one difference between novice learners and experts is not only how much they know, but also how they organize and use what they know. Examining patterns and categories also puts information into a context, making it more meaningful and memorable.

Direct students to look at the details within a bigger picture. You learned in chapter 4 that seeing patterns is rewarding, so teaching students how to create graphic organizers and requiring their use is a strategy that comes up throughout this book and is particularly helpful when encoding into long-term memory. We want to teach students how to reformat material to make it easier to remember. Creating a visual is one way, or they can make an outline or a list, or rewrite the material in their own words.

One strategy that experts use is chunking within chunks. As applied to textbook learning, for example, it would be similar to an outline. A learner might consider four sections of the unit as four chunks. Within each section, they find the key chunks and then break those into smaller chunks. Outlining, an old strategy, is also a highly effective one. It can be done individually or in groups, using traditional outline form, mind-mapping, or Venn diagrams. Let them figure out the diagram and relationships with guidance from you.

Encoding into long-term memory may sound familiar to you as the kind of study strategies we have long taught. There is evidence regarding the least and most effective strategies for recall. Psychologist John Dunlosky and his team examined the best and worst strategies and discovered that the least effective strategies were highlighting and underlining. Daniel Willingham, a professor of psychology at the University of Virginia, and his lab tested ten of the most common study strategies students use to identify which were the least and the most effective. They examined how well they worked across content areas and across individual differences and many other variables. They, too, labeled highlighting and underlining as the worst. Some techniques such as summary writing and forming mental images were rated low in part because they applied to only some conditions or research was still inconclusive, so we don't want to rule them out. Rereading was low too, but I suspect it is the type of rereading that may have been used. If the student is mindlessly rereading, then that strategy of going through the motions would not be effective.

The best strategy was practice testing and distributed practice (spacing over time). To see why, remember that the more a group of neurons fires together, the more likely they are to fire together again. Practice tests activate the network used when taking the test—the expressive pathway or getting it out and therefore reassembling the memory. Learning takes time and consolidation: distributed practice. Researcher Regan Gurung, a professor of human development and psychology at the University of Wisconsin, found that college students who said they used practice testing as a strategy had higher achievement on exams than those who didn't.

Students need to know about this research. It is important to provide your students with practice tests, making sure those tests use a format similar to that of the graded test. For example, you don't want them to practice on matching and then test them on short answer, because that would activate two different networks: recognition and recall. Perhaps you could use the tests from the previous semester as practice tests. Students can also use the questions at the end of chapters as practice tests. The important point is they are practicing what they will be required to ultimately do: reassemble the memory and produce it by activating the appropriate neural network.

Spaced repetition has been shown to be one of the most effective ways to encode information into long-term memory. We know that repetition is important, but there also needs to be some space—some time—between repetitions. The ideal amount of time is that the repetition occurs when we are about ready to forget the information, so of course that varies from student to student and it varies during the learning process. The time between repetitions should be longer each time because the networks get strengthened with each repetition so it should be able to be remembered longer as time goes on.

Since this sounds somewhat difficult to provide to students in a practical format, suggest a generic timetable. For example, teachers have long advised students to review the material later in the day it was presented and then to review it daily until the test. Good teachers have an instinct for what the brain is doing. Now we know why it was such good advice. You may suggest to students a timetable such as doing their first review the same day as the lesson, then the next day, then every two days, then every three days, and so forth until the test. As with other information about how the brain learns, explain the reasoning behind this to the students. You are helping them make the best use of their study time.

Another reason to space out studying is that the brain gets tired (referred to as *cognitive overload* or *cognitive fatigue*). You will learn more about that in chapter 7, but for now, know you need to give the brain a brief rest periodically.

Adequate sleep is important for everyone's health and is also an important factor in learning. Tell students that skipping sleep to study is not the best way to learn. Instead, they can find pockets of time during the day to review material rather than relegating studying until late at night. They could review a page or two of notes while dinner is being prepared, waiting in line, between classes, or any other time there is a break between one daily event and another. Now that we know spaced studying is efficient for the brain, these little study breaks make more sense than long bouts of studying.

A key factor in moving information to long-term memory is attention, which brings us back to where we started in this chapter: multiple pathways working together. The more pathways we use to encode information, the easier it will be to fire up the network and retrieve the information.

HOMEWORK MENU

- Create mnemonics for the material.
- Reformat the lesson in a new way, making a visual for other students.
- Create practice tests for classmates, and provide the answers.
- Create associations with a mind map or diagram.
- Describe an example of how to apply the material in real life.
- Teach this lesson via video.

SUGGESTED STRATEGIES

- Alert students to orient their attention to specific information.
- Avoid distractions in the classroom.
- Teach students how attention and memory work.
- Remind students to engage in effortful control to sustain attention.
- Avoid instructions that are too long for working memory capacity.

- Scan tests and other materials for sentences that exceed working memory capacity.
- Teach specific strategies for encoding working memory into long-term memory.

REFLECT AND CONNECT

Examine the most recent test you wrote for working memory issues. How did you do?

Write an example of a poor question. Then write a revised version more compatible with normal working memory capacity.

What encoding strategies have you explicitly discussed with or taught to students?

How have you made material more memorable to students (e.g., emotional, using humor)?

Do your homework assignments provide for encoding? Explain.

SUGGESTED READING

Dehn, M. J. (2008). *Working memory and academic learning*. Hoboken, NJ: Wiley.

Fougnie, D. (2008). The relationship between attention and working memory. In N. Johansen (Ed.), *New research on short-term memory* (pp. 1–45). Hauppauge, NY: Nova Science.

Goleman, D. (2013). *Focus: The hidden driver of excellence*. New York, NY: Harper.

Gurung, R.A.R., & Schwartz, B. M. (2008) *Optimizing teaching and learning: Practicing pedagogical research*. Hoboken, NJ: Wiley-Blackwell.

Klingberg, T. (2013). *The learning brain: Memory and brain development in children*. New York, NY: Oxford University Press.

Posner, M. I. (2004). *Cognitive neuroscience of attention*. New York, NY: Guilford Press.

Ruff, H. A., & Rothbart, M. K. (1996). *Attention in early development: Themes and variations*. New York, NY: Oxford University Press.

Sapolsky, R. M. (2005). *Monkeyluv: And other essays on our lives as animals*. New York, NY: Scribner.

Squire, L. R., & Kandel, E. R. (2008). *Memory: From mind to molecules*. New York, NY: Holt.

Wright, R. D., & Ward, L. M. (2008). *Orienting of attention*. New York, NY: Oxford University Press.

The Language and Math Pathways

What is it about word problems? I teach a formula, I give problems, and students work the problems. However, when I follow this with a word problem using the same formula, they get lost! You would think word problems would be more effective, since they put the math into a context. I can't figure out what to do differently so they do not struggle as much with word problems.

MAKING CONNECTIONS

Is it true when students say, "I know it, but can't say it"? If you have a student who speaks two languages, will this child have more difficulty learning to read? Are there subtypes of reading difficulty? Do you have students who seem to read fluently but without comprehension? What are two important math skills in early childhood that affect adult math performance? What is a major reason students have difficulty with math?

Everything you have learned so far is going to play into this chapter. What appears to be reading or math difficulty may be due instead to deficits in sensory processing, effects of emotion, motivation, and, to a great extent, attention and working memory issues. We are going to look at additional ways the skills of language acquisition, reading, and math can get off track and ways to address the resulting learning difficulties.

Obviously this book can't be a handbook on how to teach reading, language, or math or even fully explain the complexity of these processes in the brain. Instead, the intention of this chapter is to bring to your attention some of the research regarding these processes to provide an understanding of the multiplicity of brain processes affecting reading, math, and language acquisition and to examine some implications for the classroom.

LANGUAGE AND SECOND LANGUAGE

What Does the Research Say?

You have heard that language is in the left hemisphere of the brain. However, some left-handers have language in the right hemisphere and some aspects of language are processed in the right hemisphere, such as the emotional component of language. Aspects of language such as grammar, syntax, vocabulary, and pronunciation are processed in different regions; therefore, many brain regions have to work together to process language.

The first stage of language in the brain begins in the thalamus, the relay station that diverts sensory input to appropriate areas for processing (figure 6.1). At the thalamus, the brain recognizes incoming data as sound and sends it to the auditory cortex (figure 6.2). The auditory cortex then differentiates the sound as environmental or language. If it is determined to be language, it is sent to language areas of the brain for further processing, including Broca's area (speech and language production) and Wernicke's area (speech and language comprehension) (figure 6.2). If it is going to be spoken or sounded out silently, the motor area would also be activated (figure 6.2). To see how language learning is processed in the brain, we'll look at first language and then see how a second language may be different.

Even before babies are born, they hear the sounds of their mother's language while in utero. Patricia Kuhl is a psychologist and speech scientist who has made a great contribution to our understanding of how infants learn language and hear sounds. She recently discovered that infants only a few hours old can tell the

Figure 6.1 Thalamus and Corpus Callosum

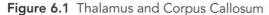

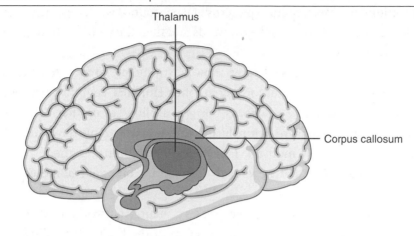

Thalamus

Corpus callosum

Figure 6.2 Some Regions Involved in Language

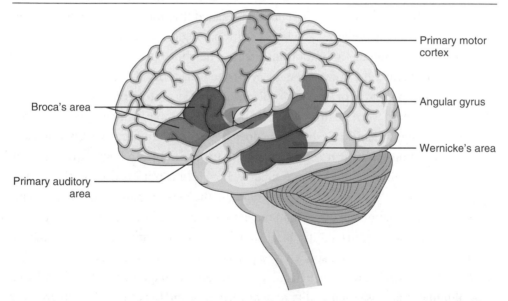

Primary motor cortex

Broca's area

Angular gyrus

Wernicke's area

Primary auditory area

difference between vowel sounds in their native language and a foreign one. They hear the prosody of language—the melody, the rhythm, the rising and falling.

Kuhl says that unborn babies learn the patterns of speech during the last ten weeks of pregnancy. As Alison Gopnik, a psychologist, says, babies are like little scientists deciphering the patterns of these sounds. Newborns continue to make neural connections and can recognize patterns of what sounds work together. Eventually the sounds come to be associated with words and then the words with objects as the neural network grows.

By nine months, infants already show a strong preference for the pattern typical of their first language, according to Johns Hopkins' cognitive neuroscientist Peter Jusczyk. Interestingly, newborns born to a bilingual mother have an equal preference for languages heard before birth, while a newborn born to a monolingual mother prefers only the mother's language. Psychologists at the University of British Columbia found that newborns born into a bilingual home can tell the languages apart.

Just as learning the first language creates a neural network, so does learning a second language. These networks can overlap in the brain, depending on when the second language is learned. Neuroscientist Denise Klein's results offer evidence that the age of acquisition is an important factor in the development of brain structures. The earlier a second language is learned, the more it uses first-language areas. Later, language learning activates additional regions.

Age of acquisition has an important effect. A newborn baby is capable of hearing every sound distinction in every language in the world, but this changes over time. As early as seven months of age, a baby begins paying less attention to sounds outside the language heard from birth. A Japanese baby, for example, can hear the difference between an English *l* and an *r*, but if she does not hear that difficult distinction early enough, the ability to hear it is pruned away. This pruning can begin around seven months and continues until around puberty. If a child is not exposed to the sounds early, some sounds may be difficult to articulate, the reason many of us have accents when speaking a language other than our native one. Kuhl has found a way to stop the brain from losing this ability: brief social interaction with a foreign speaker in infancy. Hearing the sounds spoken by a person preserved the ability.

Neuroscientist Laura-Ann Petitto, a renowned language researcher found that monolinguals may lose their ability to hear certain sounds as they approach one year of age, but bilinguals do not lose this ability. She calls this a "perceptual wedge" that keeps the window for learning sounds open. Language researchers Ellen Bialystok and Kenji Hakuta believe the only difference in the way adults and children learn a second language is a phonological one. Syntax and vocabulary don't exhibit age-related differences in acquisition.

Research studies clearly demonstrate that the earlier one learns a second language, the better. An important study in 1962 by McGill University language researchers Elizabeth Peal and Wallace Lambert found that not only did learning two languages from birth not harm language learning, bilinguals outperformed monolinguals on both verbal and nonverbal intelligence tests. The bilinguals appear to have more diversified mental abilities than monolinguals.

Substantial research now indicates that bilingualism creates structural and functional changes in the brain, resulting in a better brain in several ways. For example, Petitto has found that bilinguals have greater communication between the left and right brain hemispheres compared to monolinguals, who show more left hemisphere activation. She believes this means that bilingual brains are more efficient and use the brain's resources better, leading to better literacy. A 2013 study by Brian Gold, a neuroscientist at the University of Kentucky College of Medicine, showed that older bilinguals could perform a task-switching activity faster and use less energy (cognitive load) to do so. They are using their brains more efficiently than older monolinguals do.

Neuroscientist Cathy Price at University College London found that bilinguals had more gray matter in the posterior supramarginal gyrus (an area associated with vocabulary) in both hemispheres. Neuroscientist Ellen Bialystok at York University found that bilinguals were better at the Simon task involving working memory (recall the example of the basketball gorilla video from chapter 5). Researcher Jennifer Krizman at Northwestern University reports that bilinguals were more efficient at processing sound, and this was associated with an advantage in working memory and higher-order thinking skills. She also led a study in Nina Kraus's auditory neuroscience lab at Northwestern University that found bilingualism led to better auditory processing. This was associated with enhanced executive function, providing evidence that bilingualism improves cognitive function (chapter 7).

Being bilingual may even improve social skills (chapter 8) such as empathy according to psychologists Paula Rubio-Fernandez and Sam Glucksberg at Princeton. Thought-provoking research by linguistics and bilingualism researcher Susan Ervin-Tripp at the University of California, Berkeley, hypothesizes that two languages create a situation similar to having two different minds. Her research shows that the same material is perceived differently depending on the language in which it is presented. As you can see, almost every pathway covered in this book is affected by bilingualism.

The implications for education from neuroscience research on language learning are huge. Evidence is substantial that a second language should be taught as early as possible and that learning more than one language improves the brain overall in many ways that contribute to achievement in school. In fact, I believe that research conveys an imperative for education to create dual-language programs in early education.

I believe that research conveys an imperative for education to create dual-language programs in early education.

You have learned in the chapters in this book on other pathways about the importance of underlying invisible processes such as attention and working memory, and evidence shows that language learning improves these critical skills. Other studies find that fluent bilinguals have more cognitive resources and are better at multitasking than monolinguals. Petitto finds that bilinguals are better readers. Researchers at Northwestern University found that bilinguals can learn yet another language more easily than monolinguals can. Viorica Marian, a bilingualism researcher at Northwestern University, says it is not that some people are just better at learning language, but that being bilingual is what makes it easier.

Socioeconomic status (SES) has long been associated with academic achievement: those with lower SES have poorer skills and lower achievement. Helen Neville, a neuroscientist, has reported that low-SES children enrolled in a dual-language program outperformed high-SES monolinguals not enrolled in the program. Another study covering several countries found that low-SES children raised to be bilingual had better cognitive skills than those who are monolingual. Researchers speculate that bilingualism also improves executive function. This research provides strong support for dual-language immersion programs.

Low-SES children enrolled in a dual-language program outperformed high-SES monolinguals not enrolled in the program.

What are the implications for teaching a language new to the student? Conventional policy of teaching a foreign language in high school in fact does not make sense according to what we know now about how we best learn language. Moreover, high schoolers do not have a much better idea of which world language might be most beneficial to them than younger children do, so putting that choice off until high school for that reason does not make sense. It is convenient for schools to teach languages in secondary school because of the way we have structured school, so it can be offered as an elective. However, since learning a second language (English or foreign) makes it easier to learn another language later, we should introduce additional languages into the curriculum earlier.

My sixth-grade teacher taught us German because she knew it. There was no book or special curriculum. We did it for fun, and loved learning it. Schools need to use the language resources of teachers and include language lessons in the first or second language of the elementary teacher or change the curriculum to accommodate individual choices and offer as many languages as teachers in the school can speak. We may have to redesign curriculum from the ground up.

Within those second or foreign language learning classes, students need to be exposed to multiple speakers of the language, according to cognitive scientist David Pisoni. We learn language naturally through patterning. Exposure to one speaker only does not allow learners to experience the broad range of sounds in order to hear and pronounce them correctly. For example, an infant knows "tom ay to" and "tum ah to" are the same "a" vowel sound because every speaker operates somewhere within that vowel range to a different degree. Exposure to multiple speakers helps learners hear the patterns of language more extensively.

Leaping into the Classroom

You can imagine why it might be somewhat more difficult to learn a second language when a baby is already learning the first one even before birth. Since the brain is plastic and language is essential to survival, everyone can learn a language at any point in life. Of course when language is learned later, it can be harder to master some of the difficult sounds and achieve native fluency.

Patricia Kuhl believes language learning is a result of our social brain (see chapter 8): babies (and all other humans) have a strong desire to communicate.

If language is communication driven, then it makes sense to teach it in that context—meaningful communication rather than isolated grammar lessons. Petitto and educational neuroscientist Kevin N. Dunbar at Harvard believe that full mastery in a second language cannot be achieved through classroom instruction alone: it must include social and community activities and real-life experiences.

In chapter 1, I discussed making connections and prior knowledge. The importance of this cannot be emphasized enough for language learning. Many times English language learners have literacy or learning issues in their first language that will, of course, affect the learning of a second language. Making connections prior to the introduction of every lesson is crucial.

Focusing attention is critical to making changes in the brain. When teaching language, the focus must be on the new language. Whether you are working on sounds, meaning, syntax, or something else, direct students' attention explicitly. As they practice and work, remind them to keep their attention focused on the aspect of language you and they are working on.

Speaking is important to language learning. Speaking involves the motor pathway in the brain and must be fired and wired also. Sometimes students say, "I know it but I can't say it," and that is true: they may have comprehended the information, but they can't reassemble and articulate it. Sometimes they can't pronounce words because they can't form the articulatory loop of actually making the speech sounds. Sometimes they can't reassemble the memory itself. The more we get them speaking in the classroom, the stronger that pathway becomes.

If a student can't articulate one of the more difficult sound distinctions, such as b/d, it may be because his or her brain can't hear it. If that is the case, the speaker can't pronounce it accurately, resulting in a persistent accent. James McClelland, a psychologist and researcher at Stanford, suggests that instructors exaggerate the foreign language contrasts to help learners hear the subtle differences. Keep in mind that this difficulty may persist if the brain can't hear it.

One of the ways to get more speaking in the classroom is "to use the stand up and explain" strategy from chapter 2. Of course, the flip side of speaking is listening, and this strategy includes both skills, because half of the students are listening while the other half speaks. Another speaking activity is fact or fiction. Have a group of students listen to some text. Then one student will say something to the class that the class decides is fact (was in the passage) or fiction (student has deliberately changed it to make it wrong). This is a safe activity because if the speaker accidentally gets it wrong, there is no shame.

Various components of language are activated in different parts of the brain. Therefore, these processes must be "fired and wired" as well. One of these is *prosody*, which engages the right hemisphere and relates to the emotion, tone, and musicality of the speech and is very important to meaning. Sometimes in the classroom, we teachers forget this must also be addressed and practiced.

It is hard to get prosody if the speaking of the words itself is not fluent. Having students practice speaking a sentence until they can fluently articulate the words and *then* having them say it with the correct inflection and emotion until that becomes fluent helps to integrate the pathways. You can make this fun with exaggerated inflections by having the entire class repeat phrases with different inflections, such as *I* told you, I *told* you, and I told *you*. Other ways are to play recordings of stories, stop the recording, and have students repeat certain sentences or phrases trying to copy the inflection. Having students sing nursery rhymes in the target language can be helpful because they usually have exaggerated emotion and prosody. Choral reading and singing in general are also helpful. Ella Baccouche, an ESL middle school teacher, has used Big Books with students who have had no English exposure. The poems and short stories express an exaggerated emotion and help with the prosody of English. "Jazz chants" (those with rhythmic beats) have been helpful, too.

READING

Reading is not natural. Yes, you read that correctly. Reading is not a natural process for the brain like vision and hearing are. Instead, reading uses parts of the brain designed for other tasks. It thus creates a new pathway in the brain.

Most readers use a typical fluent pathway to read; however, some students use an alternative less fluent pathway. We say these readers have *dyslexia*: difficulty in reading fluently in spite of normal intelligence and adequate instruction. Dyslexia is not reading words backward or experiencing them jumping around on the page. The most common form is the persistent inability to sound out words. However, not all poor readers have dyslexia. They may have impairment in any of the other pathways that impede their reading performance. Let's explore the science research on reading to get a better understanding of what is happening in the reader's brain.

Neuroscience researchers have been able to use neuroimaging to look inside the brains of those with and without reading difficulty and see what regions are activated in the brains of good readers compared to those with reading difficulty or dyslexia. In good readers, scans show activation of the posterior portion of the superior temporal gyrus (figure 6.3) during phonologic processing (the sounding out of words). Poor readers had little or no activation there. Instead, they had right hemisphere activation in a corresponding area, according to neuroscientist Panagiotia Simos at the University of Texas. Sally Shaywitz and Bennett Shaywitz, well-known dyslexia researchers, have studied the brains of people with reading disability for many years. Their research indicates differences in the posterior (rear) regions of the brain between those who read well and those who don't. Fluent readers rely more on the angular gyrus (figure 6.3) and Wernicke's area (figure 6.2) and activate Broca's area more (figure 6.2).

More prefrontal activation occurred in poor readers, possibly from trying to rely on frontal lobe skills and perhaps more on working memory. Shaywitz says this puts more demand on the frontal cortex (figure 6.4) when people with dyslexia read. Since the frontal cortex is often overloaded and involved in many functions (see chapter 7), this makes it more effortful and fatiguing for those with dyslexia to read. My research measuring the frontal lobe in college students with and without dyslexia found that those with dyslexia had 11 percent larger prefrontal areas, which perhaps offers support for her findings. (This does not mean they have dyslexia, but it might predispose them to it.)

Some promising new research may lead to early diagnosis of potential dyslexia so that interventions can begin early. Neuroscientist Mark Eckert at the University of Florida and his colleagues, including Christiana Leonard, a pioneer in dyslexia research, used brain scans to look at the neuroanatomy of elementary school children with and without dyslexia. In addition to some other differences, they found that those with dyslexia had significantly smaller right anterior lobes of the cerebellum (figure 6.4), a difference that could classify whether someone had dyslexia.

As with spoken language, the first step in the brain process of reading is the thalamus, which recognizes the sensory input (figure 6.1). In this case, it recognizes

Figure 6.3 Regions Involved in Reading

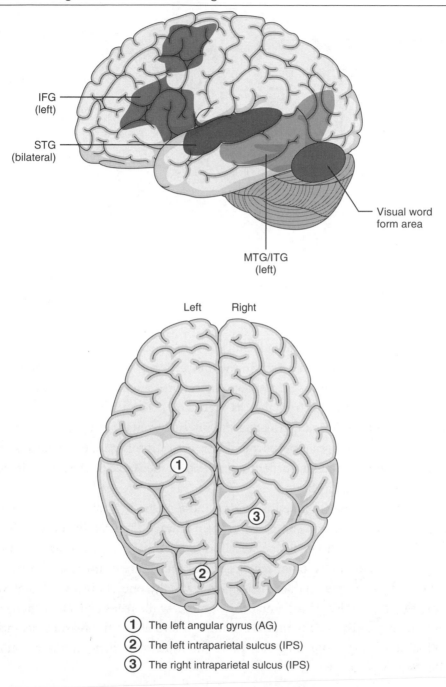

IFG
(left)

STG
(bilateral)

Visual word
form area

MTG/ITG
(left)

Left   Right

① The left angular gyrus (AG)

② The left intraparietal sulcus (IPS)

③ The right intraparietal sulcus (IPS)

Figure 6.4 Some Regions Involved in Math

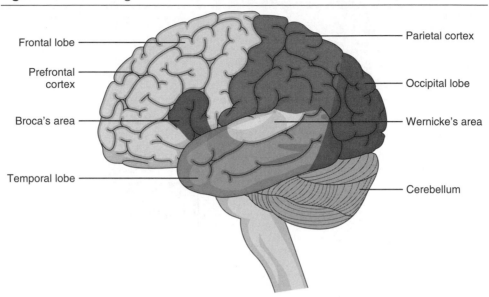

the input as something visual and sends it to the visual cortex (figure 6.2). If it is perceived as a word, it is processed in the midfusiform gyrus, the visual word form area (figure 6.3). Then it is sent to phonological processing regions in the left superior temporal and inferior frontal areas (figure 6.3). To associate meaning with the word, the middle temporal gyrus and the inferior frontal gyrus must be activated (figure 6.3). For comprehension, frontal lobe activation (figure 6.4) controls memory and attention and higher-order thinking skills. (See table 6.1.) Reading is clearly a complex process in the brain.

Students could be impaired in any of these areas. In some cases, readers are using alternative pathways compared to the pathway of typical, fluent readers. This has nothing to do with intelligence or effort. Sometimes a region is activated more strongly or in addition to other regions due to the nature of the task, the material, or the reader's unique characteristics. Interestingly, one study found that when adults read, they activate the frontal cortex more, while teens activate the amygdala (emotion) more. The adults may be thinking more about the reasons behind the emotion and being more analytical rather than just experiencing the emotion as the teens may be doing.

Table 6.1 Some Regions Activated During Reading

Region	Function
Thalamus	Recognizes input as visual or auditory and sends to appropriate area
Occipital visual cortex	Recognizes the visual pattern of the word
Broca's area	Speech and language production, some grammar and syntax, reading words aloud or silently
Wernicke's area	Speech and language comprehension
Fusiform gyrus	Visual word form area (VWFA), recognizes shapes, attuned to words, storage and retrieval of words, spelling and recognizing whole words
Angular gyrus	Bridges the VWFA and rest of language system, processes phonemes, integrates auditory and visual information
Frontal lobe	Higher-order thinking skills underlying comprehension

Fluent reading comes with communication among various regions of the brain, a process mediated by white matter. A new area of neuroscience research is looking at white matter tracts in the brain. This research shows that differences in reading difficulty may not be with the regions but with the connections among regions.

According to many models of reading, there are three pathways or routes involved in reading: the phonological, orthographic, and semantic. The *phonological* route is how readers sound out words in order to recognize them. Phonology is the sound system of language and enables readers to sound out words. Sounds of speech are critical to reading success. The most common type of dyslexia is phonological dyslexia—the inability to sound out words as tested by use of nonwords.

In a large study of college students, neuroscientist Qinghua He discovered that brain scans showed a correlation between gray matter volume and how well someone could make a connection between a new word and a sound. Some exciting research from Nina Kraus's lab indicates that reading difficulties stem from auditory processing deficits: the reader can't hear the sounds properly so can't sound out the words properly, and he or she therefore confuses letters and sounds. Early instruction in phonemic awareness is critical, as it is well documented that this skill predicts future success in reading.

The second route is the *orthographic*: recognizing words by sight, by their appearance. Sight word reading is tested by the ability to read words that are not written as they sound, such as "*island*." A reader who says *is-land* is using the phonological pathway instead of orthographic.

Learners impaired in the visual word form area (VWFA), for example, can sound out but can't recognize words: these students are impaired in the orthographic or sight word pathway but not the phonological pathway. Neuroscientist Laurie Glezer recently found the neurons in the VWFA were tuned to words, not nonwords, and this selectivity increased with experience. As children learn to read and work with words, they are fine-tuning the area that recognizes words. Like the rest of the brain, this develops in response to experience.

In addition, readers can be impaired in the third pathway—the *semantic* pathway—and have trouble figuring out words in context or associating words with their meaning, whereas good readers can use context to recognize a word they couldn't read phonetically or by sight.

Learning to read changes the brain by creating new neural pathways. One interesting study by Stanford psychology researcher Jason Yeatman and colleagues looked at the brain's white matter (connections between neurons) in good and poor readers. Although the poor readers may have started with more white matter, those who ended up as high-performing readers rapidly developed more white matter. Those who started with more white matter but ended up as low-performing readers actually lost some white matter, meaning they were not creating and strengthening pathways. Michal Ben-Shachar, a psycholinguistics neuroimaging researcher in the Gonda Multidisciplinary Brain Research Center in Israel, believes this information could be used as a diagnostic tool for early intervention.

What Does This Mean for Educators?

It is important for educators to understand that reading is a complicated process that involves the smooth integration of many structures and functions in the brain. Students could be impaired anywhere in the process. Nevertheless, students of any age, including adults, can improve their reading. Stanislas Dehaene's lab presented a significant paper showing that even literacy acquired in adulthood changes the visual and language networks in the brain.

In addition to being impaired at any point in the reading pathway, a reader can also be impaired in other pathways described in this book, and this could affect reading. The student's existing neural network of knowledge affects the reading performance. The sensory motor pathway could be impaired in that students are not properly encoding the sounds or visual appearance of the word, or perhaps they have problems with the motor skills of forming the sounds. This has nothing to do with their eyes or ears but with the visual or auditory cortex that may be impaired. We have noticed that people with dyslexia tend to have poor handwriting as well as poor reading, so the motor system does seem to be tied into the reading system beyond the mental articulation of the sounds. Attention and working memory may be impaired as well. In fact, many people with attention deficits also have reading problems. When you think about it, fluent reading is very impressive. While we may not be able to engage students in certain types of intensive intervention in the classroom to rewire the reading circuits, some of the deficits are due not so much to faulty wiring as to lack of wiring. In other words, the connections in and between the areas haven't been strengthened due to lack of appropriate instructional experience. Research clearly supports the importance of early phonemic awareness. School systems need to educate parents about the importance of using lots of language and reading to children (see chapter 9 for more on early childhood).

Early diagnosis and intervention have been shown to be critical. However, many students arrive in college with poor reading skills, so intervention at every grade level is important. We can strengthen weak networks and can help impaired students discover compensatory strategies. Furthermore, we can understand that reading differences can be complex and are not due to a lack of effort or intelligence.

Educators need to work closely with educational neuroscientists to bridge the scientific and educational research on reading. Studies of the neural underpinnings of reading can lead to better understanding of brain differences that underlie reading differences, which can lead to early diagnosis. Neuroimaging can show changes in activation as a result of intervention. Eventually interventions can be designed that could be conducted in schools and classrooms as technology evolves in a way that student work can be assigned based on individual needs.

Leaping into the Classroom

Reading involves decoding *and* constructing meaning. Obviously decoding deficits can create problems with obtaining meaning from the text. We can't say "dyslexia" or "trouble reading" because that is too broad. We want to get to the underlying deficit and intervene. While some of these are beyond the scope of the classroom, others may be overlooked in our typical reading instruction. Here are some of them:

Problems in Reading

- Decoding (application of letter-sound relationships)
- Prior knowledge, vocabulary, or concepts
- Working memory
- Frontal lobe executive functions (see chapter 7)
- Controlling attention
- Drawing inferences
- Comprehension: constructing meaning; in order to do this, all other processes must be effective

Improving reading requires understanding which processes are impeding progress.

Reading instruction needs to strengthen all three reading pathways: phonological, orthographic, and semantic. The phonological pathway requires explicit instruction in phonemic awareness early in childhood. Phonemic awareness in prekindergarten predicts reading achievement into middle school and beyond.

However, phonological deficits after adequate instruction tend to persist into adulthood. Therefore, after a certain point, asking students to acquire vocabulary through silent reading and sounding out new words is not going to work with these students. If vocabulary is important in your course, then show and say the words for the students so they can compensate by strengthening their sight word vocabulary.

Orthographic (sight words) and semantic (meaning) pathways can be strengthened through reading. The more one reads, the more one acquires vocabulary. However, initially students must be taught to learn words in context in order to acquire new vocabulary as they read.

Students who insist on sounding out words as their only reading strategy may have deficits in acquiring, storing, or retrieving words. This is another subtype of dyslexia. Students who have trouble extracting meaning from context may be exhibiting underlying working memory issues. This is why, once again, we caution against classroom diagnosis. Instead, we should provide multiple pathways to strengthen and compensate.

Reading comprehension of passages goes beyond the decoding of individual words and draws on other processes. Frontal lobes and their executive functions play an important role in reading for comprehension. As you will learn in the next chapter, these are involved in controlling attention and in working memory and specific skills important to fluent reading. Many of the tasks we call *reading comprehension skills* are actually thinking skills: predicting, making inferences, determining the main idea, and prioritizing information (see chapter 7). These skills must be taught and strengthened over time. The latest research indicates that these thinking skills start in early childhood and continue developing throughout early adulthood. Since frontal lobes are continuing to develop until around ages eighteen to twenty-five, this process of strengthening the skills should occur throughout all levels of teaching.

Sometimes poor reading comprehension goes back to a topic examined in the first chapter in this book: making connections. Students can't comprehend if they do not have sufficient neural network on the subject. Of course, material will always include new information and new vocabulary. However, a student who can't begin to find a way into the material with the existing network can easily get lost.

If the reading does not make sense to readers, it cannot be said that they actually read the material effectively. Several factors influence the ability to make sense of reading. As you require and develop metacognition in the students, ask them to stop and reflect as they read and ask if the material made sense. If not, then ask first if they understand the vocabulary. One unclear word can throw off the sense of an entire sentence or paragraph. If they understood the vocabulary and didn't misread any words, then perhaps working memory was the culprit. In a long, complex sentence or paragraph, the student may have trouble holding all the information online in working memory (see the preceding chapter) to get the sense of the entire text. Teachers need to scaffold the students to analyze their problems. Again, the goal is to teach students strategy, awareness, and control of their own learning.

Modeling the process of reading is helpful for students. We are wired to learn from others, so seeing someone read in a thoughtful way can be very helpful. Teachers can read aloud just a little from the first part of a reading assignment before turning it over to the students.

Dehaene suggests that using the gestural or motor system more might be helpful when teaching children to read, something he feels has been neglected in the teaching of reading. In the early grades as you read to the students, stand and gesture too. If someone in the story waves good-bye, for example, you can wave.

Some readers might be teaching reading across the content areas or teaching students to read textbooks. Keep in mind what you have learned about neural networks, scaffolding, and strategies. Begin with reading material on an easier grade level to provide background knowledge so the textual reading becomes more comprehensible, introduce the vocabulary and concepts as a foundation for new material, and give students a sense of fluency before tackling the more difficult material. (Did you see I broke my rule of sentences that strain working memory?) It is important to stress that the easier material is not instead of but in addition to regular curriculum.

Every teacher should be involved in teaching the strategies for reading in his or her course. A not uncommon response to this is, "I don't know how to teach reading." Nevertheless, many excellent models for approaching reading material are available. Most are elaborations of previewing and then reading. The model used in the textbook I wrote with coauthors, *College Reading: The Science and Strategies of Expert Readers*, is *Preview* (including predicting and questioning), *Study-Read*, and *Review*. This model builds on what we know about how the brain learns.

As readers, we first build the foundation through a preview, adding this more general information to our existing network and providing a foundation for details to come. We question in order to activate the brain's love of making sense or figuring things out, for example, by creating a problem to solve or a question to answer. Finally, after establishing and activating our network of knowledge, we add the new information and details. This process involves repetition and engagement with the material. Some teachers also may want to include a summary step in the process.

In the content areas, it may mean spending a couple of days early in the semester going over the reading approach you have selected as best for your course material as part of introducing the course and the textbook to students. I would like to see a schoolwide reading system reinforced by every teacher in middle schools and high schools.

As I have emphasized throughout this book, we want to use multiple pathways to both strengthen weak networks and create compensatory networks. If you want students to learn content, find ways to help the poorer readers compensate. Provide material auditorially to supplement the textbook, for example. Younger students may benefit from guided reading groups in which students are placed in ability groups with material at an appropriate reading level for each group. Refer them to YouTube videos to help them get a foundation in vocabulary and context.

Use alternative assessments that are not heavily print dependent for students who have difficulty, because we can't penalize students for brain differences. Many of these brain differences come with talents in other areas, and students can use talents and strengths to demonstrate their proficiency or to access the material. Homework menus are especially important for students with reading difficulty, because this can be associated with writing and test-taking difficulty. The visual cortex is not nobler than the auditory cortex! We see *and* hear with our brain; this is where the knowledge is processed, so it doesn't matter how the knowledge gets there. Of course, we want to teach reading, and reading is a lifelong blessing. However, for students for whom this is and will remain a challenge, we also look to compensate to help them acquire knowledge and succeed.

Use alternative assessments that are not heavily print dependent for students who have difficulty, because we can't penalize students for brain differences.Reading skill may improve over time if the reader finds a topic of great personal interest, according to research on adults with dyslexia. This usually occurs outside school or on the job. Ideally, in school we could find ways to allow students to read widely on areas of personal interest.

The bottom line is that we want to put reading into perspective, particularly at the college level. Offer instruction and provide for compensation.

MATH

You have seen throughout this book that any single mental task is not as simple as it seems. The same applies to math. Math is not one thing; it is different processes in the brain that must work together smoothly. These processes underlie the math task and are invisible to teachers. Let's look at the science and see what else may be going on.

Educators call math difficulty *dyscalculia*. According to neurologist Ruth Shalev, 5 to 6 percent of children have dyscalculia. It is not more common in boys than girls, as commonly believed. The question now is whether difficulty in this area is really math disability or whether another brain process is creating the difficulty.

Neuroscience research is showing that math is more complicated than we thought. Two main processes underlie math: estimation and calculation. It seems we are born with an innate ability for estimation. Even young children know before they can count if another child got more candy than they did. Neuroscientist Mann Keopke says this is hard-wired in us. However, calculation must be taught. A student could be impaired in either or both processes.

The parietal cortex processes numerical information (figure 6.4). The right parietal area mediates quantity processing, such as estimating how many items are in your shopping basket. Scans showed that people with dyscalculia had an abnormally short and shallow right intraparietal sulcus, a region that mediates the visualization of spatial images (figure 6.3).

The left parietal area mediates calculation, that is, basic arithmetic such as adding and subtracting. Swiss neuroscientist Karin Kucian's lab examined children with math difficulty using functional neuroimaging and found that activation in this region correlated with accuracy. Children with dyscalculia had reduced gray matter in the left intraparietal sulcus and activated the right, rather than left, intraparietal sulcus when doing math, illustrating that they are using their brains differently.

Working math problems involves logical reasoning as well as calculation. New Mexico State University neuropsychologist Jim Kroger's lab found that the reasoning was carried out in Broca's and Wernicke's language areas (figure 6.1) while the left prefrontal cortex and superior (upper) parietal lobe were more activated during calculations (figure 6.4).

Neuroimaging neuroscientist Joonkoo Park at Duke University recently found it was the strength of communication via the corpus callosum between the left and right hemisphere that predicted basic arithmetic ability (figure 6.1). It makes sense that connecting the two abilities of numerical information and arithmetic would be necessary for skill in math. In our study of the corpus callosum in students with dyslexia, we found differences in the size of subsections of the corpus callosum that correlated with specific reading skills. Perhaps similar differences may be found if we measured it in those with math difficulty.

Researchers Elizabeth Brannon and Joonkoo Park discovered an intervention to improve symbolic math skills, such as adding or subtracting two- and three-digit numbers. They found that the ability to "guesstimate" quantities was related to math skills. They trained adults in estimating quantities of dots, and after ten weeks of this practice (during which they became better), their math abilities improved compared to those who did not receive this intervention.

Limits of working memory are a significant contributor to math difficulty. To perform a math operation, information has to be held "online" long enough to work the problem. Vinod Menon, a Stanford University School of Medicine neuroscience researcher, found that younger children require more working memory, attentional resources, and demand on regions involved in memory during mental arithmetic than older students do. His lab suggests that as students become more fluent at math, the brain regions become more specialized to the left inferior parietal cortex and make less demand on other areas.

Reading expert Usha Goswami's research at the Centre for Neuroscience in Education at St. John's College, Cambridge, indicates using one's fingers to learn to count may be an important developmental step. A fascinating study using neuroimaging by neuroscientist Marie-Pascale Noel shows that the brain may be mentally using finger representation in the brain as a child does when learning math. Noel found being able to tell which fingers were being touched (*finger gnosis*) was a strong predictor of mathematical ability in children and adults.

What Does This Mean for Educators?

According to the US Center for Educational Statistics, one in five adults in the country can't do eighth-grade math. Although math deficits are not usually diagnosed until around fifth grade, problems show up much earlier. Psychologist David Geary studied math performance in children from kindergarten to high school and saw that children with the least number system knowledge early on were still the lower performers in high school. Number system knowledge is more than knowing how to count; it is a deeper understanding that the number symbols represent actual quantities. It also means students understand that larger numbers means greater quantities (magnitude) and that numbers can be broken into parts—that 6 is also two groups of 3. This number sense ability was not related to IQ or attention. Cognitive neuroscientist Kathy Mann Koepke stresses the importance of early intervention and suggests that in early childhood, we should teach more than counting aloud and include attaching numbers to items and to talking aloud about numbers.

This number sense ability was not related to IQ or attention.

Neuroscientists are just beginning to study math, the brain, and learning, and specific strategies for intervention are still unclear. However, based on what we have learned so far about the brain, we can make some leaps into classroom practice.

Leaping into the Classroom

When students perform poorly in math, teachers and the students themselves often believe they "can't do math" when actually several different cognitive deficits may be involved, varying with the person. These include numerosity, estimation, difficulty remembering verbal information, trouble with working memory in general, or all of these. Addressing underlying deficits is more helpful than simply giving more practice on problems.

As usual, we can't attribute difficulty to lack of effort or intelligence. While neuroscience might not help us right now to know what interventions to use, research may lead to early diagnosis and targeted interventions for those with math difficulty. Park suggests that tasks could be developed to strengthen communication between the left and right parietal area to improve the processing necessary for skilled math performance.

Improving Performance

Create games in which students guess quantities—the number of gumballs or pennies in a jar or guessing which picture has the most dots in it, for example. As students get better at this, they will improve their basic math skills according to recent research.

Working Memory

Just as in writing and reading, math is heavily dependent on good working memory capacity (chapter 5). Michele Mazzocco, a developmental psychologist and education researcher, and her colleagues investigated the role of working memory in mathematical performance. They discovered that some students quickly forget verbal information or can't hold information long enough in working memory to complete a math problem. Bill Thompson, a math professor at Red Rocks Community College, recalls he once wrote out each step for a math problem requiring a student to add two mixed numbers (e.g., $1\,^3/_4 + 2\,^1/_2$). The number of steps was around thirty. This would create a large load on working memory and require a lot of planning and keeping track of the process. Many students cannot follow the process from beginning through to completion, and this is not even algebra yet; it is an eighth-grade arithmetic skill (or lower).

Rather than teachers simply drilling on the skill itself, they can begin by addressing the potential underlying source: poor working memory capacity (see chapter 5). The memory strategy of "chunking" is often used; however, new research indicates the amount of material we can hold in working memory is more like four items, not the five to seven as previously believed. The more fluent a person is with the material, the bigger the chunks can be and the more information can be held online in working memory. However, some math problems have such long and complex calculations that the chunks are large and there may be more than four steps. Thompson points out that while chunking might help, the person has to order and process the chunks. This might decrease the load on working memory, but it increases the load of executive processing because there is now another level in this process—the metachunks, if you will.

As with other learning difficulties, teachers can address this in the classroom by showing students how to break down long problems into shorter chunks and perhaps make notes as they go through the process. Teacher Ella Baccouche reminds us to use pictures along with the words to take advantage of the visual memory from the visual-spatial sketch pad and to speak aloud to use verbal memory from the phonological loop.

Working memory deficits predict poor math achievement. The more fluent the calculation, the less demand on working memory. This is where fluency and rote memorization can be helpful. Flash cards and lots of practice can help students with poor working memory capacity.

Working memory can be affected by math anxiety.

Working memory can be affected by math anxiety (see chapter 3) and impair performance. This must be addressed. Students with anxiety as well as attentional or working memory issues are going to need more time to complete tests. In some way, this must be provided for but can be challenging because many tests take an entire class period. One solution is to make two shorter tests and give them on two days. Some schools have a testing center or lab that can give makeup tests. An alternative is to allow students to take a comparable version in the center or lab, using all the time they need. Perhaps your department can brainstorm ways students can be relieved of the time pressure of math tests. Many times a student can perform the work, just not in the time allowed. Ask yourself if it is really necessary that the student be fast at the math, or just able to do it, and then design assessment accordingly.

Retrieval

Not only does working memory pose a problem, but retrieval from long-term memory can be a problem for students. If they have not properly encoded (stored in long-term memory) prior knowledge such as multiplication tables, they will find the subsequent material problematic.

Acronyms are especially helpful in math. (You may want to review the information about encoding memory in chapter 5.) All math teachers know PEMDAS (Please Excuse My Dear Aunt Sally) to help remember the correct order for the long string of operations. Strategies like this are especially helpful for students with working memory issues and support what we know about memory for all learners: the normal limits of working memory and chunking as a tool for extending the limits.

Psychologist Daniel Willingham's investigation of the best and worst study practices found that for math, interleaved practice, in which various problems are mixed in together, is the best. More than one formula may be presented with practice. It was found that students performed better and were better at knowing when to apply a given formula. West Virginia University researchers Kristin Mayfield and Philip Chase investigated the teaching of college algebra and found that a three-step process was most effective. First, students are introduced to a certain type of problem. Then they practice that problem until they are fluent. Finally, they practice the problem on work that includes other types of problems (interleaved). It was this final cumulative practice that led to higher achievement and faster performance. While students may have some difficulty in this final practice stage, test results were better.

Memorization

Typical instruction in math involves having students memorize a formula and then apply it to problems. As we learned in chapter 4, inductively reasoning how the formula works from examples may be a better approach. I am not against memorizing. Students need their multiplication tables often in real life, and it is not desirable that they should pull out their smart phone for simple calculations. However, students with memory impairment may need to rely on such devices as tablets and smart phones their entire lives. Since these devices are almost always available, allowing some students to rely on those is not significantly different from allowing those who are having difficulty walking to use a cane . . . until they can walk better, if ever. At the same time that we want to strengthen weaknesses, we want to provide some compensatory strategies until they get better. We can do both. Neuroscience has indicated some of these difficulties are due to brain processing weaknesses or deficits, and these may persist through adulthood.

Another consideration when thinking about what needs to be memorized is that the world has changed dramatically since many of those who are adults today were taught math. We have access to technology that can do lengthy calculations for us. Rather than memorizing a formula and knowing how to calculate it, perhaps now our goal might be to help students understand when and why a formula must be used rather than mindlessly memorizing formulas. Teaching math in a problem-solving format in which a student figures out what needs to be calculated, what information needs to be inputted, and what formula would be most appropriate is far more valuable in life than temporarily memorizing formulas and working the problem manually. Perhaps we should put the focus more on meaning, transfer, and application than on memorizing.

Word Problems

Word problems are challenging for many students. Long word problems pose a challenge to the limits of working memory in that a student can't hold the beginning information "online" in their memory long enough to process it with the later material. In addition, many students have a reading difficulty, so reading the problem, not the math, poses the difficulty. Students with attentional issues struggle with something in which close sustained attention must be paid. Those with anxiety or learned helplessness struggle in the face of something more challenging. Those with executive function (higher-order thinking) deficits have trouble with the planning and organization required by word problems. Another issue with story problems is neural network or prior knowledge. No wonder students have trouble with word problems. Their difficulty isn't with the "math" itself but other pathways.

Check the story problems in the assignments and especially on the test to make sure there is nothing in them that could be affected by lack of prior knowledge. If a story problem refers to a metronome, for example, make sure students understand what a metronome is prior to the test or assignment or eliminate that problem from the assignment or test (or change the wording to something they are familiar with).

Scaffolding and Strategies

As in other areas, we use scaffolding in math to help students compensate for weaknesses. If underlying weaknesses in attention or working memory pathways are part of the problem, we can anticipate and try to offset them. We can teach the math by breaking it into parts for them at first and eventually introduce longer and more complex problems that they are able to break down for themselves. They can use writing or talking aloud (under appropriate circumstances) to help them deal with long and complex material.

Teaching math thinking style and strategies is critical. Researchers at the University of Munich found that math achievement is more related to motivation and study strategies than IQ. Students need to know this good news. Once again, this is something that they can control. These researchers caution that IQ is important when developing math skills in the early stages; later, these other factors are important to growth in math over time. The researchers identified skills such as summarizing, explaining, and making connections to other materials were important.

In any subject, good executive function is important. Determine if the student has an underlying weaknesses in executive functions such as planning, organizing, or budgeting time on tests. Teach the executive function skills as they apply to math. Start the semester by scaffolding the students with shorter assignments with more direction and by using blank graphic organizers to help them plan and work through the material. Then progress to less direction and more independence. Researcher Liane Kaufman, a specialist in neuropediatrics at Innsbruck Medical University in

Austria, suggests not discouraging the use of fingers when learning or struggling with math. Using fingers can be an intervention for children and adults with mathematical difficulty.

Modeling is as important in math as in other skills. As you write the examples on the board, talk aloud to yourself as you work them, anticipating the stumbling blocks the student may have. Seeing other students work problems on the board is also helpful, especially if the student working them is struggling with the problem and the rest of the class is helping. Remind the students there is nothing wrong with struggling; they are creating neural networks.

Engage the social brain and the motor system with "human math" problems by distributing paper with numbers and signs to students. Call students up and have them hold up a number or sign as they stand in a row so that a math problem and solution is visible. Ask students if it is correct. If not, ask them who (what number?) needs to come up to make it correct. Students will see they can change the numbers in the problem *or* in the solution to create a correct answer. This strategy gets students up and moving, which is important, and it helps them visualize the math.

Using Meaningful and Realistic Material

Engage the reward pathway by making the material as meaningful and as close to real life as possible. Sometimes it is hard to explain to students how they will use the material later in life, but we are teaching it so that they can, so we should be able to find good examples. Good videos on YouTube can provide such examples. This link to real life is important at any grade level.

Since most math problems we encounter in life are not presented to us with the math written out and a blank for our answers, transfer is important. One reason we teach word problems is to transfer math skills from numerical problems to "real-life situations." Unrealistic word problems don't seem to do the trick. Unfortunately, most word problems don't sound particularly meaningful or based on real life. One solution is to use real-life issues to work with the math.

Pose a problem to students that the math will solve. For example, tell them that they are sales representatives selling equipment but aren't sure if the floor load will handle the equipment that the client wants. If the equipment causes the floor to fail, those below it in the building will be killed. Then say to the students, "You are responsible for both selling your client the equipment and making sure that it will be safe once it is installed. What information would you need to know, and how would you calculate it?" Younger children could determine how many children a tree fort could hold. Or have students measure their living room and determine how much flooring to buy, then compare pricing from ads to find the best deal. Make the examples relevant to their culture and experience, and let them figure it out. They can work in groups and then as a class. In this way they see the relevance to real life and don't have to memorize formulas because they understand the process.

There are always many community issues to investigate with math. For example, maybe the local zoo is holding a fundraiser because it wants to expand. Students could brainstorm ways to make more money and how much it would take to earn what the zoo needs. If admission to the zoo was raised by, say, one dollar, they would need to know how many visitors there are per year to figure how much that would generate. If they come up with an answer that is not enough or is too much, then determine what exactly the increase would need to be. Using the name of the local zoo and posing a real-life scenario is more meaningful to the brain than problems out of context.

Multiple Pathways

The ideal way to teach math is to use multiple pathways when teaching, practicing, and assessing. See it, say it, model it, apply it, draw it, analogize it, and so forth. Keep in mind the purpose of teaching the material. If the purpose is for the student to understand when to use a formula, know the formula, apply it correctly, and get a correct answer, then how the student demonstrates that is not the significant issue. If a student demonstrates it through creating a model, a poster, multiple real-life applications, or a video to explain it, then that may be as effective as simply taking an objective test. If at all possible, provide an alternative assessment for students. One homework option can be to build a representation of the formula for the area of a rectangle, for example.

HOMEWORK MENU

Because this chapter covers three content areas, it is beyond the scope to address the typical content assignments in these domains. Use those, but add as many of the homework menu options from the other chapters as would apply.

SUGGESTED STRATEGIES

Language

- Get students speaking as much as possible.
- Provide multiple speakers of the language being taught, so students can use the natural language learning process of pattern recognition.
- Sing songs to create more time speaking aloud.
- Use materials with noticeable prosody, such as rhymes, songs, and choral readings.
- Expose children to speakers of other languages as early in infancy as possible.
- Create dual-language programs for all students.

Reading

- Explicitly teach phonemic awareness.
- Determine whether difficulties in reading occur in phonology, orthography, or semantics and target interventions.
- Use materials with low working memory demands to test comprehension.
- Show words while pronouncing them for students.
- Teach context clues.
- Address comprehension issues related to prior knowledge.

Math

- Provide activities on both number sense and calculation.
- Make math visible and tangible.
- Use YouTube videos to supplement instruction.
- Encourage students to talk problems through.
- Address missing neural networks—the prior knowledge necessary to work the problem.
- Let students use their fingers to count.

- Use songs and mnemonics to remember formulas.

- Use human math problems to make processes visible and to encourage movement.

- Reduce strain on working memory by writing down interim steps.

REFLECT AND CONNECT

How will you engage multiple pathways discussed so far in your language instruction?

How will you address working memory problems that could underlie reading or math?

Case study: Describe a student who has exhibited one of the problems discussed in this chapter (such as knowing it but can't say it, can't pronounce a sound, reading comprehension problems, trouble remembering math formulas). How did the student behave? What did you believe the problem to be? How did you address the problem? What would you do differently now?

SUGGESTED READING

August, D., Short, D., & Genesee, F. (2010). *Improving education for English learners: Research-based approaches*. Sacramento: California Department of Education Press.

Bialystok, E., & Hakuta, K. (1994). *In other words: The science and psychology of second-language acquisition*. New York, NY: Basic Books.

Davis, R. D., & Braun, E. M. (2010). *The gift of dyslexia*. New York, NY: Penguin.

Dehaene, S. (1997). *The number sense: How the mind creates mathematics*. New York, NY: Oxford University Press.

Dehaene, S. (2009). *Reading in the brain: The new science of how we read*. New York, NY: Penguin.

Doidge, N. (2007). *The brain that changes itself: Stories of personal triumph from the frontiers of brain science*. New York, NY: Viking.

Forsten, C. (2010). *Step-by-step model drawing: Solving word problems the Singapore way*. Peterborough, NH: Crystal Springs Books.

Gopnik, A., Meltzoff, A. N., & Kuhl, P. K. (1999). *The scientist in the crib: What early learning tells us about the mind*. New York, NY: HarperCollins.

Lems, K., Miller, L. D., & Soro, T. M. (2010). *Teaching reading to English language learners: Insights from linguistics*. New York, NY: Guilford Press.

Shaywitz, S. (2005). *Overcoming dyslexia: A new and complete science-based program for reading problems at any level*. New York, NY: Vintage.

Sobanski, J. (2002). *Visual math: See how math makes sense*. New York, NY: LearningExpress.

Willingham, D. (2009). *Why don't students like school?* Hoboken, NJ: Wiley.

Wolf, M. (2007). *Proust and the squid: The story and science of the reading brain*. New York, NY: HarperCollins.

Zadina, J. N. (2008). *Neuroanatomy of dyslexia: A behavioral-anatomic study of dyslexia subtypes and controls*. Saarbrucken, Germany: VDM Verlag.

Zadina, J. N., Smilkstein, R., Daiek, D. B., & Anter, N. M. (2013). *College reading: The science and strategies of expert readers*. Boston, MA: Wadsworth Cengage.

7

The Frontal Lobe Executive Function Pathway

Danny is my most problematic student. His notebook is a mess, and he can't find the day's assignment. He misses deadlines and doesn't seem to think of the consequences. I am frustrated with him speaking out of turn in class and not following directions. He isn't doing well in reading or math and acts like he just doesn't care. I don't understand. Is this from poor parenting, or is he just a student who doesn't care and can't learn from his mistakes?

MAKING CONNECTIONS

What behavior in the primary grades has recently been shown to predict achievement years later? Why are some students so disorganized? Why can't some college students think critically?

Maybe Danny has executive dysfunction, a problem with the frontal lobe. So far you have learned about many pathways and processes in the brain. Now we turn to a part of the brain that controls and orchestrates those pathways in addition to mediating some functions critical to academic achievement. The frontal lobe can consciously control intention and arousal, as when you decide you need to be more alert and are involved in regulating emotion. In chapter 4, you learned that it is rewarding and motivating for students to figure things out for themselves, a process involving the frontal lobe. In chapter 5, you learned the academic importance of attention and working memory, two functions mediated by the frontal lobe. Assuming all of your pathways and processes discussed so far are working well, you need to get them all to work *together*, to bring them "online" when needed, and to suppress certain ones at times. In addition, you need to be able to think about your thinking and monitor your behavior (metacognition). Welcome to the frontal lobe, the conductor of the "orchestra." Let's look at how the frontal lobe in the brain develops and its role in learning.

What Does the Research Say?

Executive functions is a term associated with the behaviors mediated by the frontal lobe of the brain. The frontal lobe is in the front of each hemisphere of the brain, behind your forehead. You have a left and a right frontal lobe. Frontal lobe functions begin to be seen in early infancy and develop throughout the school years, finishing their development at approximately ages eighteen to twenty-five. In adolescence they go through a pruning and regrowth period as the brain adapts to new needs and experiences.

The frontal lobe (figure 7.1) has often been called the executive part of the brain because it is responsible for functions similar to what an executive might engage in—getting everything to work together to achieve a goal; that is, helping other parts of the brain execute effectively. An important part of the frontal lobe is the prefrontal cortex (figure 7.2). It is, as it sounds, in the frontal lobe and it interacts with parietal (sensory integration and language) and the anterior cingulate cortex (attention) (not shown) when performing executive functions.

Critical to Academic Performance

Frontal lobe executive functions underlie academic performance across the curriculum. Performing math problems puts a high demand on the frontal lobe, as information must be held in working memory. Skilled readers engage the frontal lobe along with the language pathways. The frontal lobe has been shown in brain

Figure 7.1 The Frontal Lobe

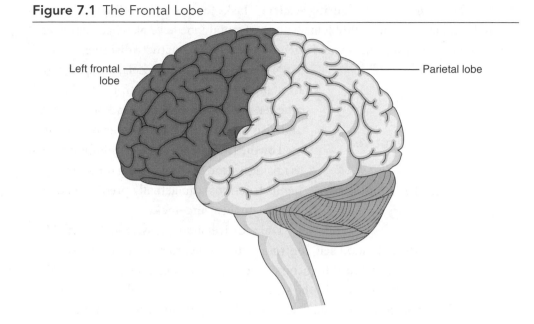

Left frontal lobe

Parietal lobe

Figure 7.2 The Prefrontal Cortex

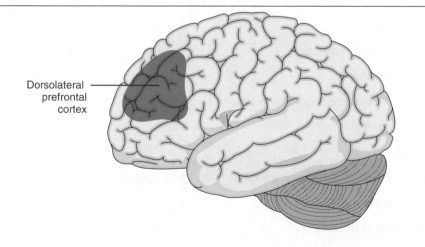

Dorsolateral prefrontal cortex

scans to be heavily activated during academic tasks for less fluent bilinguals, such as second-language learners. Problems with the frontal lobe have also been associated with conduct disorder, autism, and attention-deficit hyperactivity disorder.

Neuroscientist Philip Zelazo reports that frontal lobe executive function in childhood is a better predictor of school readiness than IQ and also predicts SAT scores. Behaviors mediated by the frontal lobe in early childhood, such as raising a hand to speak, lining up, and following instructions, can actually predict academic and life quality outcomes.

Frontal lobe executive function in childhood is a better predictor of school readiness than IQ.

Duke University neuroscientist Terrie Moffitt notes that early childhood self-control predicts outcomes at age thirty-two that include a person's physical health, income, and even drug dependence and criminal convictions. Since the children in the study were matched on childhood socioeconomic status and intelligence, it does appear that their life success was influenced by their early frontal lobe functioning.

Functions

The term *executive functions* describes the higher-order thinking processes orchestrated by the frontal lobe and include these:

- Planning
- Analysis and synthesis
- Organization
- Control of attention and emotion
- Metacognition
- Judgment
- Mental flexibility—shifting strategies and adjusting to change
- Working memory
- Delaying gratification
- Handling ambiguity and uncertainty
- Intrapersonal skills and insight

- Recognizing and selecting relevant information
- Initiating and sustaining activity over time
- Time management

You can see how these skills, similar to higher-order skills in Bloom's taxonomy, are critical to achievement.

One study of executive function created two groups of students. One group received more math instruction, while the other group had a discussion about the planning aspects of doing math, that is, the frontal lobe functions. The group that did better was the one emphasizing the role of the frontal lobe in math: planning.

Cognitive Load

The frontal lobe is metabolically expensive: it uses more than its share of the body's fuel. That is why prolonged attention can be so exhausting. We can feel as exhausted after a long period of mental activity as from physical activity, though in a different way. Brain imaging studies have revealed increased blood flow to the frontal lobe during tasks requiring intense intellectual effort. Brain scans show the brain is working harder when learning a new task as opposed to performing a task that has been practiced.

This initial state of learning creates increased *cognitive load*—the amount of effort required by the brain at a given moment. Holding information in working memory also increases cognitive load. Distractions and multitasking add to the cognitive load. More effort—that is, more cognitive load—means fewer resources are left over for other tasks. As you learned when taking the Stroop task in chapter 4, more cognitive load can lead to more mistakes, fatigue, and longer task completion time.

The brain conserves its resources automatically for survival. This may be why we don't always make the mental effort we could. Sometimes we have to be stirred out of our inertia to do the more challenging mental tasks.

What Does This Mean for Educators?

As we used to say in the lab, "Good frontal lobe, good life." People who have a well-functioning frontal lobe are better at using good judgment, budgeting time and money, delaying gratification, self-monitoring, and the other skills described earlier. The good news is that these thinking skills can be taught. Rosemary Tannock, an attention-deficit hyperactivity disorder expert at the University of Toronto, suggests intensive cognitive behavior training can improve executive functions, such as teaching children to think about their behavior and control their attention. These skills develop over time, so they must also be taught at every grade level, including college.

Importance of Early Intervention

Early executive function abilities predict later outcomes. The research of Clancy Blair, a cognitive psychologist at New York University, and colleague Rachel Razza suggests that student achievement can be improved through curricula designed to improve self-regulation skills. Phillip Zelazo, a neuroscientist, encourages educators to begin building good executive functions in children prior to their entering school. He believes there is a window of opportunity during preschool that can be used to prepare students for the increased demand on executive functioning that kindergarten requires (controlling behavior and maintaining attention). James Heckman, an economist, investigated the effects of early childhood experiences on achievement outcomes in adolescence and adulthood. He reports in the prestigious journal *Science* that we get a better return on our educational investment with interventions in preschool. This has strong implications for early childhood education. (See chapter 9.)

You build these cognitive skills in the same way the brain develops other skills: through use. Zelazo reports success in training children in executive functions through computer software and found that after training, their brains then looked more like those of older children.

Deficits

Many students diagnosed with learning differences show impairments in the executive functions performed by the frontal lobe. In addition to deficits in areas that work with the frontal lobe, students may have deficits in the frontal lobe functions themselves, known as executive dysfunction. The person may be born with deficits in these functions or injury may damage this lobe. These deficits may not show up right away.

In late elementary or early middle school, education puts more demand on frontal lobe functions; consequently, this is when deficits may begin to appear in terms of academic performance. As the curriculum requires more and more of these abilities, some students who are highly intelligent and have had good academic performance to that point may start to falter as their weakness in executive function begins to become a problem for them. Often students get by until they begin college, and suddenly the increased workload and demand on executive functions lead to failure. Because these students have not had specific problems before, it can look as if they have suddenly become lazy or unmotivated. Parents may believe their son or daughter is not trying.

Development

The frontal lobe is the last part of the brain to come fully online. Frontal lobe executive functions carry the person from adolescence into full adulthood. Individual executive functions may have different developmental trajectories, so you can't expect a student to be equally good at all of the functions, even though he or she may excel at some. It is important for educators to understand that the functions listed earlier are not activated in the brain in the same way in children, adolescents (including many college-age students), and adults (those over age twenty-five). Keep in mind that from approximately ages ten to twenty-five there is a great deal of variability in maturation of the frontal lobe. Like other brain processes, frontal lobe processes develop as a result of age and experience. Expecting all students to be at the same developmental milestone at the same time is one major mistake in our current educational system. All children do not learn to read at the same time, nor do they develop higher-order thinking skills at the same time. We can't measure students by one test at one point in developmental time.

Leaping into the Classroom

What we as teachers are capable of orchestrating may not be entirely feasible yet for our students. Our job is to get them to the high-functioning state so they can budget their time, organize their materials, meet deadlines, control their emotions, and make good decisions. Teachers may complain that their students can't do those things or say they can't "think critically." Your job is to help them get there; they will not be as good at it as you are until they have fully developed that part of the brain.

Learners may have temporarily reached the limits of their ability to manage these functions. I say temporarily, because one of the goals of educators from primary and secondary schools through college is to facilitate the development of executive functions. Therefore, you are a critical factor in helping students create a satisfying life through a high-functioning frontal lobe by giving them tasks that require frontal lobe activity, teaching them strategies that enable them to perform the tasks listed above, giving them scaffolding as they learn to get better at those tasks, teaching them skills to compensate for weaknesses in those processes, and remaining aware that it is a developmental *process* of acquiring good executive function. (Notice I am breaking the working memory rule from chapter 4. I am leaving it here as a cautionary tale.)

Recognizing Executive Function Weakness

What can poor executive function look like in the classroom?

- Poor reading comprehension
- Difficulty with math
- Trouble meeting deadlines or completing assignments
- Difficulty writing due to the steps involved, such as planning and organizing material
- Apathy, boredom, lack of motivation

You may not know whether a student's difficulty is executive function impairment or other deficits. What might appear to be frontal lobe executive function weakness or deficits might be a process that works with or is regulated by the frontal lobe, such as reading, working memory, or attention. Many developmental disorders, such as dyslexia, attention deficit disorders, and autism, may include deficits in executive skills, although not always. Impaired executive function can also be caused by stress, anxiety, or depression.

Sometimes poor frontal lobe function appears to be apathy or lack of effort, and frustrated teachers and parents may berate the learner for being lazy. Neuroscientist Martha Denckla says calling students lazy, irresponsible, or unmotivated is "adult name-calling" and traumatizing to children. You can imagine that labeling a student in this way would make these conditions, and thus executive function, more impaired. Struggles with executive function lead students to feelings of defeat and perhaps impaired self-efficacy. Some students are resilient, but others are not and become embroiled in a downward spiral of low self-efficacy, or learned helplessness. These states then can diminish effective executive functioning on a downward spiral. The emotional pathway is affecting the performance of the frontal lobe pathway.

One underlying concept of this book is that many brain processes work together and involve multiple pathways. Diagnosing a student would be neither appropriate nor feasible for a teacher to do in the classroom. Of course, you try to determine where a student is getting off track or what his or her problem may be, but the teacher's role is not to diagnose a learning disorder or label a student. Since you can't specifically diagnose or usually remediate with targeted interventions for each student, you can use a multiple pathways approach to address the multitude of differences between students by providing multiple options for instruction, assignments, and assessments.

Early Education

Start addressing executive function in early childhood. Harvard psychiatrist and neuroscientist Enrico Mezzacappa found that the early childhood environment has an impact on executive capacity later in life. Since executive function skills develop in response to experience, the appropriate early experiences may not have been provided to some children. This deficit will continue to affect them because their executive skills remain underdeveloped.

Early childhood and elementary teachers can provide stimulating activities that require students to use these skills, while keeping in mind that these children are still developing those abilities. Teaching young children to self-regulate by raising a hand to speak, be silent when asked, or follow instructions is critical to providing students with the skills for success later in school and in life.

High School and College Students

From middle school through college, instructors need to consciously include activities and assignments requiring executive function skills. In addition, instructors need to factor in the transfer of executive skills so what students learn about planning on one task, for example, will be independently applied on the next task. Familiar tasks need to be included as scaffolding, but novel tasks must also be included that require the student to make a connection between earlier tasks and new tasks. Novel tasks can put more demand on executive skills, thus helping the student develop those skills more fully.

Instructors need to consciously include activities and assignments requiring executive function skills.

Students with executive function deficits require more scaffolding, as well as instruction in compensatory strategies so they can scaffold themselves later with strategies and technical support. For traumatized students, executive function may be diminished, as emotional processes use more of the brain's resources and these students find it harder to engage in higher-order skills. Again, they require additional support. College students' skills may not have evolved to the point that some professors may expect. Professors who do not understand frontal lobe development or executive function impairment may also believe a student isn't trying. They may not understand that the student is impaired in his or her ability to execute a long process or multiple demands or hasn't learned the skills.

Often high school and college students have helicopter parents who hover over them and get overly involved in their academic life. These parents are trying to act as their child's frontal lobe! This does not help their child develop good executive function. Would you put your child in a wheelchair when young so he or she didn't fall down in the process of learning to walk? No; children fall, get up, and eventually get better at walking.

Children have to be given opportunities to fail, as well as succeed, in order to develop their frontal lobe. I am not talking about failing a course. I mean they fail to meet a deadline, receive consequences, and learn from their mistakes. Learning from mistakes is part of creating good executive functions. A classroom needs some freedom to fail. For example, I suggest students get one "get out of jail free" card. They can get a two-day extension on one assignment during the semester, for example. Or they may be allowed one make-up test. In other words, there is a safety net while they are learning to manage these skills.

Modeling

Of course, teachers must model good executive function themselves. Arriving late to class, promising to return papers on a given date and failing to do so, or failing to control emotions all exhibit poor executive function. Of course, things happen, but a pattern of this does not model good executive function. Alternatively, saying something such as, "Since it was raining today, I had to leave a half an hour early to get here on time," models good planning and forethought for students.

Teaching Executive Functions

As I emphasize throughout this book, teaching students specific strategies is important. One executive function deficit is trouble managing an assignment. You can demonstrate the steps to do so. A timetable could be helpful here for longer projects. If the project takes more than one day, help students break it down into manageable pieces. You would also include any content-specific strategies as well, such as their guideline for the reading process if the assignment is to read a textbook chapter.

Scaffolding and Strengthening

One of the ways I scaffolded executive functions such as planning was with a monthly calendar. My developmental reading students were required to read a book during the semester in addition to their regular classroom assignments and readings. First, I divided the number of pages in the book by the number of class days available to us. It came out to around ten to fifteen pages of reading per day to keep up. I plotted that on the calendar so they had a daily reading assignment to keep up with. If they didn't have time to read one day, they knew they had to read more another day. They knew explicitly whether they were on target by looking at the calendar. Then I plotted chapter deadlines on the calendar along with test dates and journal collection dates. This helped us all stay on track. My hope was they would learn this strategy of planning and apply it in their future courses. In addition, since uncertainty increases anxiety, making deadlines explicit reduces unhealthy stress in the classroom.

You have learned to create a homework menu that enables students to work with their strengths. Early in the semester, pick one of the options that demands good executive function, such as a project requiring multiple steps or carried out over time, and make it a scaffolded project. The student will get a breakdown of the steps required to carry out the project—a checklist and a timetable. As the semester goes on, scaffolding can be reduced.

Teachers should slow down their speech and repeat information to assist with normal limits of working memory.

The frontal lobe mediates working memory. Tannock suggests that teachers should slow down their speech and repeat information to assist with normal limits of working memory.

Cognitive Load

One of the most important concepts neuroscience has provided to education is that of cognitive load, the amount of brain effort required by a task. Just as a person can lift only a certain amount of weight, the brain can put limits on the amount of effort that can be put forth at any given moment. This effort fatigues the brain just as lifting weights fatigues the body after a certain amount of time.

We can actually see with brain scans when the brain is working harder. You want to create an environment in which ideal learning can take place so you must always be aware of the approximate cognitive load of any given situation, task, assignment, or assessment. In the lab, we sometimes deliberately create cognitive load to stress the system and see how it can perform under high-cognitive-load situations. But it is not fair to do that in the classroom. Teachers who understand cognitive load theory can design lessons, assignments, and assessments that do not create unnecessary cognitive load.

You can understand the effect that distractions in the classroom have in increasing cognitive load. You can be careful that tests do not in themselves create additional cognitive load by requiring too many items to be held in working memory, such as when matching formats have too many items or questions use unnecessarily long sentences (see chapter 4 on working memory). If readers have a strong neural network on the material being presented and are fluent readers, they can handle long complicated sentences, such as the ones you find in this book. Our students are probably already struggling with the content. You do not need to stress their cognitive system further by unnecessarily increasing the cognitive load through compound or complex sentences.

Multitasking increases cognitive load. One way in which multitasking does not create much additional cognitive load is when one of the tasks is a habit or a highly fluent task such as driving a car. Driving a car is so automatic that your mind is free to do other tasks, including the dangerous one of texting. Repetition drives the fluent and repetitive tasks into the basal ganglia so they can take over, thus freeing the brain for other thinking tasks—to give more attention to something else. That is why you can drive without thinking as much as when you learned to drive and why you might arrive somewhere and realize you don't even recall the drive because your mind was a million miles away. Therefore, an important goal is to make some tasks fluent and automatic, and thus reduce cognitive load, before introducing the next step or new material. This is the purpose of flash cards. In learning a second language, an important goal is to turn the effortful and conscious searching for the correct word or pronunciation into an automatic response—fluency.

Keep an eye on cognitive load during a lesson. When presenting information, do not throw too much new information at the student at once. Have a clear structure for your lesson, and make this structure explicit to the students with a general outline or graphic organizer they complete. Use visuals instead of lengthy explanations where possible to simplify a complex topic into a picture easier to manipulate in working memory. Another way to reduce cognitive load is to write things down. This same technique holds true when too much extraneous information is on your mind while working on a task. Stop and make a to-do list, which removes it from your mind, and then focus on one task at a time.

One way to reduce the cognitive load is to teach a strategy by applying it to material that is very easy for them—perhaps below their reading level or on content with which they are already fluent. In this way, students can focus on the strategy itself. Then the next step is to apply the strategy to the textbook material—the more challenging material. In other words, have them create a neural network on the strategy before raising their cognitive load by applying it to new material.

For example, if a student is learning the concept of summary, don't begin with having them summarize a difficult reading passage. Ask students to tell you the plot of a movie they saw using five sentences that tell about the entire movie—beginning, middle, and end. Then pick the best examples to read to the class and tell them, "This is a summary." Then ask them to write a summary of what happened to them the day before. These are easy tasks that focus on the concept of summary rather than trying to comprehend challenging material while learning the concept. Finally, bring them to the step of summarizing the material in the textbook. Introduce one step at a time. Otherwise if a student is trying to learn *and* apply a new strategy to new or difficult material, you won't know whether the problem is a lack of understanding of the strategy itself or a lack of understanding of the material.

Since cognitive load is the highest early in the learning process and when students struggle with other learning issues that increase cognitive load, such as working in a second language or struggling with a learning difference, you can diversify your strategies according to the timeline of the learning process. This means to be conscious of reducing the cognitive load early in the sequence and then bring in more complex tasks later in the process. More challenging tasks are best scheduled earlier in the class period, with more interactive or less attention-intensive activities scheduled later in the class period. This is true for all ages and becomes even more important when classes are ninety minutes or three hours in length.

Students need to know that certain activities are going to be more effortful than others—for example:

- Learning new material
- Performing executive functions when they are stressed
- Applying a new strategy
- Carrying out a long-term project
- Checking for errors
- Thinking metacognitively about performance and where to improve it

Metacognition

Metacognition is the act of thinking about your own thinking and is one of the skills of the prefrontal cortex (see figure 7.1). If the brain is an orchestra and the frontal lobe is the conductor, think about the mental processes of the conductor to understand the role of metacognition. The conductor doesn't just tell the orchestra what to do; he must be aware of how the musicians are doing it. Does one instrument come in too loud, too fast, or sound off-key? How did this performance compare to the last one? How is player A performing compared to player B, and should their roles be switched (similar to switching strategies)? How successful was the practice? Are you ready for the performance (the test)? If a conductor doesn't think about the performance, observe it, evaluate it, and make adjustments accordingly, the orchestra would not be successful and the conductor would probably get fired. Share this metaphor with your students.

Being able to be metacognitive is important to all parts of life, including learning. Being in tune with what your mind is thinking enables your prefrontal cortex to take more control. If you are aware you are no longer paying attention to a lecture, you can redirect your attention. Students who stop to reflect on their processes as they read may discover they did not understand the passage, but just mindlessly moved their eyes across the words. The frontal lobe can then alter the behavior, bring in more attention, and enable the student to reread the passage with understanding. Being metacognitive means you can determine which strategies are effective for the specific material and for your individual strengths and weaknesses profile and adjust strategies accordingly.

Keep in mind that you must teach students how to be metacognitive. This is a skill that develops with age and experience. Teaching the process of metacognition is important at every grade level. Students need to learn how the brain learns and, just as important, how to evaluate how their own brain is learning. The brain develops according to how it is used, so requiring students to engage in metacognitive tasks will make them more metacognitive and enable them to use their frontal lobe more effectively. Include metacognitive tasks as part of an assignment. One question on the assignment can be, "What strategies do you plan to use?" Follow up with questions about what strategies they actually used, how well they worked, and what they could have done differently. This feature is as important as any other part of an assignment: you are teaching your students to be better thinkers and learners and to be insightful about their learning. It should be part of any discussion or assignment.

Metacognition is a high-cognitive-load task, that is, it puts a high demand on the brain's resources. Keep these activities brief and alternate them with activities that engage different processing, such as group work, drawing, and listening. Although all of these tasks do put demands on the brain, they do so in different ways.

Reflection

Reflection is an important frontal lobe skill similar to metacognition. In metacognition, one is thinking about one's thinking or performance. Reflection is thinking about material from a more personal standpoint, such as how the material fits in with what is already known (existing neural network of the individual), what it means to one's own life, or a personal or emotional response to material. We saw in chapter 1 that reflection is critical to making connections. At the beginning of a unit, you make explicit connections to upcoming material. During or at the end of a lesson, you allow for reflection to consolidate learning and facilitate the connection of the recently learned material to the learner's existing network. The 10/80/10 rule suggests spending 10 percent of time on making connections, 80 percent on content, and 10 percent on reflection. Now that you understand more about how the brain learns, you see the necessity of providing for reflection. Build in moments approximately every ten minutes for simple reflection:

- Draw something relevant to what was learned.

- Doodle.

- Create or add to a mind map.

- Write in a journal about their understanding of what was covered.

- Write or share how the material relates to real life or to them personally.

- Write or share their emotional reaction to the material.

- Write down a question to work on later in groups.

- Write or discuss how the material relates to previously learned material.

Frontal Lobe Fatigue

Part of enhancing the frontal lobe is knowing when to give it a rest. You not only need to activate the frontal lobe; you also need to be able to turn it off. Understanding that the brain can get exhausted, just like the physical body, helps in designing more effective lessons. You wouldn't teach a gym class with continuous exercises with no rest, and you shouldn't teach content that way either. If you are exhausting the brain prior to an important mental task such as a test, you are not being wise. So you can see that cramming right before a test is not a good idea. Understanding the needs and constraints of the brain can keep us from harmful practices stemming from a lack of understanding of the brain.

Understanding that the brain can get exhausted, just like the physical body, helps to design more effective lessons.

Many tasks are high in cognitive load, and students need to know these require effort and may have to be spaced out with rest periods. When students get stuck on a problem or feel that they are not making any progress, advise them to take a quick break and let the unconscious mind process the information. This break should not be anything that is heavily frontal lobe, such as checking e-mail or playing Words With Friends. It should be downtime, such as going for a walk, loading the dishwasher, taking a shower, or walking the dog.

Problem solving is another area that can sometimes be helped by tamping down frontal lobe activity. The conscious mind can search for solutions to a problem, but sometimes the solution is still elusive. "Sleeping on it" is also ideal, whether it be a nap or going to bed at night. Students will be surprised at how often the brain can solve a problem seemingly on its own. Suddenly the problem doesn't seem so difficult.

Doing an activity that doesn't require so much prefrontal cortex activity, such as when showering, walking, driving the car to a familiar location, or just waking up in the morning, can lead to better creativity. That may be when you get some of your best ideas. Momentary breaks in content can give the brain some time to consolidate learning and form those neural networks. Daydreaming and doodling can help with this too, so maybe you shouldn't get too worried if a student appears to be daydreaming. He or she may be searching for connections, being creative with the information, or just resting his or her brain.

You can introduce some humor or a simple story or metaphor illustrating what was taught. Laughter is a great break too. Engage the students in mindfulness activities such as the ones covered in chapter 5. Mindfulness is a helpful tool for improving attention and also for resting the brain and being able to use it more effectively. If you put students in groups for an activity, this can serve as the break—the change of state. Scientist Jack Naglieri, speaking at a Learning and the Brain Conference, reports that ten minutes of math problems, then ten minutes of discussion about planning and approach, and then ten more minutes of math led to the best achievement, especially in the lower-performing students. Use the stand up and explain strategy (explained in chapter 2) whenever appropriate because it increases arousal (alertness) and socially engages students.

Just a slight break or change in activity will rest the frontal lobe. Students can doodle or reflect on what they just learned. In one interesting study, researchers taught a large group of students some new material. Then they divided the group and put them in two different rooms. One group was given fifteen minutes to study for the subsequent test. The other group was told to doodle for fifteen minutes. Then students were reunited and given a written test. Doodlers did better. In another study, cognitive psychologist Jackie Andrade found that those who doodled while listening to material recalled 29 percent more than those who just listened.

Our frontal lobe is critical to having a quality life in general and to being successful in school, and it must be developed and enhanced through experience and age. In academic settings (and the workplace too), it must be given a rest in order to perform well. Curriculum is like life: we need balance. Using multiple pathways for instruction in the classroom is good for brain performance as well as for learning. The frontal lobe also helps us engage more effectively with others, as you will see in the next chapter on the social pathway.

HOMEWORK MENU

- Write one of the following:
  - — Reflection
  - — Analysis
  - — Critique
  - — Outline
  - — Comparison/contrast
  - — Summary
- Create a graphic organizer with the most important relationships.
- Create a chart.
- Design a PowerPoint that illustrates the steps in carrying out a problem, project, or product.
- Create a timeline of the events.
- Design your own project, submit the proposal, get approval, and execute it.

SUGGESTED STRATEGIES

- Scaffold executive functions.
- Teach executive functions explicitly throughout a course.
- Discuss planning the aspects of doing assignments, including math assignments.
- Build in time for reflection.

- Begin with lessons that
  - Are highly structured
  - Are brief
  - Contain checklists for every step
  - Are written out for the student in steps
- Move students toward more independence:
  - Teach them how to plan.
  - Practice during class setting assignments with fifteen-minute deadlines.
  - Set deadlines at longer intervals.
  - Assign longer-term assignments.
  - Teach students how to break projects down and set intermediate deadlines.
  - Provide directions that do not include as many detailed steps.
  - Require metacognition of progress:

    At what steps did the student falter: not starting on time, failure to plan, failure to organize, not budgeting time?

    At what steps did the student succeed: starting the assignment, persevering, allowing enough time?

    What strengths did the student exhibit in the project that can be used in future assignments: good writing skills, good reading skills, organization skills?

    What progress was made during this period of intermediate independence?
- Require students to become independent:
  - Assign a long-term assignment.
  - Set a final deadline.
  - Provide the assignment without explicit intermediate steps.
- Reduce cognitive load:
  - Use the ten-minute rule.

— Avoid distractions, unnecessary information, and unnecessary visuals, such as clip art (see chapter 2).

— Use appropriate visuals to simplify material.

— Obtain fluency before proceeding.

REFLECT AND CONNECT

What instruction in executive functions have you built into your syllabus and lesson plans?

Describe a student you have now or recently taught who might have executive function deficits. What can you do to help this student strengthen and compensate?

SUGGESTED READING

Bartlett, F. C. (1932). *Remembering*. Cambridge: Cambridge University Press.

Cooper-Kahn, J., & Dietzel, L. C. (2008). *Late, lost and unprepared: A parents' guide to helping children with executive functioning*. Bethesda, MD: Woodbine House.

Cooper-Kahn, J., & Foster, M. (2013). *Boosting executive skills in the classroom: A practical guide for educators*. San Francisco: Jossey-Bass.

Dawson, P., & Guare, R. (2010). *Executive skills in children and adolescents: A practical guide to assessment and intervention* (2nd ed.). New York, NY: Guilford Press.

Fuster, J. M. (2003). *Cortex and mind: Unifying cognition*. New York, NY: Oxford University Press.

Goldberg, E. (2001). *The executive brain: Frontal lobes and the civilized mind*. New York, NY: Oxford University Press.

Hall, T. E., Meyer, A., & Rose, D. H. (2012). *Universal design for learning in the classroom: Practical applications*. New York, NY: Guilford Press.

Meltzer, L. (2007). *Executive function in education*. New York, NY: Guilford Press.

Sohlberg, M. M., & Mateer, C. A. (2001). *Cognitive rehabilitation: An integrative neuropsychological approach*. New York, NY: Guilford Press.

8

The Social Pathway

I am a very upbeat teacher. I know positive emotion is important in the classroom, so one day when I came to school very stressed out, I put on my happy face and taught as usual. Wouldn't you know the students picked that particular day to really act up, including Gina, a girl who has always been a pleasure. I pulled her aside and asked her why she was behaving inappropriately and contrary to her usual behavior. She told me that I was mad at her and she didn't know why. I wasn't, and why would she say that? I guess we all have those days, but this one was really tough. What is the best way to handle this?

MAKING CONNECTIONS

How relevant is our social nature to learning? What are the cognitive effects of social rejection and bullying? Are emotions contagious? Is group work always a good thing? Is technology rewiring children's brains? Is online teaching brain compatible?

That the brain is highly social affects every pathway addressed in this book. Patricia Kuhl, a prominent psychologist who studies language learning in children, hypothesizes that language learning depends on the social brain. Of course, emotions play a role in social interaction. The frontal lobe helps us regulate attention in ways affecting social interaction.

Our social pathway may be the strongest of all the pathways, such that we may even prefer social contact over food. In the 1950s, in a study that garnered worldwide attention, Harry Harlow, a psychologist, found that infant monkeys separated from their mothers preferred a wire "mother" to food, indicating that our social needs are a separate need and a critical pathway. Even earlier, in the 1920s, psychologist Lev Vygotsky promoted the view that learning is inherently social. It turns out that we may be wired to learn from others. Let's look inside the brain and see how this may have an impact on our practice.

SOCIAL STATUS AND SOCIAL REJECTION

The brain is highly social. We seem wired to learn from others, with the brain activating differently in response to humans versus objects. The brain is so connected to others that changes in social status affect brain chemistry, and social rejection is perceived as pain.

What Does the Research Say?

Social interaction activates multiple brain regions (see figure 8.1). There is a special place in the brain just for faces: the fusiform face area (FFA). This area is relatively large because faces are important to our survival. The temporoparietal junction (TPJ) (the junction of the temporal and parietal lobes) helps us understand what others may be thinking (theory of mind). We understand the movements of others with activation in the posterior superior temporal sulcus (pSTS). The medial prefrontal cortex (mPFC) mediates personality and social behavior.

During adolescence, these areas go through some renovation as structures develop and synapses and connections are reorganized. These areas peak in size around puberty and then decline until the mid-twenties, when they stabilize in size. The anterior temporal cortex (ATC), involved in applying our general social knowledge to a specific situation, peaks a little later and finishes developing a little later than the other areas. Of course, emotional areas are involved in our social thinking. We hope it is the reward pathway with positive emotion, but sometimes it is fear activation in the amygdala.

Our social nature is critical to our well-being and survival, as evidenced by the fact that social ostracism is one of the worst punishments we can give others.

Figure 8.1 Some Brain Regions Involved in Social Interaction

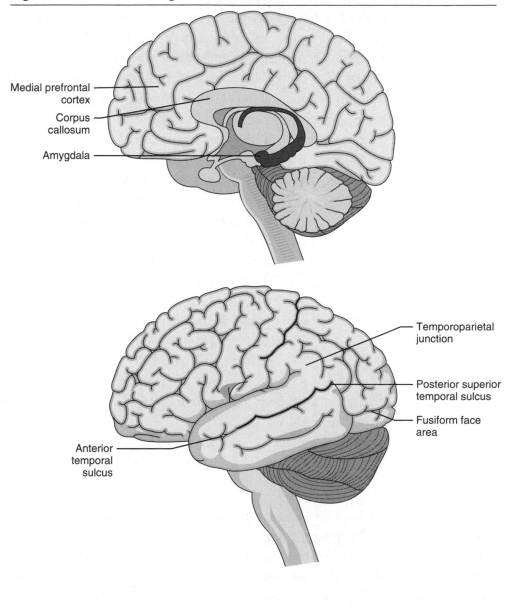

Medial prefrontal cortex

Corpus callosum

Amygdala

Temporoparietal junction

Posterior superior temporal sulcus

Fusiform face area

Anterior temporal sulcus

A recent theory, the social pain/physical pain overlap theory, was formulated by Naomi Eisenberger and Matthew Lieberman, researchers in the Social Cognitive Lab at the University of California, Los Angeles. It argues that the networks for social and physical pain overlap in the brain, meaning that social pain can feel like physical pain. Social pain can convey the same amount of brain response in the brain as being burned with a cigarette. Jaak Panksepp, a researcher in the Integrative Physiology and Neuroscience department at Washington State University, found opiate pain medication actually helped relieve social pain. This may be one reason drugs of abuse are so addictive.

Social pain can convey the same amount of brain response in the brain as being burned with a cigarette.

The good news is that neutral or positive social interaction is very rewarding, contributing to good health, well-being, and longevity. Social learning may be rewarding to the brain partly because it involves cooperation. Using MRI brain scans, neurobiology researcher Jean Decety and colleagues at the University of Chicago found that cooperation and competition, compared to working alone, increased arousal (see chapter 1) by increased activation of the anterior insula. However, cooperation, not competition, also activated the reward pathway with left medial orbitofrontal cortex activation (chapter 4), resulting in a reward of feel-good chemicals.

Social Status

In many species, social activity and social hierarchies play a role, and this is particularly true of humans. You have probably heard the terms *alpha male* and *alpha female*, roughly translated as "top dog" because dogs, primates, and other animals, as well as humans, react to status. Social status can affect immunity and health, as well as learning. Researchers in Japan found that social "pleasure" or reward, such as having a good reputation, activated the striatum in the brain just as monetary rewards did.

Robert Sapolsky, a professor of biology and neurology at Stanford, describes in his book *Monkeyluv* his studies of status issues in baboons, which, like humans, have social stress. He found status can be measured by chemical levels in the brain. Those whose status was unstable—whose status might go somewhat up or down—were the ones most negatively affected. Changes in status can affect human's stress hormones as well. Sapolsky also found that social connectedness was more important than rank itself.

Social Rejection

Social rejection increases stress and changes the brain. This becomes more extreme in cases of bullying, which can cause social pain to the extent of suicide. Isabelle Quellet-Morin, a Canadian researcher at the Centre for Studies on Human Stress, found that bullying changes the structure around a mood-regulating gene in the victim, and this can affect this person's mental health throughout his or her life. It can cause reduced connectivity and reduce the growth of new neurons. Stress hormones such as cortisol are released, which affect learning and, if they are high enough, can even kill neurons (chapter 3). The trauma from bullying compares to that of child physical and sexual abuse.

Neuroscientist Martin Teicher found that verbal abuse was as damaging to adolescents as physical abuse, and bullied teens had more depression, anxiety, and psychological disorders. Neuroimaging revealed that the corpus callosum, connecting the left and right brain, in bullied teens also had less myelin (the coating that speeds communication), which also has an impact on learning. According to psychologist Tracy Vaillancourt, bullied teens performed worse on working memory tasks, a skill critical to achievement (see chapter 3).

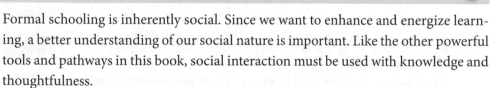

What Does This Mean for Educators?

Formal schooling is inherently social. Since we want to enhance and energize learning, a better understanding of our social nature is important. Like the other powerful tools and pathways in this book, social interaction must be used with knowledge and thoughtfulness.

Social Status and Its Effects

Social status has been shown to affect academic performance. This has been pronounced in math performance, particularly because females have to counter the gender bias (stereotype threat) in math performance and their subsequent lower status in the classroom as perceived by society. Educators need to be aware that status issues can affect learning and be careful not to exacerbate those issues. Providing enough variety in club activities and sports can help more students find areas where they can succeed rather than these activities being the domain of the top-status students.

Social Rejection and Its Effects

Bullying causes brain damage as well as emotional damage. Just as schools would not allow students to be violently beaten, they cannot allow bullying and dismiss it as teasing, hazing, or rites of passage.

Bullying or even social ostracism can be a serious problem in the classroom. The brain processes social pain as if it were physical pain, as indicated by many of our metaphors: "felt like I was kicked in the gut," "heartache," "ouch!" and "made me sick." As teachers, we must be cognizant of the serious ramifications of hurtful social behavior. This is an issue at every grade level, from kindergarten through graduate school. It is not enough for schools to have explicit policies addressing bullying; they must be proactive in preventing it.

Some interesting new research by psychologist Joseph A. Durlak at the University of Chicago found that when students were given social and emotional training, their behavior improved along with their academic achievement. The increase in achievement was similar to purely academic interventions. You might reflect on which course would help a student get a better job, have better relationships, and make better decisions leading to an overall better life: algebra 1 or a course in social and emotional behavior? Of course, I am not advocating doing away with algebra, only comparing the impact on a successful life and emphasizing the importance of including social and emotional behavior in the curriculum.

Leaping into the Classroom

One way to tap into the powerful reward pathway is to increase positive social interaction. We can create environments that deliberately foster inclusion of all students.

One of the most amazing principals I ever met was at a high school in Covington, Louisiana. Because of the temperate weather most of the year, many of the high school students hung around outside before and after school and on lunch breaks. The school had picnic tables and areas with seating and trees around most of the perimeter of the school. Every clique had its special place to hang out. Of course, cliques create hierarchies, which affect status and therefore stress chemicals for some students. One day the principal noticed that a group of students who were considered outcasts by the other students hung out at the very back of the school, where there was no seating or nice landscaping. He considered those students an important part of the school as well and immediately landscaped a lovely area where they hung out and provided picnic tables for them, making them a part of the school and sending a message to them that they counted as much as the popular students.

We must provide for the social needs of our students because these needs are related to emotions and emotions affect learning. Elementary English as a Second Language teacher Grace Quagliariello agrees, reporting that when her students feel safe and connected to their classroom and when their culture and language are accepted and celebrated, they learn better.

We must provide for the social needs of our students because these needs are related to emotions and emotions affect learning.

It is not enough for schools to have explicit policies addressing bullying; they must be proactive in preventing it.

Social Status and Group Work

A common way to include the social aspect in the classroom is to have students collaborate or work in groups. As we learn more about the brain, we understand both the advantages and disadvantages of group work. Everyone varies on a continuum from extrovert to introvert, and the amount of social interaction they need and want. Most students like to work in groups. However, this is not the case with all students. Some thrive in groups, and others get bullied or get stressed. Neuroscientist Naomi Eisenberger says that working with others can be good or bad, depending on whether an individual even thinks there is a chance of social rejection. Therefore, group work can be threatening to some students.

What about students in the classroom who are left out of groups? Once I had a student no one wanted in the group. His numerous piercings and tattoos set him apart from the rest of the students. He did his project option by himself, an amazing drawing illustrating the lesson. The other students were so impressed they all wanted him in their group the next time. It really changed things for him. Had he been forced to be in a group, his voice may have been ignored and his talent never discovered. If a student wants to work alone, I allow that in almost every case.

Author Susan Cain in her book *Quiet: The Power of Introverts in a World That Can't Stop Talking* addresses the mentality that everyone must work in groups to learn to get along in life. Although the pendulum swung too far toward privileging the extroverts, we are again recognizing the advantages of those who are introverts rather than extroverts. We need to be aware that both types exist and have different needs for learning. Very bright and motivated students may be slowed down by a group. In one interesting study, researchers at Virginia Tech found that working in groups made people "dumber." The premise is that in the group dynamics of coming to consensus and moving the group along, some of the more innovative thinkers may have to "tone it down" or get voted down by the majority. I think the point here is there is no one best solution. The more we know, the more we realize that group work is not to be taken lightly, but with knowledge and forethought, as with our other practices.

I do believe group work is important in general. Sometimes it takes another student to see where the gap is in our neural network. I had some outstanding statistics professors, but it was the other students who helped me the most when I struggled. They could see where I was missing out and helped me fill in those gaps. Directions to "discuss what you learned" or "discuss a topic" is wasting time in the classroom in order to engage in the popular practice of collaborative learning unless the directions are specific enough to make the activity meaningful. Since class time is limited, we need to combine the group time with purposeful work.

One of the most effective experiences I had was when the test that came with the developmental reading textbook my class was using was far too difficult for my developmental readers. On the day of the test, I announced they would be able to take it in groups. The excitement and motivation were astonishing. I had never before seen students work so hard with such urgent engagement. I didn't put much weight on that grade, and then a week later, I gave them a more realistic test I had made. The previous group test had helped them prepare and gave them a sense of positive expectation that they could handle the next test or motivated them to become more prepared. They saw the other members of the group succeed or struggle and saw their process of taking the test.

Other purposeful group activities are to solve a problem, generate ideas, answer questions, or complete an assignment. Many of these activities can take less than five minutes, thus providing a change of state, social interaction, arousal, and motivation before starting the next portion of a lesson.

As with earlier information, an awareness of status issues is important. It would do us well to be cognizant of status issues in the classroom. In any class, there will be a struggle for the position of alpha male and alpha female. Hopefully, it is you! Within a class or within a group, someone establishes dominance over peers. This struggle will invisibly or, unfortunately, sometimes visibly, play out among the students. When we put students into groups, they begin establishing the pecking order. An alpha "dog" emerges and, typically, so does someone with obviously low status in the group, and the others fall in between. When students change groups, status must be reestablished among the members. These relationships may need to change, thus upsetting the established balance. I am not saying not to change groups, just to be aware that this can be somewhat disruptive and present a feeling of threat to some students.

To address status issues during group work, it may be helpful to assign the group membership rather than let students pick their own groups, which makes status issues embarrassingly obvious to others and is stressful for all but high-status students. You can have students draw names out of a hat or use other random selection strategies. You can find random student selection tools on the Internet. I caution against changing group membership for the sake of changing, however. I think it is a good idea to change groups occasionally during the semester but not frequently. Try to find a balance between stability and novelty.

Since status is important in groups, one way in which all students can feel some status is to assign various roles in the group and base the role assignment on each student's strengths. In this way status does not depend on who you are but what you do in the group—your role. Assign people in groups so you end up with a variety of strengths. One person can be the moderator and direct the activity. Another, perhaps a quiet student with good verbal skills, can be the note taker. Another may be the listener who extracts the ideas from the brainstorming and recaps them. One may be the reporter who reports the results to the class. Someone good at planning may draft a long-term schedule for completion of a project. Someone good with technology may create the PowerPoint, for example, or someone more artistic may create a poster, as assignments warrant. Another may be the messenger who visits other groups and brings ideas back. Each of these roles taps into various skills that students may have. Everyone can be good at something in the group and have status.

Social Status and Classroom Activities

Many activities in class visibly affect a student's status. Getting called on and being right gives an instant status boost, as does getting the highest score on the test. Being wrong or being embarrassed can cause someone's status to feel threatened. As you may have noticed, people have a strong need to be right. However, in the classroom, students are often wrong in their answers. Teachers have found ways to work around this. With younger students, teachers sometimes use small whiteboards and have students hold up their answers so only the teacher sees them. For older children, some instructors have the students text their answers during class.

When an answer is incorrect, make the strategy wrong, not the student. You can ask, "How did you come to that answer?" and then suggest an alternative process. Your approach should be in a way that maintains the student's respect. We can take the sting out of being wrong by reminding students that making mistakes is just part of the learning process and nothing to be embarrassed about. Set the stage before students begin answering in class, such as in the first few days of a semester. Explanations of the learning process to students should include that it is effortful and that mistakes are naturally part of the process. An atmosphere of effort and struggle is better than an atmosphere of being right or being faster.

Explanations of the learning process to students should include that it is effortful and that mistakes are naturally part of the process.

Discussing results with a student in terms of progress rather than number correct is also face saving to students and reduces threat. You can point out that the student earned x number of points more than last time, indicating he or she is getting stronger at applying strategies, or study skills, or acquiring the skills necessary in the course. We almost always win when we play against ourself and don't lose status if we don't beat a previous score. Remember from chapter 4 that a sense of progress is rewarding to the brain, as is winning. But a student doesn't have to beat another student to get reward in the brain. I think one reason many people like the computer game Draw Something is that the progress of both players is tied together. As long as both succeed, they move forward. If one fails, they start over together. Teamwork in the classroom could be along those lines.

Service-learning projects can enhance the status of all members of the class as they gain self-esteem from helping others. One of the reading teachers at the community college where I taught had the developmental reading students read to the children in the on-site day care center. This benefited both groups. Students could read to those in assisted living homes as well. Since Hurricane Katrina, Tulane University requires all students to participate in community service projects. (I would like to see more of this in our institutions.)

Setting the Classroom Tone

There are several ways we can set the tone in our classroom that negative social interaction will not be tolerated. Most important, we must model this behavior. Under no circumstances should a teacher use sarcasm directed toward a student. Even making undermining remarks about a colleague who is not present is a threat to students because they know they may be next. It sets a bad example as well. It is also important we state this policy overtly on the first day of school: "Bullying or unkind social interactions will not be tolerated. The consequences are spelled out in your paperwork." Of course, you may not be able to discipline small negative interactions, and this is where your behavior and modeling come in. You could also make a countering statement: if a student mocks another's work, you can say something like, "In this class, we don't make judgments like that." Never let it go unchecked.

Social/Emotional Learning

Emotional intelligence can be taught and needs to be taught. If the school does not provide for social/emotional learning (SEL) in the curriculum, then we must provide it in our classrooms, ideally in the first week of school. Students can be taught to improve their skills in self-management, empathy, and cooperation. This can be accomplished through new materials that have been developed to teach students about their social/emotional lives. Include reading materials that exhibit emotional intelligence, and discuss them explicitly with students. Ask students why a character's behavior demonstrated good emotional intelligence. Build questions about emotional intelligence into lessons throughout the semester.

At the college level, this is more difficult but can be done. This topic must be included in student success courses and can be incorporated into reading, writing, and psychology courses. All content teachers can address these issues the first day or first week of the semester as they introduce the procedures and consequences or expectations in their class—for example:

- This classroom values cooperation over competition and respects all persons.

- Mistakes are a sign of thinking and learning.

- We respect the opinions of others.

And of course, we teachers must model emotional intelligence.

MIRROR NEURONS

What Does the Research Say?

Figure 8.2 What Happens When You Look at This Picture?

Look at figure 8.2 for a minute. What happened? Did you mirror the action by yawning? Humans (and primates) appear to have special neurons in the inferior frontal gyrus and inferior parietal cortex that react to the actions of other individuals. Scientists named these *mirror neurons* because they enable us to mirror or mimic another person's actions.

Neuroscientist Scott Frey at the University of Oregon looked at the mirror system using brain scans of college students who simply watched someone perform an action versus those who intended to copy the action. Different brain areas lit up for the two conditions. There was more brain activity if they intended to copy, and this predicted their accuracy in copying the action. This takes us back to chapter 1 where we explored the importance of students' setting intentions.

Some research has indicated that mirror neurons are more active when engaging with people more similar to us. Neuroscientist Elizabeth Losin at UCLA identified a gender-imitation bias: watching someone of the same gender activated the reward pathway in the brain, thus encouraging us to continue mirroring. Other research has demonstrated that mirror neurons are more active when watching someone from the same culture as opposed to someone from a different ethnicity or culture. Some experts in autism research suggest that the mirror neuron system may be deficient in those with autism.

We mirror others in another way: our emotions. When we see someone who looks sad, our brain activates a similar network in our brain in order to comprehend it. This activation can actually cause us to feel the emotion behind the expression. This may be how we experience empathy. It may also make some emotions "contagious."

What Does This Mean for Educators?

Mirror neurons suggest the importance of modeling. Many have suggested an apprenticeship model. You have also heard of hands-on learning. Both of these paradigms understand the importance of modeling and of learning by watching and then doing. If the brain has a natural tendency to model, then it makes sense to incorporate that into our pedagogy on many levels.

Mentoring and relationships foster achievement and retention. The National Institutes of Health studied 443 students in Texas, with results supporting earlier studies showing that student achievement is linked to the quality of student-teacher relationships.

Schools should endeavor to have enough diversity in their faculty (e.g., diversity in ethnicity/culture, first language, personality, interests) so that every student can find someone to relate to. Students don't have to like every teacher, and teachers should not try to make everyone in the class "like" them. However, all students should have one teacher they like best and someone they feel is like them. The more diversity there is in faculties, the more likely this is to happen. In this way, faculty can serve as role models.

Leaping into the Classroom

Many courses can incorporate less text and more apprenticeship and modeling. We are often so locked into the model of textbooks and tests as the means of learning that sometimes we forget the nature or purpose of what we are teaching. A teacher of yoga at a community college once mentioned something to me about the written test for his yoga class. I thought, *A written test for yoga!?* "Oh," said the teacher, "but of course they must have a written test and understand the history and terminology of yoga to pass the class." Really? I am guessing most students in the class are taking yoga for health and enjoyment and not to become a yoga teacher. Shouldn't the grade be based on progress in the course based on an individual's starting ability, not on memorization of facts? Isn't yoga performance based? This is a good example of a course in which learning by watching is integral. Many technical courses and courses in the arts can have a similar foundation.

We know the advice to "show, don't tell," but do we think of that when we are writing lesson plans? Ask yourself how can you can show students the desired outcome of what you are teaching. This is easy in courses in the arts and trades, but it is increasingly more accessible to the rest of us than we have thought, especially with the availability of YouTube videos, Kahn Academy, and other sources of videos for teachers.

Even when you are teaching learning strategies, you can demonstrate the strategy using the material and talking aloud. You can make your own videos demonstrating the important learning strategies for your classroom, such as note taking, reading strategies, organizing strategies, and study strategies. Students who need scaffolding can watch these videos outside class; you don't lose any class time teaching the study skills at the beginning, and you can use the lesson over and over. Better yet, let a student who is exemplary in one of these areas make the video as a homework option and then you can use it as a teaching tool. Posting videos on YouTube can be one of the many homework menu items in this book (although they should never be required due to privacy issues for our students).

In math class, demonstrate the working of a problem, and have the students immediately do it themselves. Remember, though, that your ways of thinking, seeing, and working are not everyone else's way. Students who have a different way of working the problem but still get it correct can also demonstrate their way to their classmates. The more different ways you can demonstrate something, the better you will reach diverse learners. The ultimate goal is not for students to learn *our* way as *the* correct way, but to learn how to do it correctly in their own way.

We can model ways of thinking, behaving, and working. We let students see our thinking strategies and our struggles with writing or handling long-term projects and how we achieve successful outcomes by sharing the process with the students as we go along. Model how to approach people, tasks, projects, writing, and discouragement. Instructors can share their own writing process. You can use Track Changes during your draft and print that out for students. They will be surprised because students only see final versions. This shows them it is a process and that you struggle just as they do. Show them how you welcome criticism by having another person comment using Track Changes. Most students think their teacher can just sit down and whip out a finished project in one sitting (unfortunately, some of us expect students to do that). Model the process, the struggle, for students.

One way my coauthors and I used modeling in our reading textbook is by drawing little thought bubbles next to a paragraph illustrating an ideal reading/thinking process. Make

Model the process, the struggle, for students.

copies of a page in a book where you have made annotations. Let them see your thinking process, or create one based on one of their reading assignments. Use bubbles of your thoughts to model a thinking process.

Another way to provide models for students is to offer texts and videos about people who are good role models because they have overcome hardship or demonstrate expertise in the task being taught. Some studies have shown that reading about others who have overcome hardships has a positive effect on struggling students' achievement and effort.

Priming is an effect that makes a mental response more likely to happen because certain trigger words were presented (see chapter 3). In one interesting study by

Ap Dijkersterhuis, an expert in unconscious thought at the Behavioral Science Institute at Radboud University, half of the students taking a test based on Trivial Pursuit were primed by the presentation of the words *professor* and *intelligent* prior to the test. The other group was primed with the words *soccer-hooligans* or *stupid*. The group primed to think of a positive example such as a professor performed better. You can have young students think of someone they think is really smart or pretend they are the teacher when they take a test. Some research indicates it is the students closest in achievement one step up who can often be the best role models for struggling students. In other words, a failing student may be more inspired by someone who is now getting a C than by one getting an A, as an A may seem out of their reach or there is too great of a difference to model. If you are in the practice of praising effort, progress, and strategies rather than outcome, you can select all types of students as exemplars.

Mirror Neurons and Emotional Climate

Keeping in mind that mirror neurons may make emotions contagious, be careful of what emotion you bring into the classroom. It is often the strongest emotion that is most contagious. Unfortunately, that can often be negative emotions. We don't want that starting in the classroom and spreading like the flu. Instead, try making your positive attitude the strongest emotion in the room.

Since you are the authority figure, your emotions are already most likely to be seen as strongest and to carry the day. If you come to school in a stressed state (and who hasn't?), then students may pick up on an underlying state of stress, feel it, feel stressed, and, worse yet, think it is directed at them. This can start a negative spiral.

Deborah Christie, a teacher with one of the most positive attitudes I have ever met, told a story about the time she was highly stressed by the time she got to school. She tried to be her usual perky and upbeat self in spite of inner turmoil. However, shortly after class started, a typically ideal student started acting up. She called the girl out in the hall and asked her what was wrong with her. The girl replied, "You are mad at me, and I don't know why." When we unconsciously pick up emotions, we may think they are directed at us because we feel those emotions as well. The lesson from this is we have to handle our stress so we do not carry it into the classroom. Our emotions have an impact on the emotional climate of our classroom and on student learning.

Whether it is mirror neurons, empathy, biology, social cues, or other factors, we are affected by the behavior of others. We need to be conscious of our role as models. Teachers are often discussed as role models, but do we think about what we are actually modeling in the classroom? We need to be careful because we are likely to get back what we give out. If our voices are loud or we are angry, we may be more likely to arouse that in our students. Model the behavior and attitudes you want to see from students.

Model the behavior and attitudes you want to see from students.

TECHNOLOGY

I have included technology in the social chapter because the subject usually comes up when I am speaking about the social pathway. At first, classroom technology seemed the antithesis of brain compatible because it did not address this strong social pathway. However, technology developments now enable us to be social outside the classroom as well as in, and it can be used to activate some of the other learning pathways.

What Does the Research Say?

Technology is rewiring the brain because whatever we do changes the brain. School-age children are spending upwards of ten hours a day using various technologies, and that is going to change the wiring. During adolescence, brains go through a process whereby what isn't used as much gets pruned away and connections used a great deal are strengthened. What adolescents do most of during this time of life is restructuring their brain accordingly. What you do less of also changes the brain in that it does not get the activation it would have. In other words, students may not be engaging in as much one-on-one social activity in which they see faces and eyes and hear inflections in voices as previous generations do. Therefore, their brains are going to be different from those of earlier generations.

According to neuroscientist Gary Small, although we can't stop this increasing technology use in society, we can deliberately create and make time for face-to-face interactions to help balance this out. He does express concern that digital natives are becoming addicted to technology through the dopamine reward system. But Small also says, Google is making us smarter, an assertion based on his brain scans of older adults who had more frontal lobe activation when doing a Google search than when reading a book. He believes this may help with working memory, a function mediated by the frontal lobe.

Computer learning games can activate the reward pathway and be motivating. However, multitasking can impair learning, and too often we engage in technology in a multitasking manner. Another danger of technology is that the frontal lobe needs rest and downtime. The always-on nature of technology robs us of that.

Neuroscientist Jordan Grafman believes that technology can help develop children's brains if it is used carefully. If technology is not used instead of face-to-face interactions but in addition to it, it can enhance the social pathway. Technology is neither good nor bad in itself: it is how we use it.

What Does This Mean for Educators?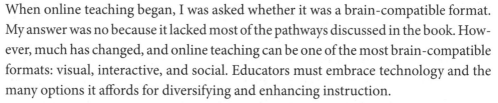

When online teaching began, I was asked whether it was a brain-compatible format. My answer was no because it lacked most of the pathways discussed in the book. However, much has changed, and online teaching can be one of the most brain-compatible formats: visual, interactive, and social. Educators must embrace technology and the many options it affords for diversifying and enhancing instruction.

Computer scientist Manuel Cebrian at the University of California, San Diego, recently found that students who are more interactive online are more academically successful than those who don't interact as much online. Unfortunately, they also found that higher-performing students from the beginning exclude lower-performing students from their interactions, forming their own elite circle, and those excluded students were more likely to drop out. There are many complex interactions in this study, so cause and effect are not well established. However, being aware of this potential behavior can help teachers identify at-risk students and find ways to bring them into the learning community.

Leaping into the Classroom

Technology is revolutionizing education. From what you have learned in this book, you can see how technology can make your instruction more brain-compatible in many ways:

- Build prior knowledge with material from the Internet.

- Increase arousal and motivation with videos rather than text.

- Take advantage of those more expert than you in content areas through video.

- Heighten sensory input as students both see and hear information.

- Provide a dopamine reward with games and challenges.

- Individualize instruction.

- Enhance memory with sites that create flash cards and puzzles.

- Help students with dyslexia and language learners hear phonemes more accurately.

- Enable students to pronounce vocabulary words with auditory input.

- Enable language learners to hear multiple speakers.

- Support executive function with planning and organization software and sites.

- Increase social interaction with e-mail, instant messaging, Skype, and other social media.

If you don't know a great deal about technology, create homework menus offering technology options, and you will learn it as the students do it. One homework option can be for students to create and upload a video with the stipulation that they do it with you. (Students will love teaching you!) Instead of fighting the technology of cell phones in class, some teachers are creating lessons that work with smart phone technology. It is beyond the scope of this book to teach this technology or to present all the options. Instead, the purpose is to illustrate that using technology is now very brain compatible and can and should be used to enhance and energize instruction.

CONCLUSION

When I started teaching developmental reading and English at a community college, I read Mike Rose's book *Lives on the Boundary*, which gave me tremendous insight into my students. He writes about the role of relationships in achievement and retention. Students are more likely to stay in school if they have a strong relationship with just one adult. In order to have a relationship that isn't playing favorites in the classroom, we have to interact with students outside the classroom, which means being available outside the classroom. We can pass through the lunchroom, cafeteria, or coffee shop and say hello. When we are outside our classroom between classes, students can come up with a personal question. We remain after school briefly and arrive early, perhaps having coffee in a common area. We go to the library during our preparation period or keep our office door open as much as possible. I admire the ESL teachers so much because they plan and engage in extracurricular multicultural events for their students. My high school English teacher, James Fulcher, changed my life dramatically by encouraging me to go to college. He selected me to be his unpaid assistant, which meant that during my free period, I made copies and did other tasks for him. During this time, he would ask me what I was reading outside class and then suggest the next book. When teachers interact with students, they change lives. Sometimes they save lives.

HOMEWORK MENU

- Design and participate in a service-learning project.
- Collaborate with other students on a project.
- Conduct an interview.
- Teach a lesson to others in a video.
- Present the lesson in a skit you create with other students.

SUGGESTED STRATEGIES

- Provide for our social nature:
  — Use pair-share activities
  — Group work
  — Projects

- — Community service learning
- — Students teach students
- Create a positive social environment:
  - — Have a verbal and a printed explicit policy against negative social interactions.
  - — Teach social and emotional skills.
  - — Model positive social behavior.
  - — Make sure all students are included who want to be.
  - — Take responsibility for your emotions and the effect they have on the class.
  - — Provide examples to students of exemplars who have made progress or overcome hurdles.
- Incorporate our natural tendency to mimic and model:
  - — Use demonstrations wherever possible.
  - — Include strategies based on apprenticeship learning.
  - — Model the strategies and processes for students:

    Include examples of your own process.

    Demonstrate how you think and read the material.

    Include videos that demonstrate someone carrying out desired actions, such as learning strategies or the procedures being taught in the course.
- Provide for the effects of social status:
  - — Do not diminish a student's social status.
  - — Correct the process or the strategy, not the student.
  - — Keep an emphasis on progress, not competition with others.
- Assign group work carefully:
  - — Be clear about the product and purpose of the group interaction.
  - — Assign group membership rather than have students choose their own team.
  - — Give students a clear role in group interaction.
  - — Provide for introverts and those who learn better alone.

- Use technology to enhance learning:
  — Take advantage of multiple pathways by using Internet resources such as videos.

  — Keep online courses social with Skype or your picture, voice, or video.

  — Use e-mail, instant messaging, Facebook, Twitter, and other forms of social interaction.

  — Take advantage of technology to build background knowledge.

REFLECT AND CONNECT

What are you doing to provide for the social needs of your students beyond putting them into groups?

How are you handling negative social behaviors?

Give three examples of behaviors you model.

What kind of relationships do you build with students outside class time?

What are you going to do differently now that you know about the social pathway?

SUGGESTED READING

Beane, A. L. (2011). *The new bully free classroom: Proven prevention and intervention strategies for teachers K-8*. Minneapolis, MN: Free Spirit.

Cain, S. (2012). *Quiet: The power of introverts in a world that can't stop talking*. New York, NY: Crown.

Chen, X., & Rubin, K. H. (2011). *Socioemotional development in cultural context*. New York, NY: Guilford Press.

Coloroso, B. (2003). *The bully, the bullied, and the bystander: From preschool to high school: How parents and teachers can help break the cycle of violence*. New York, NY: HarperResource.

Cozolino, L. (2006). *The neuroscience of human relationships: Attachment and the developing social brain*. New York, NY: Norton.

Goleman, D. (2006). *Emotional intelligence: Why it can matter more than IQ*. New York, NY: Random House.

Rose, D. H., & Meyer, A. (2002). *Teaching every student in the digital age: Universal design for learning*. Alexandria, VA: ASCD.

Rose, M. (2005). *Lives on the boundary*. New York, NY: Penguin.

Sapolsky, R. M. (2005). *Monkeyluv: And other essays on our lives as animals*. New York, NY: Scribner.

Tronick, E. (2007). *The neurobehavioral and social-emotional development of infants and children*. New York, NY: Norton.

Zadina, J. N., Smilkstein, R., Daiek, D. B., & Anter, N. M. (2013). *College reading: The science and strategies of expert readers*. Boston, MA: Wadsworth Cengage.

Zins, J. E. (2004). *Building academic success on social and emotional learning: What does the research say?* New York, NY: Teachers College Press.

9

The Big Picture

I read about some schools where overall achievement is higher. They don't teach to the test, yet students perform well on standardized tests. We have outstanding teachers and we spend a great deal of time preparing students for these tests, yet we are not seeing these kinds of results. Do they know something we don't?

MAKING CONNECTIONS

Does the body play a role in learning? Should males be taught differently from females? What interventions have been shown to raise achievement? Where can our educational dollars get the best return on investment?

We started this book with the big picture: how the brain learns. Then we examined individual (although interactive) pathways involved in learning. Let's zoom out again to the big picture and look at some powerful broader factors involved in learning that do not fit well into one specific pathway but affect, and are affected by, all of the pathways.

PHYSIOLOGY

Of course, the body is involved in learning. In fact, the body often helps us learn by telling us through arousal mechanisms what to pay attention to. We feel some excitement when we hear something new and interesting, and that excitement makes the connection stronger and more likely to stabilize: it fires more strongly and is more likely to wire. Let's look at the physiological science that applies to learning.

What Does the Research Say?

We have come a long way since Descartes' error (the duality of mind and body), as Antonio Damasio called it in his groundbreaking book by the same name. The sciences are showing us just how closely linked are the body and brain/mind and how the body affects learning.

Sex Differences

Are there sex differences in learning abilities? While some write about such differences, neuroscience research does not support educators' differentiating instruction by gender. A 2013 study by data analyst Bobbi Carothers at the University of Rochester looked at 122 characteristics in over thirteen thousand people by analyzing data from many previous studies and found no sex differences, even in terms of empathy (often associated with females) and math ability (often associated with males). However, this may not be true across other cultures, and that remains to be studied. Since individual differences are great, the differences between male and female on any single item average out. Psychologist Janet Hyde calls it the "gender similarities hypothesis." A better approach is to address multiple learning differences in the classroom with a multiple pathways approach.

Sleep

Unquestionably sleep is linked to a better brain and better learning. Adolescents have a different sleep cycle than children or adults do. Sleep researchers Mary Carskadon and Bill Dement found that adolescents need as much sleep as children—and maybe more. Their sleep cycle starts later, hence late nights, but goes later into the morning, hence the need for late-morning sleep. Sleep also affects the ability to consolidate the learning—for the brain connections to strengthen—according to neuroscientist Robert Stickgold at Harvard. Students need sleep before a test and after learning new material. A nap during extended studying for a test may be the best use of time. Neuroscientist Clifford Saper presented his research on this topic at the 2012 Society for Neuroscience conference in New Orleans. He found that sleep deprivation not only affects alertness, and thus test scores, it can even affect empathy. His advice for students is to "learn, sleep, repeat."

Fuel

The brain requires fuel, as does the rest of body, and it is metabolically expensive; it is approximately 3 percent of your body weight but uses 20 percent of the body's fuel. That is why prolonged attention can be exhausting. You can feel as exhausted after a long period of mental activity as from physical activity. Keeping the brain fueled is as important as resting the frontal lobe (chapter 7). However, it should be the right kind of fuel. Sugar gives a quick burst of energy, but it is followed by a very low energy slump that is not only unhealthy but has a negative impact on learning. New evidence is suggesting that Alzheimer's disease is actually a type of diabetes, a kind that can be prevented or controlled by diet if caught early enough.

The brain and body are connected, and what is healthy for the body to eat is healthy for the brain. It is not appropriate to suggest specific dietary recommendations here, but overall we want foods rich in omega 3, such as salmon, and antioxidants, such as blueberries. Avoid high-fat, high-sugar foods, especially those containing transfats (partially hydrogenated).

Exercise

Exercise contributes to a better brain. One way is by increasing blood flow, which energizes and fuels the brain. German neuroscientist Bernward Winters's research showed that three minutes of aerobic exercise improved both short- and long-term memory. Neurocognitive kinesiologist Charles Hillman and colleagues saw a positive relationship between physical activity and school achievement, including improved standardized test scores. Harvard psychiatrist John Ratey designed an intervention in which students who exercised at the beginning of the school day had better academic performance: the better that elementary school children performed on physical tests, the better they scored on achievement tests regardless of socioeconomic status.

A great deal of research supports exercise as an intervention against stress. We know that stress damages the hippocampus and has a negative impact on learning. This research suggests ways in which we can improve the life and learning ability of our students far more than a focus simply on academic content. Neuroscientist Cyrus Raji at UCLA found that even older adults who engage in more physical activity have more gray matter in important areas such as the hippocampus, an area important to learning. He makes the strong statement that no drug can have this kind of effect on the brain. As neuroscientist Helen Neville suggests, we should determine interventions that enhance plasticity. Exercise appears to do that.

What Does This Mean for Educators?

Because our learners are not just a brain but are in a body, and the body and brain work together, we must take the body into consideration when planning school environments and curriculum. Educators need to be informed about how the body can affect learning.

The Importance of Sleep

If you are an educational leader, you can make global changes based on this information. I met a principal in Covington, Louisiana, who pushed back the high school start time because research indicated that adolescents need late-morning sleep. This was not well received by some bus drivers and parents, but he did what he deemed best for the students' learning. If high school or college students must take early morning classes, then they should not schedule early morning work or other activities on the weekends.

Research indicated that adolescents need late-morning sleep.

The Importance of Fuel

Meals, including breakfast, are important for learners. Schools need to provide breakfast for all learners. One study showed that middle school children who ate sugary breakfasts (sugared cereal, toaster snacks, and pastries) performed on tasks of memory and attention at the level of seventy-year-olds. However, those who were given a breakfast of beans on toast performed well. Now you may not want a classroom on beans, but a breakfast with protein, fiber, good fats, and good carbs can make a difference.

When I was teaching at both the high school and community college levels, I ate breakfast at the school. We had a large array of choices, but it was not pastries and sweets. It was bacon, eggs, potatoes, and fruits. However, recently I was speaking on a college campus and decided to eat breakfast there because the hotel's "hot breakfast" was waffles, pastries, and other junk food. Much to my surprise, the college campus breakfast consisted of a choice of pastries or hugely fat and caloric-intense burritos. This is unacceptable given what we know now about the impact of nutrition on learning and health. As educators, part of our job is to educate students, parents, and our schools about the importance of a good breakfast. Hospitals and schools should be a place where we are teaching the public about good choices and offering a variety of healthy foods.

Furthermore, food needs to be available throughout the day. A schedule of very early or very late lunch can create low blood sugar at some point in the day, a condition as dangerous for the brain as high blood sugar and bad for health. Vending machines can have yogurt, apples, and nuts available all day long, and breaks between classes need to be long enough to access bathrooms or vending machines. If we want to improve learning and raise achievement, we cannot ignore this important research in favor of school convenience.

The Importance of Exercise

School curriculum choices have often been made based on budget cuts and an uninformed belief about what is and is not important to learn. Neuroscience is revealing that some of these cuts may not be in the best interest of the brain, with the best interest being a healthy brain that learns well. Unfortunately, exercise has been cut out of some curricula even at the pre-K level. All students need exercise and all students need recess, a time to rest their frontal lobe.

Why do we have gyms at school that go unused in the early morning, at night, and on weekends, and students and parents have to pay to go to a fitness center to work out? Communities should open the gym and school workout center to residents at night and holidays, which can be financed by charging a nominal fee to parents and students and more to nonresidents. Yoga, meditation, tai chi, golf, tennis, and other classes can be taught at schools in the evenings. Hire your instructors from the community if necessary. Work with the YMCA and share resources. Students can attend free as part of physical education requirements. Offer some options offsite after school, such as bowling, swimming, or tennis. Let students sign up for these after school instead of physical education if they are so inclined.

The Importance of Environment

Provide retreat areas where students who are losing control of their emotions can go to de-stress. Some calming music in a relaxed atmosphere can teach students to provide their own "time-out" and ways to gain control of their emotions. Provide a nature retreat outdoors with a sitting area and plantings somewhat separated from other areas or a quiet room with calming music and comfortable furniture. Just as has been done in hospitals and nursing homes, service animals are being brought into schools to work with students learning to read or to provide stress relief. In some private schools, the headmaster brings his or her dog to school, and this friendly mascot around the school is a reassuring presence to students who have to come to the office to discuss discipline or academics.

Schools that want higher achievement for their students can look to the evidence from neuroscience for solutions.

Providing a schoolwide environment that addresses the entire student, mind *and* body, should be a priority. The evidence is clear-cut with relation to achievement: schools that want higher achievement for their students can look to the evidence from neuroscience for solutions.

Leaping into the Classroom

Although as a classroom teacher you may not have any control over students' sleep, diet, or exercise, your knowledge of physiology relevant to learning can help you advise and guide them. Teach your students this information just as you teach them how the brain learns. Special education teacher Jan Sundmark advises that adequate sleep, a nutritious diet, and regular exercise need to be modeled to young people by the adults in their lives.

CURRICULUM AND ASSESSMENT

Curriculum must take into account the developmental trajectory of brain processes. Some cognitive skills are more developmentally based than others. You learned in chapter 4 that a second language is more readily learned early in life, although a language can be learned at any time. Reading is a skill with a wide developmental window, with some children ready earlier than others. The frontal lobe continues developing until the midtwenties. Understanding brain development can ensure that our curriculum takes these stages into account.

What Does the Research Say?

David Rose and Katherine Rose, two educators from Harvard interested in educational neuroscience, argue that curriculum can actually *create* disability. Just as dyslexia is a print-based disability that would not exist without the requirement of accessing print, curriculum design can create a disability when it works against what we know about brain development. They believe that educational demands on the frontal lobe executive functions move faster than executive function skills develop (see chapter 7). This varies greatly from student to student and can cause some students to fall behind early while others hit the wall later in their education, even into college. Rose and Rose point out that although there are explicit interventions for some difficulties such as dyslexia, this area is often overlooked. David Rose proposes his "universal design for learning" as one way to address this problem.

The Arts

Exercise and recess are not the only curricula cut as budgets drop: the arts are also fast to go even as we discover that they are also important to developing a brain that learns well. Learning to play an instrument can change the anatomy and the function of the brain, such as when guitar players have a larger thumb representation in the brain.

You have probably heard about the Mozart effect in which playing Mozart's music prior to testing improved achievement. This got blown out of proportion by the media into the idea that listening to music improved intelligence, and it led to many misuses of music in education. However, recent research suggests ways we can use music effectively. A study at the Stanford University School of

Medicine showed that classical music activates the hippocampus and areas of the cerebral cortex involved in memory and attention. Perhaps the music stimulates brain regions so they perform more efficiently for a period of time afterward. Glenn Schellenberg, a specialist in cognitive developmental issues in the auditory system, further researched the relationship between music and cognitive abilities. He found that listening to music gave only a short-term benefit; however, music lessons in childhood were associated with long-term cognitive benefits unrelated to other factors, such as socioeconomic status.

Music lessons appear to provide cognitive benefits to the brain and learning. We know that learning to play music strengthens the auditory system in the brain not only for hearing music but for other listening tasks, including language tasks, just as using other parts of the brain or body strengthens them. Studies have shown a relationship between the ability to keep a beat and reading ability. Nina Kraus, a specialist in bilingual and auditory research, suggests that music training strengthens the auditory system, which leads to better phonology and better reading. The lab of research specialist in language Ellen Bialystok studied children who were assigned to a twenty-day program in either music or visual arts. They found that both groups improved in phonological awareness (important to language and reading), but those with music also improved more on a visual-auditory learning task. This has implications for benefits in reading and language learning. Neuroscientist Michael Posner and colleagues researched how training in the arts improved attention. Vanderbilt psychologist Sohee Park and colleagues found that trained musicians had greater frontal lobe activity and enhanced divergent (creative) thinking. Other research has shown that being musically trained early in life predicts brain performance and thinking skills in older adults.

You have learned that working memory is critical to academic achievement. Cognitive psychologist Michael Franklin and colleagues found trained musicians had greater verbal working memory capacity and better long-term memory. An exciting new study by Northwestern University researchers Erika Skoe and Nina Kraus suggests that taking music lessons early in life can improve working memory. Unlike earlier studies that looked at professional musicians who continued to play music, they looked at those who had studied music early in childhood but not afterward and found that the changes persisted.

What Does This Mean for Educators?

Curriculum must be designed based on what we know about how the brain learns and the natural developmental trajectory of the brain and various cognitive functions. The implications of neuroscience for education need to be part of teacher preservice training programs at universities. As well, teachers need access to ongoing professional development in this area. School systems and universities can hire or consult with an educational neuroscientist who can provide information and guidance.

While early intervention for learning difficulties is desirable, we must balance that with a caution about assuming a child has learning differences when he or she may just not be developmentally ready for some cognitive tasks. All students are on a different developmental path for various skills. Because of this, we want to avoid labeling. We can offer students extra support with skills without labeling them as deficient or disabled.

Content

Early childhood music training confers benefits throughout life and must be included in curriculum. Psychologists Joseph Piro and Camilo Ortiz at Long Island University initiated an intervention program that included three years of music lessons for elementary school children and found that those with music lessons had better vocabulary and verbal sequencing performance compared to those without during that time.

Music within an individual classroom can enhance learning too. Music researcher Katie Overy and Karen Ludke, a specialist in music and second language learning, published a study in the journal *Memory and Cognition* reporting an intervention that can help language learners. Two groups of learners had words spoken to them. The group that either sang or rhythmically said the words back scored higher on the test than the group that just repeated the words. In another study, researchers at the University of Edinburgh found that those who sang in another language while learning did twice as well at speaking the words later than those who did not sing them.

In chapter 1 you read that learning means making connections in the brain and the importance of prior knowledge to making those connections. I would like to see more thematic curriculum in the schools enabling students to make connections across curriculum, such as using math in science classes and reading about history in reading or English class. More depth and less breadth allow students to make more connections and develop skills and executive functions at deeper levels. Many courses taught in a linear way, such as history, could also be taught in a thematic way. For example, throughout a given area of history, certain themes emerge. Looking at multiple historical issues in relation to a theme allows students to do more than memorize: they can make connections between multiple historical events and see the deeper, underlying connection. They can talk and write about those themes and discover where in our world today these same themes play out. Constantly changing topics, fragmented readings, and isolation of content is not conducive to deep thought, focused attention, and higher-order thinking.

Research Application

We are negligent if we ignore this new research. So much money is put into new programs, and yet too often, this research is ignored. This may be partly due to a lack of a bridge between the latest developments in psychology, medicine, neuroscience, and educational research. Creating a position for an educational neuroscientist in colleges or school systems would bridge that gap. An educational neuroscientist can discern what new interventions are credible and available and consult on curriculum design.

Educating Parents

Another important role for curriculum planning through sixth grade is parent education. New research is emphasizing that learning begins from birth, and sometimes even before. Much evidence indicates the role of environment in learning, especially in the early years; ignoring this important factor—the early environment of the home—is certainly a sin of omission. The effort put into a child's early years can have payoffs throughout the child's education and, indeed, throughout life. Superintendent David Burleson in Burke County, North Carolina, sent out a letter to

The effort put into a child's early years can have payoffs throughout the child's education and, indeed, throughout life.

parents of the graduating class—the class of 2025! He obtained a list of birth certificates in the area and, knowing those would eventually become his kindergarten students, sent a letter to parents inviting them to attend a year-long series of educational meetings years before these babies would be kindergartners.

When parents know better, they can do better. Educating parents to provide the appropriate language and learning experiences from early on can make a big difference when children start school. Informed parents make better decisions about diet, sleep, nutrition, environmental noise, rich first- and second-language experiences, play, exploration, emotion, and the importance of human social interaction.

Leaping into the Classroom

Course outlines and class lesson plans need to be designed not only with course requirements in mind but also with the constraints of the brain in mind. Throughout this book, you have learned much about how the brain learns best and acquired numerous strategies. Putting these into your overall course design and individual lesson plans requires a little more information, as well as a review of what you have learned.

Addressing Learning Differences

It is critical for teachers to understand that learning differences are not a matter of preference but of brain wiring. Learning differences are caused not only by deficits in specific brain regions; they can be caused by problems in connections between regions. Learners may be using an alternative network of regions in the brain to process functions such as reading. Realizing that brain differences can lead to behavioral differences is important. Knowing students' brains and behavior can change over time encourages us to work with students to strengthen weaknesses. Students need to fire and wire different ways of behaving through interventions targeting specific deficits as well as general behaviors. We are at the tip of the iceberg with neuroscience informing us of the underlying nature of these differences and determining targeted interventions. In the meantime, we learn about the differences from neuroscience and apply what we know from psychology and education to address learning differences.

Teachers face a broad variety of individual brain, environmental, and educational differences in their classroom, so it is impossible for them to diagnose and address learning differences with specific, targeted interventions for every student. Therefore, we must create a teaching design that allows a variety of approaches, strategies, and interventions so each student may have an approach that works. In the classroom, we can take a shotgun approach, providing multiple pathways for achievement. Throughout this book, I have suggested options for multiple pathways of instruction and homework in a twofold approach: strengthen weaknesses *and* provide compensatory strategies for mitigating weaknesses through using strengths. This approach does not suggest less rigor or lowering our standards. It suggests altering our approach and methods in order to reach more students.

It is essential that all students, and especially those with learning difficulties, learn how to learn and understand that they can change their brain. The first step in addressing individual differences is making that sure all students understand the material presented in chapter 1 in this book: how their brain learns. It is also essential that students understand that although they may have weaknesses, they also have learning strengths. Teach them to determine their strengths and use them to compensate.

It is essential that all students, and especially those with learning difficulties, learn how to learn and understand that they can change their brain. Throughout the book, I have emphasized scaffolding and strategies, another area to keep in mind. Rather than labeling a student as "learning disabled," consider that the problem may be that the tasks required are ahead of the student's neuropsychological development. Provide instruction, scaffolding, and strategies. The developmental window is wide and varies from skill to skill, and yet we place students in grade levels and expect them all to reach the same milestones at the same time. Our curriculum needs a dramatic overhaul, but until then, we can accept students where they are and move them forward individually. If we leave students better off than when we found them, we have succeeded. When we leave them frustrated, defeated "failures," we have done them a disservice.

Planning for Instruction

Typically when we prepare lesson plans, we may be thinking strictly in terms of content. We determine the most logical order of presentation and balance the content in terms of how much time we have. We then come up with homework assignments for students to do outside class and plan to cover content during class. This is the traditional model. However, with knowledge comes responsibility, so now we have to factor in some other variables. Instead of a focus on logical order of content only, think in terms of brain activity when deciding what to include and when. For example, you learned the importance of making connections (chapter 1) and of reflection (chapter 7). We should think first of brain processes, then content.

In addition to developing daily, weekly, or unit lesson plans, reflect on the structure of assignments over the entire semester or year. Scaffold students' frontal lobe executive functions throughout the year, starting with a great deal of support and moving toward independence later in the year (see chapter 7). Look at all of your assignments together, and revise them according to dependence on autonomy, meeting deadlines, prioritizing, organizing, and other higher-order skills. Move from more explicit instruction and circumscribed assignments to more options and flexibility for students. If you see students faltering after attempting to make this transition, provide structured materials to support those students, keeping in mind that some deficits in executive function are not remediable in one course, one semester, or even one year. Communicate this with your students regularly so when extra support is withdrawn, there are no surprises. In this way, we are helping them develop their executive function skills over time.

A delicate balance is required here. Some students thrive in a constructivist approach that uses problem solving and homework options. However, those with executive function deficits or a high sense of threat might thrive under more traditional instruction, with each step clearly defined. We want to reach all types of learners.

Assessment

Just as we provide multiple pathways of instruction and practice, we want to provide multiple pathways of assessment. Tests cannot always measure the true understanding of a student, especially students with learning differences.

An issue in test performance is failure to transfer: students do well on homework and in class but perform poorly on the test or can't apply what they learned to new material. Why? Students with weak executive functions may perform poorly on tests because they perform poorly prior to the test itself. Perhaps they fail to pay attention to cues from the instructor about what is on the test or how to prepare for it.

They might have trouble with note taking or budgeting time to study for the test. Or they fail to predict questions or recognize signals of important information in the textbook.

Sometimes the problem lies in the test itself or a mismatch between the type of assessment and an individual student. Sometimes a student may know the material, but due to deficits in executive functions, may not be able to demonstrate mastery in the manner required by the test. For example, an essay test is heavily dependent on executive functions: planning, organizing, budgeting time, and controlling attention. An essay test is also more taxing for those with language differences, whether second-language issues or reading impairment. Many objective tests are poorly written and tax working memory capacity. Students can't hold lengthy question stems in their mind while reviewing the options and making a decision.

Test anxiety is a concern for many students. If students are highly stressed before a test, they may go into fight-or-flight mode: the body diverts energy from the thinking brain to the body for fighting, fleeing, or freezing (chapter 3). It is imperative that instructors treat this as part of their instruction to students at any age. When students understand what is happening in their brain, body, and mind when they are anxious and how that affects their performance, they can realize they can do something about it.

Often important tests in math or reading are timed in order to test the fluency of the student's ability, but many students with executive function deficits, second language, reading difficulty, or anxiety do not do well on timed tests. That does not mean they would not succeed in the next course, albeit they may have to spend more time on homework. When I taught community college, we were allowed to give students with a documented learning disability additional time on tests. That was uncomfortable for me because it was often the students who were financially well off and could afford the expensive testing who were able to obtain the paperwork and it looked as if I was playing favorites. I knew other students needed additional time as well due to differences that were either not documented or not considered legitimate (such as high stress). I suggest we need to rethink the use of timed tests. I am not convinced they ensure proper placement in courses or represent actual performance in other circumstances.

Another concern in test taking is the nature of the questions. We need to explicitly teach test-writing strategies to teachers. Some questions put too much stress on working memory in that they contain many clauses and phrases (see chapter 5). The format is key. When is the first time the students worked with the information in the testing format, such as matching words with definitions or explaining a concept in their own words? The test? The expressive pathway must be fired and wired also. Students should practice dealing with the information in the test format prior to the test. This is not teaching to the test; this is ensuring that tests cover information in a format that is familiar. If you ask short-answer or long-answer questions, students should do those in class or on homework as well. In math, similar types of problems are grouped together in homework or practice, but on the test, different types of problems and processes may be mixed up. Yes, students should be able to recognize and apply their learning, but allowing them to practice that format is essential. We are not making tests easier; we are making them fair.

If you are writing comprehension questions, make sure they really test understanding of the material and not memory, unless memorization is critical to what has been taught. This is particularly important in reading tests. You may have good readers who are missing questions that are actually testing details based on memory rather than understanding. There is a difference between good reading and good memory. What are you testing for?

What, then, is the best way to test? That depends on each student. And since our students are all wired differently, our tests must offer multiple pathways to demonstrate their achievement of the learning objectives. This puts more demand on your time and energy to construct many types of tests for every unit; nevertheless, it must be done.

The test should not be the final step in the process of learning. Students need to know that learning and progress are a process, not a point in time, and we must provide for and model that. Require students to turn in the test with a brief essay on the back about what strategies they used to study for the test and to take the test. What worked and didn't work?

The test should not be the final step in the process of learning.

What will they do differently next time? Ideally, print those questions on the back of the test, so students know they will always be there and will be held accountable for their strategies before and during the test. This awareness strengthens their executive function skills, increases their sense of control, and reinforces their strategy skills. Keep the focus on progress and process.

Using Music

Of course, we should have music instruction in our curriculum. What about music in the classroom? In my presentations on educational neuroscience, I caution about the use of music in the classroom. Certainly it can be a powerful tool, but it must be used with knowledge and caution or it could interfere with learning. A study at Penn State University found that when students listened to classical music for ten minutes prior to a test, they scored nine points higher on an IQ test: however, this is probably a transient effect. Since music is pleasurable and reduces stress and may improve performance, it appears that it would behoove us to play classical music prior to intensive bouts of selective attention or frontal lobe activities, such as testing, studying, or working problems. If you are going to play a little music prior to a test, it should be the right kind of music, such as classical music, at least until we learn more about this.

Perhaps the music could play as students enter the classroom, like a theme song. You can use music with or without words to create an optimal arousal level and positive emotion by selecting a theme song to play each day as students enter the room. Select something positive, however, not, say, "Wasted Days and Wasted Nights" or "We Gotta Get Outa This Place"!

Sometimes music may be played in the background for concentration. If you are going to use music while students work, it is imperative to use the right kind of music. First, it should not have words if you are playing it while they are working with a verbal task to prevent a Stroop effect with two tasks competing. Music while exercising can have words, of course. Second, it must have the right number of beats per minute (BPM) so we do not get too much or too little arousal. Our heartbeats entrain to the beat of the music, and a normal heartbeat, a rate conducive to concentration, is 60 to 80 BPM. Therefore, music played for concentration should be within that range. If you can't find the BPM on the CD insert, here are some ways you can determine it:

- For digital music, log onto MixMeister.com, download the free BPM Analyzer, and drag your songs into the program. It will determine the BPM. If you use iTunes, download iTunes 2.1.14 (at Apple.com), and it will calculate and assign a BPM for every song in the library.

- If your music is not digital, use a stopwatch. Start the music and count as you tap out the drumbeats for fifteen seconds. Then multiply by four to get the BPM.

For those of you who can have students participate in exercise, if you play music with 120 to 140 BPM while students are exercising, their endurance will increase by 15 percent, and performance on mental tasks afterward was found to be a stunning 200 percent better according to a study done at Ohio State University-Columbus.

We know that words set to music are much easier to remember, so one effective way to use music is to use songs that teach a lesson. I believe this extends beyond language learning to the learning of other vocabulary words or even facts. You can find sources for purchasing lessons put to song online and make a homework option to write a song teaching the lesson. Then you can reuse them in the future.

EARLY CHILDHOOD

Let's end at the beginning—where it all begins. The latest neuroscience research indicates that our best education investment is often before the child enters school or in early grades. Longitudinal studies indicate interventions made early on result in higher achievement throughout the learner's education. Therefore, I provide some of this recent research that suggests future directions in early childhood instruction for our education system. The small sampling presented here lends strong support to the importance of early childhood education.

What Does the Research Say?

New, more child-friendly neuroimaging technology now allows researchers to look into the brains of young children. This research supports the critical nature of early childhood education and lifelong learning.

Stimulation and Environment

According to her new research presented at the 2012 Society for Neuroscience conference, neuroscientist Martha Farah finds that cognitive stimulation at age four seems to have a greater impact than at age eight. We are talking about stimulation of the normal sort prevalent in language-rich homes and where the child experiences creative play, such as playing with building blocks or imaginative play as opposed to sitting in front of an electronic babysitter (DVDs and television). Early cognitive stimulation with language, numbers, and behavior is important.

Although working memory and attention can be damaged by early childhood poverty even into adulthood, prominent neuroscientist Bruce McEwen notes that training in early childhood has been shown to improve these functions. Again we see the importance of investing in diagnosis, intervention, and strategic activities in early childhood as an investment in better outcomes in adulthood.

Exercise is critical to all students, and starting in early childhood and elementary school is especially important. We know this will improve their brain function later in life. A study by education researcher Robyn Jorgensen found that toddlers who learned to swim achieved other skills earlier than those who didn't. She believes this would confer an advantage on entering school. It also seems to lessen the impact of low socioeconomic status (SES) because even those with low SES outperformed those with high SES who didn't learn to swim.

Evidence also shows the detrimental effects of a loud environment on the later auditory system of children. We know that for children to succeed in reading, they must be able to associate sounds with letters—phonological awareness. However, they can't do this if they do not accurately hear the sounds. An environment very noisy with, for example, a blaring TV or loud music on all of the time or even a loud air-conditioner or other white noise in the baby's or child's room can impair the developing auditory system. Early childhood centers should not have unnecessary background noise, and day care centers should not be playing music for the caregivers' own entertainment. Children need to hear quiet sounds, such as those in nature, to finely tune their auditory system. They need to hear lots and lots of language—from humans, not from a TV or radio, so they can decipher the sounds and develop language skills. Of course, it is appropriate to play music for the children and to encourage singing, but not to use music as constant background.

Psychologist John Protzko at New York University reviewed numerous studies of raising the intelligence of children from birth to kindergarten. He discovered that three interventions were effective. The first was adding fish oil to the diets of pregnant mothers and to the newborns because it is important to neuron development. The second intervention was for economically disadvantaged children to be placed in quality preschool programs. (Other socioeconomic levels were not studied.) The reasoning is that it exposes these youngsters to complex and stimulating environments that they might not have at home. The researchers did not find earlier intervention was more helpful than at the preschool age. The third intervention was to teach parents to read to and interact with their child. This did not apply to children over four years old. Apparently this early interaction stimulates language learning. Reading books with pictures may be most helpful.

Language

The importance of extensive language exposure in infancy and early childhood cannot be overstated. Researcher Dilara Deniz, working with language researcher Patricia Kuhl at the University of Washington, found in a groundbreaking study that more gray and white matter in two regions in the brain in infants could predict their language abilities at one year of age. The areas were the hippocampus, known for its relation to memory, and the cerebellum, typically associated with motor learning. Kuhl says this makes sense because the infants memorize sounds and then move their mouth to create the sounds. New research at Northwestern University indicates that children who hear words (as opposed to tones) associated with a picture learn to form categories as early as three months of age. The authors speculate that words promote attention, which leads to category recognition, an important cognitive skill.

Frontal Lobe Executive Functions

In chapter 7 you learned about frontal lobe executive functions. Psychologist Lindsey Richland at the University of Chicago finds that children as young as four and a half years old begin to show signs of higher-order thinking skills related to reasoning skills in adolescence. Her study is the first to show that executive function in children helps develop later complicated analytical thinking, such as planning, controlling attention and emotion, and organization. Just as certain activities strengthen executive function in older children, research shows that executive function can be strengthened in early childhood through appropriate experiences. This has been shown in studies of preschool children through impulse control training. A study in Italy by neuroscientist Jacques Mehler showed that seven-month-old bilingual babies (those who had heard two languages spoken) had an advantage in the executive function skill of stopping and starting actions—that is, they had cognitive flexibility—even though they couldn't yet speak.

Math

Young children are taught to recite their numbers in preparation for math skills later on. As it turns out, it is not reciting the numbers that is important but counting.

According to educational researcher Luis Manfra at the University of Missouri, helping preschoolers prepare for math is best achieved by practice in counting objects. Psychologist David Geary, also at the University of Missouri, found that a single specific skill in first grade was correlated with performance on adult tests of math (a seventh-grade math skill level) and better math performance in adolescence: number system knowledge, that is, the understanding that a number represents quantity and that there are systematic relationships between numbers. Students who might have trouble counting could make that up later and do fine, he said, but those who fell behind in number system knowledge stayed behind. He believes this deficit creates problems in school and lifelong problems with employment, debt, and money management.

What Does This Mean for Educators?

This information indicates that more is going on in infancy than previously thought and strongly suggests that schools need to provide instruction for parents as well as students. Since parents provide the environment that contributes significantly to a student's success, bringing preschool and elementary children's parents into this conversation about the brain and learning is imperative. Colleges can also work information about good parenting into some courses, such as reading, writing, and psychology.

Leaping into the Classroom

Maybe the most important skill an early childhood educator can teach is executive functions, thus setting the stage for a better quality of life and learning. Provide activities that require executive function skills, such as teaching children to plan, budget time, monitor progress, control attention and emotion (impulse control at this age), and organize materials. Explicitly teach good executive function, such as the ability to wait your turn to talk or stand quietly in line or control impulses.

Early childhood teachers need to design their curriculum and activities based on what we know about creating better learners:

- Start language instruction in another language in first grade, preferably in a dual-language program. If this can't be formally done, but you know even a little bit of another language, teach the children "just for fun." Get parents to speak to the children in another language and teach them a few words just for fun. This can enhance the auditory system as the children are exposed to new sounds and perhaps create Petitto's perceptual wedge (see chapter 6), which will set the stage for better later language learning.

- Include exercise. If your school doesn't provide time for recess or exercise, then get the students up and moving in the classroom as much as possible.

- We understand the importance of music instruction in early childhood. If this isn't provided for the students, then expose the children to all types of music, including classical and opera. Have them sing. Perhaps the school can afford inexpensive recorder flutes and you can teach students to play without concerns about quality.

- You probably have no control over your students' nutrition, but you can teach students about good nutrition. You can also provide homework with information about nutrition that teaches the parents as well as they work with their child on the homework.

- Keep the environment free of extraneous noise and use lots of language. You want students to develop good phonemic awareness, and using lots of language with students helps. However, the environment must be quiet enough that students can effectively hear all the nuances of sound. Do not use constant background noise, whether music or white noise.

- Work with both counting and understanding how numbers relate to each other. Have students talk about their manipulatives and how quantities relate. Encourage them to use their fingers when counting.

- Have students engage in activities that require sustained attention and memory. Ask them to memorize and perform songs.

- Let students get absorbed in activities, and don't necessarily change tasks according to the clock. If students are deeply absorbed, let that activity continue, thus enhancing their attentional skills.

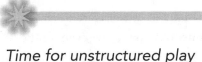

Time for unstructured play must be built into the curriculum.

Of course, all of these can be made fun. In addition, time for unstructured play must be built into the curriculum.

Teachers struggle with many learning differences over the years of schooling. Early diagnosis and understanding about underlying processes can help educators and scientists work together to design targeted interventions early on, leading to more success at higher academic levels. You learned in the first chapter that our brains can change through experience—*plasticity*. That means intelligence can change. Of course, the earlier we apply what we know about improving our intelligence the better.

CONCLUSION

You have seen that many pathways are involved in learning, and the more modalities by which we encode learning, the more significant the learning is. We want to create large, multisensory networks. Curriculum should be built with multiple instructional, homework, and assessment options.

You have learned in this book that not everyone uses the same pathways in the brain. For example, not everyone reads by the same brain pathway. Neuroimaging research shows the brains of those who learn, read, or think differently. Although we are far from translating much of this understanding into diagnosis and remediation of individuals, it helps us literally see that we are all wired differently. Now we know for certain that curriculum must address the myriad learning differences among individuals, not just those who are diagnosed as having a particular learning difference. Learning a second language poses certain challenges and confers benefits. The "language of math" may be affected by underlying processes that seem to be math but aren't. Our curriculum must account for these alternative pathways.

You have explored the importance of the reward and survival pathway in the brain and numerous factors affecting it. Curriculum should be constructed in such a way that students figure out patterns and problems for themselves. A focus on progress rather than results is more rewarding to the brain, an understanding that changes our approach. Lessons that engage readers and are relevant and rigorous are more rewarding than those that don't. Some formats are more rewarding to the brain, such as narrative and metaphor; therefore, curriculum should include those formats.

There has been a trend toward collaboration in the classroom, supported by research illustrating the social nature of our brain. Technology is changing our curriculum greatly too, helping us to make both online and in-person classes even more brain compatible. It also makes implementing all of the pathways in this book easier. For example, Google Images makes it easy to incorporate visuals, and YouTube makes it easy to provide prior knowledge.

One of the most important findings in recent neuroscience research is that some difficulties that seem to be reading, math, or motivation problems are actually problems in underlying processes, such as attention and working memory. These limitations have not been addressed much in terms of lesson and curriculum design in the past, but we are getting to the point where these new understandings allow us to make some changes based on the research. Because new research indicates that people might be able to chunk only about four items at a time, or fewer, we must readjust. We check our instructions and materials and tests for items that stress working memory. We build into the school curriculum activities that strengthen attention and working memory.

Research is also elucidating the best methods for studying, as various disciplines contribute to this understanding. We can help students make the most of their time and use research-based strategies. When students understand these strategies are taught because research shows they work the best, we may get our students to use their study skills.

Another area in which current neuroscience research has illuminated our thinking is in research that shows the impact of cognitive load and of multitasking. Our lives are changing quickly, and we must adjust to the more fast-paced and multiple-intrusion way of life. Understanding the limits of our brain is important to maximizing our abilities.

Finally, the most important pathway of all has emerged as a new discipline in neuroscience: emotion research. We have learned that emotional intelligence is also required for good learning, and high stress has a negative impact on learning. We understand that sarcasm and put-downs inhibit learning. Research on various populations has shown us that not only soldiers or victims of natural disaster have symptoms of stress that obstruct learning, so this must become a factor in curriculum design in the classroom and in the school itself.

The most important neuroscience discovery for educators is the discovery that the brain is plastic: it changes as a result of experience. This knowledge inspires us to create curriculum that will change students' brains for the better through programs in the school that create better brains and happier, healthier students. This goes from meals that are provided to exercise classes, arts, and curricula that develop body, mind, and brain. For the classroom, it means we must design the curriculum and individual lesson plans based on best practices from research.

Experience changes the physical structure of the brain: cells that fire together, wire together. You are creating firings in your students' brains and wirings in their brains. The honor, the privilege, the blessing of being a teacher is that you know you change lives. Sometimes you even save a life by altering the path of a student. But more than that, you are changing your students' brains. Keep up the great work!

REFLECT AND CONNECT

Examine one of your recent lessons and address the following questions based on what you have learned in this book:

How does the lesson provide for mental breaks?

What kind of information or skill will be fired and wired? Is this the desired outcome? What changes do you want in the students' brains as a result of this lesson? This is not the same as learning outcomes (e.g., "the student will be able to list ways that . . ."). This is about what changes take place. You are looking for real learning.

How will your eventual assessment measure the change? All three items must be in alignment: the desired change, the activity, and the assessment.

How will those with learning differences have an opportunity for differentiation? How will that affect eventual assessment?

How are you addressing reward by creating the right level of difficulty for each student?

Which pathway is the one you have most overlooked? Review that chapter, and describe how you could incorporate that information and the strategies into your practices.

What is the single most significant change you will make as a result of reading this book?

SUGGESTED READING

Cozolino, L. J. (2008). *The healthy aging brain: Sustaining attachment, attaining wisdom.* New York, NY: Norton.

Damasio, A. R. (1995). *Descartes' error: Emotion, reason, and the human brain*. New York, NY: HarperCollins.

Healy, J. M. (1994). *Your child's growing mind: A guide to learning and brain development from birth to adolescence*. New York, NY: Doubleday.

Horstman, J. (2012). *The* Scientific American *healthy aging brain: The neuroscience of making the most of your mature mind*. San Francisco, CA: Jossey-Bass.

Levitin, D. J. (2006). *This is your brain on music: The science of a human obsession*. New York, NY: Dutton.

Logan, A. C. (2007). *The brain diet: The connection between nutrition, mental health, and intelligence*. Nashville, TN: Cumberland House.

Medina, J. (2011). *Brain rules for baby: How to raise a smart and happy child from zero to five*. Seattle, WA: Pear Press.

Michalko, M. (2001). *Cracking creativity: The secrets of creative genius*. Berkeley, CA: Ten Speed Press.

Patel, A. D. (2008). *Music, language, and the brain*. New York, NY: Oxford University Press.

Perret, P., & Fox, J. (2004). *A well-tempered mind: Using music to help children listen and learn*. New York, NY: Dana Press.

Ratey, J. J. (2008). *Spark: The revolutionary new science of exercise and the brain*. New York, NY: Little, Brown.

Rose, D. H., & Meyer, A. (2002). *Teaching every student in the digital age: Universal design for learning*. Alexandria, VA: ASCD.

Rose, D. H., & Meyer, A. (2006). *A practical reader in universal design for learning*. Cambridge, MA: Harvard Education Press.

Rose, D., Meyer, A., & Hitchcock, C. (2005). *The universally designed classroom*. Cambridge, MA: Harvard Education Press.

Sacks, O. W. (2008). *Musicophilia: Tales of music and the brain*. New York, NY: Vintage Books.

Siegel, D. J. (2007). *The mindful brain: Reflection and attunement in the cultivation of well-being*. New York, NY: Norton.

Wasserman, L. H., & Zambo, D. (Eds.). (2013). *Early childhood and neuroscience: Links to development and learning*. New York, NY: Springer.

Bibliography

The following resources may be helpful to you in pursuing your interest in the topics. This is not a comprehensive reference list of all studies relevant to the discussion or mentioned in the chapters, but rather an overview of some references as a starting point for your continued investigation of the topics.

CHAPTER 1: HOW THE BRAIN THINKS AND LEARNS

Bennett, E. L., Diamond, M. L., Krech, D., & Rosenzweig, M. R. (1964). Chemical and anatomical plasticity of brain. *Science, 146,* 610–619.

Blackwell, L. S. (2002). *Psychological mediators of student achievement during the transition to junior high school: The role of implicit theories.* Doctoral dissertation, Columbia University.

Diamond, M. C., Krech, D., & Rosenzweig, M. R. (1964). The effects of an enriched environment on the histology of the rat cerebral cortex. *Journal of Comparative Neurology, 123,* 111–120.

Draganski, B., Gaser, C., Kempermann, G., Kuhn, G., Winkler, J., Büchel, C., & May, A. (2006). Temporal and spatial dynamics of brain structure changes during extensive learning. *Journal of Neuroscience, 26*(23).

Frey, S. H., & Gerry, V. E. (2006). Modulation of neural activity during observational learning of actions and their sequential orders. *Journal of Neuroscience, 26*(51), 13194–13201.

Grèzes, J., Costes, N., & Decety, J. (1999). The effects of learning and intention on the neural network involved in the perception of meaningless actions. *Brain*, *122* (Pt. 10), 1875–1887.

Hubel, D. H., & Wiesel, T. N. (1970). The period of susceptibility to the physiological effects of unilateral eye closure in kittens. *Journal of Physiology*, *206*(2), 419–436.

Maguire, E. A., Gadian, D. G., Johnsrude, I. S., Good, C. D., Ashburner, J., Frackowiak, R. J., & Frith, C. D. (2000). Navigation-related structural change in the hippocampi of taxi drivers. *Proceedings of the National Academy of Sciences*, *97*(8), 4398–4403.

Mayer, R. E. (1983). Can you repeat that? Qualitative effects of repetition and advance organizers on learning from science prose. *Journal of Educational Psychology*, *75*, 40–44.

Merzenich, M. M., Nelson, R. J., Stryker, M. P., Cynader, M. S., Schoppmann, A., & Zook, J. M. (1984). Somatosensory cortical map changes following digit amputation in adult monkeys. *Journal of Comparative Neurology*, *224*(4), 591–605.

Nader, K., Schafe, G. E., & Le Doux, J. E. (2000). Fear memories require protein synthesis in the amygdala for reconsolidation after retrieval. *Nature*, *406*(6797), 722–726.

Perry, B. (2000). How the brain learns best. *Instructor*, *11*(4), 34–35.

Toni, N., Buchs, P. A., Nikonenko, I., Bron, C. R., & Muller, D. (1999). LTP promotes formation of multiple spine synapses between a single axon terminal and a dendrite. *Nature*, *402*(6760), 421–425.

Wen, J. A., DeBlois, M. C., & Barth, A. L. (2013). Initiation, labile, and stabilization phases of experience-dependent plasticity at neocortical synapses. *Journal of Neuroscience*, *33*(19), 8483–8493.

CHAPTER 2: THE SENSORY MOTOR PATHWAY

Banai, K., Hornickel, J., Skoe, E., Nicol, T., Zecker, S., & Kraus, N. (2009). Reading and subcortical auditory function. *Cerebral Cortex*, *19*(11), 2699–2707.

Eckert, M. A., Leonard, C. M., Richards, T. L., Aylward, E. H., Thomson, J., & Berninger, V. W. (2003). Anatomical correlates of dyslexia: Frontal and cerebellar findings. *Brain*, *126*(Pt. 2), 482–494.

Golestani, N., Molko, N., Dehaene, S., LeBihan, D., & Pallier, C. (2007). Brain structure predicts the learning of foreign speech sounds. *Cerebral Cortex*, *17*(3), 575–582.

Haller, S., & Radue, E. (2005). What is different about a radiologist's brain? *Radiology*, *236*, 983–989.

Harris, S., Sheth, S. A., & Cohen, M. S. (2008). Functional neuroimaging of belief, disbelief, and uncertainty. *Annals of Neurology*, *63*(2), 141–147.

Hedden, T., Ketay, S., Aron, A., Markus, H. R., & Gabrieli, J. D. (2008). Cultural influences on neural substrates of attentional control. *Psychological Science*, *19*(1), 12–17.

Hornickel, J., & Kraus, N. (2013). Unstable representation of sound: A biological marker of dyslexia. *Journal of Neuroscience*, *33*(8), 3500–3504.

Moreno, S., Marques, C., Santos, A., Santos, M., Castro, S. L., & Besson, M. (2009). Musical training influences linguistic abilities in 8-year-old children: More evidence for brain plasticity. *Cerebral Cortex*, *19*(3), 712–723.

Strait, D. L., Hornickel, J., & Kraus, N. (2011). Subcortical processing of speech regularities underlies reading and music aptitude in children. *Behavioral and Brain Functions*, *7*(44), 1–11.

Strait, D. L., & Kraus, N. (2011). Playing music for a smarter ear: Cognitive, perceptual and neurobiological evidence. *Music Perception*, *29*(2), 133–146.

Wang, J., Nicol, T., Skoe, E., Sams, M., & Kraus, N. (2009). Emotion modulates early auditory response to speech. *Journal of Cognitive Neuroscience*, *21*(11), 2121–2128.

Whitehouse, A.J.O., Maybery, M. T., & Durkin, K. (2006). The development of the picture-superiority effect. *British Journal of Developmental Psychology*, *24*, 767–773.

Yue, G., & Cole, K. J. (1992). Strength increases from the motor program: Comparison of training with maximal voluntary and imagined muscle contracts. *Journal of Neurophysiology*, *67*(5), 1114–1123.

CHAPTER 3: THE EMOTION PATHWAY

Bandura, A. (1977). Self-efficacy: Toward a unifying theory of behavioral change. *Psychological Review*, *84*(2), 191–215.

Baumeister, R. F., Bratslavsky, E., Finkenauer, C., & Vohs, K. D. (2001). Bad is stronger than good. *Review of General Psychology*, *5*(4), 323–370.

Baumeister, R. F., & Leary, M. R. (1995). The need to belong: Desire for interpersonal attachments as a fundamental human motivation. *Psychological Bulletin*, *117*, 497–529.

Brown, K. W., & Ryan, R. M. (2003). The benefits of being present: Mindfulness and its role in psychological well-being. *Journal of Personality and Social Psychology*, *84*(4), 822–848.

Chen, Z., Williams, K. D., Fitness, J., & Newton, N. C. (2008). When hurt will not heal: Exploring the capacity to relive social and physical pain. *Psychological Science*, *19*(8), 789–795.

D'Argembeau, A., Comblain, C., & Van der Linden, M. (2002). Phenomenal characteristics of autobiographical memories for positive, negative, and neutral events. *Applied Cognitive Psychology*, *17*(3), 281–294.

Darnon, C., Harackiewicz, J. M., Butera, F., Mugny, G., & Quiamzade, A. (2007). Performance-approach and performance-avoidance goals: When uncertainty makes a difference. *Personality and Social Psychology Bulletin*, *33*(6), 813–827.

Eisenberger, N. I., Lieberman, M. D., & Williams, K. D. (2003). Does rejection hurt? An FMRI study of social exclusion. *Science*, *302*(5643), 290–292.

Erk, S., Kiefer, M., Grothe, J., Wunderlich, A. P., Spitzer, M., & Walter, H. (2003). Emotional context modulates subsequent memory effect. *Neuroimage*, *18*(2), 439–447.

Felten, P., Gilchrist, L. Z., & Darby, A. (2006). Emotion and learning: Feeling our way toward a new theory of reflection in service-learning. *Michigan Journal of Community Service Learning, 12*(2), 38–46.

Gray, J. A. (1990). Brain systems that mediate both emotion and cognition. *Cognition and Emotion, 4*(3), 269–288.

Gray, J. R., Braver, T. S., & Raichle, M. E. (2002). Integration of emotion and cognition in the lateral prefrontal cortex. *Proceedings of the National Academy of Sciences, 99*(6), 4115–4120.

Guiso, L., Monte, F., Sapienza, P., & Zingales, L. (2008). Diversity, culture, gender, and math. *Science, 320*(5880), 1164–1165.

Hamann, S. (2001). Cognitive and neural mechanisms of emotional memory. *Trends in Cognitive Sciences, 5*(9), 394–400.

Hampshire, A., Highfield, R. R., Parkin, B. L., & Owen, A. M. (2012). Fractionating human intelligence. *Neuron, 76*(6), 1225–1237.

Harlow, H. F., & Zimmerman, R. R. (1959). Affectional responses in the infant monkey: Orphaned baby monkeys develop a strong and persistent attachment to inanimate surrogate mothers. *Science, 130*(3373), 421–432.

Hedden, T., & Gabrieli, J. D. (2006). The ebb and flow of attention in the human brain. *Nature Neuroscience, 9*, 863–865.

Hinton, C., Miyamoto, K., & Della-Chiesa, B. (2008). Brain research, learning and emotions: Implications for education research, policy and practice. *European Journal of Education, 43*(1), 87–103.

Hyde, K. L., Lerch, J., Norton, A., Forgeard, M., Winner, E., Evans, A. C., & Schlaug, G. (2009). Musical training shapes structural brain development. *Journal of Neuroscience, 29*(10), 3019–3025.

Hölzel, B. K., Ott, U., Gard, T., Hempel, H., Weygandt, M., Morgen, K., & Vaitl, D. (2008). Investigation of mindfulness meditation practitioners with voxel-based morphometry. *Social Cognitive and Affective Neuroscience, 3*(1), 55–61.

Ironson, G., Wynings, C., Schneiderman, N., Baum, A., Rodriguez, M., Greenwood, D., & Benight, C. C. (1997). Post traumatic stress symptoms, intrusive thoughts, loss, and immune function after Hurricane Andrew. *Psychosomatic Medicine, 59*(2), 128–141.

Johns, M., Schmader, T., & Martens, A. (2005). Knowing is half the battle: Teaching stereotype threat as a means of improving women's math performance. *Psychological Science, 16*(3), 175–179.

Koven, N. S., Roth, R. M., Garlinghouse, M. A., Flashman, L. A., & Saykin, A. J. (2011). Regional gray matter correlates of perceived emotional intelligence. *Social Cognitive and Affective Neuroscience, 6*(5), 582–590.

Lazar, S. W., Kerr, C. E., Wasserman, R. H., Gray, J. R., Greve, D. N., Treadway, M. T., & Fischl, B. (2005). Meditation experience is associated with increased cortical thickness. *Neuroreport, 16*(17), 1893–1897.

Li, H., Penzo, M. A., Taniguchi, H., Kopec, C. D., Huang, Z. J., & Li, B. (2013). Experience-dependent modification of a central amygdala fear circuit. *Nature Neuroscience, 16*(3), 332–339.

Lieberman, M. D., Eisenberger, N. I., Crockett, M. J., Tom, S. M., Pfeifer, J. H., & Way, B. M. (2007). Putting feelings into words: After labeling disrupts amygdala activity in response to affective stimuli. *Psychological Science, 18*(5), 421–428.

Lutz, A., Greischar, L. L., Rawlings, N. B., Ricard, M., & Davidson, R. J. (2004). Long-term meditators self-induce high-amplitude gamma synchrony during mental practice. *Proceedings of the National Academy of Sciences, 101*(46), 16369–16373.

Mather, M., Mitchell, K. J., Raye, C. I., Novak, D. L., Greene, E. J., & Johnson, M. K. (2006). Emotional arousal can impair feature binding in working memory. *Journal of Cognitive Neuroscience, 18*(4), 614–625.

Mineka, S., & Henderson, R. W. (1985). Controllability and predictability in acquired motivation. *Annual Review of Psychology, 36*, 495–529.

Nummenmaa, L., Hirvonen, J., Parkkola, R., & Hietanen, J. K. (2008). Is emotional contagion special? An fMRI study on neural systems for affective and cognitive empathy. *Neuroimage, 43*(3), 571–580.

Pessoa, L. (2008). On the relationship between emotion and cognition. *Nature Reviews Neuroscience, 9*(2), 148–158.

Phelps, E. A. (2006). Emotion and cognition: Insights from studies of the human amygdala. *Annual Review of Psychology, 57*, 27–53.

Porges, S. W. (2004). Neuroception: A subconscious system for detecting threats and safety. *Zero to Three, 24*(5), 19–24.

Rauscher, F. H., Shaw, G. L., & Ky, K. N. (1993). Music and spatial task performance. *Nature, 365*(6447), 611.

Santorelli, F., Urbanowski, F., Harrington, A., Bonus, K., & Sheridan, J. F. (2003). Alterations in brain and immune function produced by mindfulness meditation. *Psychosomatic Medicine, 65*(4), 564–570.

Schmader, T., & Johns, M. (2003). Converging evidence that stereotype threat reduces working memory capacity. *Journal of Personality and Social Psychology, 85*(3), 440–452.

Steele, C. M., & Aronson, J. (1995). Stereotype threat and the intellectual test performance of African Americans. *Journal of Personality and Social Psychology, 69*(5), 797–811.

Swearer, S. M., Espelage, D., Vaillancourt, T., & Hymel, S. (2010). What can be done about school bullying? Linking research to educational practice. *Educational Researcher, 39*(1), 38–47.

Tang, Y. Y., & Posner, M. I. (2008). The neuroscience of mindfulness. *Neuroleadership Journal, 1*, 33–37.

Teasdale, J. D., Pope, M., & Segal, Z. V. (2002). Metacognitive awareness and prevention of relapse in depression: Empirical evidence. *Journal of Consulting and Clinical Psychology, 70*(2), 275–287.

Teicher, M. H., Samson, J. A., Sheu, Y. S., Polcari, A., & McGreenery, C. E. (2010). Hurtful words: Association of exposure to peer verbal abuse with elevated psychiatric symptom scores and corpus callosum abnormalities. *American Journal of Psychiatry*, *167*(12), 1464–1471.

Uchiyamaa, H. T., Saitoc, D. N., Tanabec, H. C., Haradad, T., Seki, A., Ohnoe, K., … Sadato, N. (2012). Distinction between the literal and intended meanings of sentences: A functional magnetic resonance imaging study of metaphor and sarcasm. *Cortex*, *48*, 563–583.

Vaillancourt, T., Duku, E., Decatanzaro, D., Macmillan, H., Muir, C., & Schmidt, L. A. (2008). Variation in hypothalamic–pituitary–adrenal axis activity among bullied and non-bullied children. *Aggressive Behavior*, *34*(3), 294–305.

Vaillancourt, T., Hymelb, S., & McDougall, P. (2003). Bullying is power: Implications for school-based intervention strategies. *Journal of Applied School Psychology*, *19*(2), 157–176.

Varela, J. A., Wang, J., Christianson, J. P., Maier, S. F., & Cooper, D. C. (2012). Control over stress, but not stress per se increases prefrontal cortical pyramidal neuron excitability. *Journal of Neuroscience*, *32*(37), 12848–12853.

Wang, J., Nicol, T., Skoe, E., Sams, M., & Kraus, N. (2009). Emotion modulates early auditory response to speech. *Journal of Cognitive Neuroscience*, *21*(11), 2121–2128.

Wild, B., Erb, M., & Bartels, M. (2001). Are emotions contagious? Evoked emotions while viewing emotionally expressive faces: Quality, quantity, time course, and gender differences. *Psychiatry Research*, *102*, 109–124.

Yerkes, R. M., & Dodson, J. D. (1908). The relation of strength of stimulus to rapidity of habit-formation. *Journal of Comparative Neurology and Psychology*, *18*(5), 459–482.

CHAPTER 4: THE REWARD PATHWAY

Baumeister, A. A. (2000). The Tulane Electrical Brain Stimulation Program: A historical case study in medical ethics. *Journal of the History of the Neurosciences*, *9*(3), 262–278.

Baumeister, R. F., Bratslavsky, E., Finkenauer, C., & Vohs, K. D. (2001). Bad is stronger than good. *Review of General Psychology*, *5*(4), 323–370.

Baumeister, R. F., & Leary, M. R. (1995). The need to belong: Desire for interpersonal attachments as a fundamental human motivation. *Psychological Bulletin*, *117*, 497–529.

Berridge, K. C., & Kringelbach, M. L. (2008). Affective neuroscience of pleasure: Reward in humans and animals. *Psychopharmacology (Berlin)*, *199*(3), 457–480.

Chiao, J. Y., Bordeaux, A. R., & Ambady, N. (2003). Mental representations of social status. *Cognition*, *93*(2), 49–57.

Coe, B., Sakagami, M., & Hikosaka, O. (2002). Feature-based anticipation of cues that predict reward in monkey caudate nucleus. *Neuron*, *33*(3), 463–473.

Darnon, C., Harackiewicz, J. M., Butera, F., Mugny, G., & Quiamzade, A. (2007). Performance-approach and performance-avoidance goals: When uncertainty makes a difference. *Personality and Social Psychology Bulletin, 33*(6), 813–827.

Decety, J., Jackson, P. L., Sommerville, J. A., Chaminade, T., & Meltzoff, A. N. (2004). The neural bases of cooperation and competition: An fMRI investigation. *Neuroimage, 23*(2), 744–751.

Eisenberger, N. I., Lieberman, M. D., & Williams, K. D. (2003). Does rejection hurt? An FMRI study of social exclusion. *Science, 302*(5643), 290–291.

Gunderson, E. A., Gripshover, S. J., Romero, C., Dweck, C. S., Goldin-Meadow, S., & Levine, S. C. (2013). Parent praise to 1- to 3-year-olds predicts children's motivational frameworks 5 years later. *Child Development, 84*(5), 1526–1541.

Harlow, H. F., & Zimmerman, R. R. (1959). Affectional responses in the infant monkey; orphaned baby monkeys develop a strong and persistent attachment to inanimate surrogate mothers. *Science, 130*(3373), 421–432.

Izuma, K., Saito, D. N., & Sadato, N. (2008). Processing of social and monetary rewards in the human striatum. *Neuron, 58*, 294.

Kounios, J., Frymiare, J. L., Bowden, E. M., & Beeman, M. (2008). The origins of insight in resting-state brain activity. *Neuropsychologia, 46*(1), 281–291.

Kringelbach, M. L. (2010). The hedonic brain: A functional neuroanatomy of human pleasure. In M. L. Kringelbach & K. C. Berridge (Eds.), *Pleasures of the brain* (pp. 202–221). Oxford: Oxford University Press.

Kringelbach, M. L., & Berridge, K. C. (2010). The functional neuroanatomy of pleasure and happiness. *Discovery Medicine, 9*(49), 579–587.

Lieberman, M. D., Gaunt, R., Gilbert, D. T., & Trope, Y. (2001). Reflection and reflexion: A social cognitive neuroscience approach to attributional inference. In M. Zanna (Ed.), *Advances in experimental social psychology* (pp. 199–249). New York, NY: Academic Press.

Losin, E. A., Iacoboni, M., Martin, A., & Dapretto, M. (2012). Own-gender imitation activates the brain's reward circuitry. *Social Cognitive and Affective Neuroscience, 7*(7), 804–810.

Mineka, S., & Henderson, R. W. (1985). Controllability and predictability in acquired motivation. *Annual Review of Psychology, 36*, 495–529.

Olds, J., & Milner, P. (1954). Positive reinforcement produced by electrical stimulation of septal area and other regions of rat brain. *Journal of Comparative Physiology, 47*(6), 419–427.

Panksepp, J., Herman, B., Conner, R., Bishop, P., & Scott, J. P. (1978). The biology of social attachments: Opiates alleviate separation distress. *Biological Psychiatry, 13*, 607–618.

Prat, C. S., Mason, R. A., & Just, M. A. (2012). An fMRI investigation of analogical mapping in metaphor comprehension: The influence of context and individual cognitive capacities on processing demands. *Journal of the History of the Neurosciences, 38*(2), 282–294.

Rodin, J., & Langer, E. J. (1977). Long-term effects of a control-relevant intervention with the institutionalized aged. *Journal of Personality and Social Psychology, 33*(12), 897–902.

Schultz, W. (1999). The reward signal of midbrain dopamine neurons. *News in Psychological Sciences, 14*(6), 249–255.

Subramaniam, K., Kounios, J., Bowden, E. M., Parrish, T. B., & Jung-Beeman, M. (2009). Positive mood and anxiety modulate anterior cingulate activity and cognitive preparation for insight. *Journal of Cognitive Neuroscience, 21*, 415–432.

Tabibnia, G., & Lieberman, M. D. (2007). Fairness and cooperation are rewarding: Evidence from social cognitive neuroscience. *Annals of the New York Academy of Sciences, 1118*, 90–101.

Wolfe, P. (2006). The role of meaning and emotion in learning. In S. Johnson and K. Taylor (Eds.), *New Directions for Adult and Continuing Education,* no. *110*, 35–41.

CHAPTER 5: THE ATTENTION AND MEMORY PATHWAYS

Alloway, T. P., Gathercole, S. E., Kirkwood, H., & Elliott, J. (2009). The cognitive and behavioral characteristics of children with low working memory. *Child Development, 80*(2), 606–621.

Barot, S. K., Chung, A., Kim, J. J., & Bernstein, I. L. (2009). Functional imaging of stimulus convergence in amygdalar neurons during Pavlovian fear conditioning. *PLoS One, 4*(7), 6156.

Brefczynski-Lewis, J. A., Lutz, A., Schaefer, H. S., Levinson, D. B., & Davidson, R. J. (2003). Neural correlates of attentional expertise in long-term meditation practitioners. *Proceedings of the National Academy of Sciences, 104*(27), 11483–11488.

Chiesa, A., & Serretti, A. (2010). A systematic review of neurobiological and clinical features of mindfulness meditations. *Psychological Medicine, 40*(8), 1239–1252.

Chun, M. M., & Turk-Browne, N. B. (2007). Interactions between attention and memory. *Current Opinion in Neurobiology, 17*(2), 177–184.

Cowan, N. (2001). The magical number 4 in short-term memory: A reconsideration of mental storage capacity. *Behavioral and Brain Sciences, 24*(1), 87–185.

Dhamani, I., Leung, J., Carlile, S., & Sharma, M. (2013). Switch attention to listen. *Scientific Reports, 3*, 1297.

Dumontheil, I., & Klingberg, T. (2012). Brain activity during a visuospatial working memory task predicts arithmetical performance 2 years later. *Cerebral Cortex, 22*(5), 1078–1085.

Dunlosky, J., Rawson, K. A., Marsh, E. J., Nathan, M. J., & Willingham, D. T. (2013). Improving students' learning with effective learning techniques: Promising directions from cognitive and educational psychology. *Psychological Science in the Public Interest, 14*(1), 4–58.

Fuster, J. M. (2009). Cortex and memory: Emergence of a new paradigm. *Journal of Cognitive Neuroscience, 21*(11), 2047–2072.

Gazzaley, A., & Nobre, A. C. (2012). Top-down modulation: Bridging selective attention and working memory. *Trends in Cognitive Sciences, 16*(2), 129–135.

Gober, F., & Clarkson, G. (2004). Chunks in expert memory: Evidence for the magical number four . . . or is it two? *Memory, 12*(6), 732–747.

Hahn, T. T., McFarland, J. M., Berberich, S., Sakmann, B., & Mehta, M. R. (2012). Spontaneous persistent activity in entorhinal cortex modulates cortico-hippocampal interaction in vivo. *Nature Neuroscience, 15*(11), 1531–1538.

Hampshire, A., Highfield, R. R., Parkin, B. L., & Owen, A. M. (2012). Fractionating human intelligence. *Neuron, 76*(6), 1225–1237.

Kane, M. J., Brown, L. H., McVay, J. C., Silvia, P. J., Myin-Germeys, I., & Kwapil, T. R. (2007). For whom the mind wanders, and when: An experience-sampling study of working memory and executive control in daily life. *Psychological Science, 18*(7), 614–621.

Karpicke, J. D., & Bauernschmidt, A. (2011). Spaced retrieval: Absolute spacing enhances learning regardless of relative spacing. *Journal of Experimental Psychology: Learning, Memory, and Cognition, 37*(5), 1250–1257.

Karpicke, J. D., & Roediger, H. L., III. (2007). Repeated retrieval during learning is the key to long-term retention. *Journal of Memory and Language, 57*, 151–162.

Kornell, N., Castel, A. D., Eich, T. S., & Bjork, R. A. (2010). Spacing as the friend of both memory and induction in young and older adults. *Psychology and Aging, 25*(2), 498–503.

Kraus, N., Strait, D., & Parbery-Clark, A. (2012). Cognitive factors shape brain networks for auditory skills: Spotlight on auditory working memory. *Annals of the New York Academy of Sciences, 1252*, 100–107.

Krüttner, S., Stepien, B., Noordermeer, J. N., Mommaas, M. A., Mechtler, K., Dickson, B. J., & Keleman, K. (2012). Drosophila CPEB Orb2A mediates memory independent of its RNA-binding domain. *Neuron, 76*(2), 383–395.

Lazar, S. W., Kerr, C. E., Wasserman, R. H., Gray, J. R., Greve, D. N., Treadway, M. T., & Fischld, B. (2005). Meditation experience is associated with increased cortical thickness. *Neuroreport, 16*(17), 1893–1897.

Leeming, F. C. (2002). The exam-a-day procedure improves performance in psychology classes. *Teaching of Psychology, 29*, 210–212.

Lutz, A., Greischar, L. L., Rawlings, N. B., Ricard, M., & Davidson, R. J. (2004). Long-term meditators self-induce high-amplitude gamma synchrony during mental practice. *Proceedings of the National Academy of Sciences, 101*(46), 16369–16373.

Mather, M., Mitchell, K. J., Raye, C. I., Novak, D. L., Greene, E. J., & Johnson, M. K. (2006). Emotional arousal can impair feature binding in working memory. *Journal of Cognitive Neuroscience, 18*(4), 614–625.

McElree, B. (2001). Working memory and focal attention. *Journal of Experimental Psychology: Learning, Memory, and Cognition, 27*(3), 817–835.

Miller, G. A. (1956). The magical number seven, plus or minus two: Some limits on our capacity for processing information. *Psychological Review*, *63*(2), 81–97.

Posner, M. I., & Petersen, S. E. (1990). The attention system of the human brain. *Annual Review of Neuroscience*, *13*, 25–42.

Schmader, T., & Johns, M. (2003). Converging evidence that stereotype threat reduces working memory capacity. *Journal of Personality and Social Psychology*, *85*(3), 440–452.

Shiffrin, R. M., & Nosofsky, R. M. (1994). Seven plus or minus two: A commentary on capacity limitations. *Psychological Review*, *101*(2), 357–361.

Smith, C. N., & Squire, L. R. (2009). Medial temporal lobe activity during retrieval of semantic memory is related to the age of the memory. *Journal of Neuroscience*, *29*(4), 930–938.

Strait, D. L., & Kraus, N. (2011). Can you hear me now? Musical training shapes functional brain networks for selective auditory attention and hearing speech in noise. *Frontiers in Psychology*, *2*(113), 1–10.

Swanson, H. L. (1999). What develops in working memory? A life span perspective. *Developmental Psychology*, *35*(4), 986–1000.

Tang, Y. Y., Ma, Y., Wang, J., Fan, Y., Feng, S., Lu, Q., & Posner, M. I. (2007). Short-term meditation training improves attention and self-regulation. *Proceedings of the National Academy of Sciences*, *104*(43), 17152–17156.

Taylor, K., & Rohrer, D. (2010). The effects of interleaved practice. *Applied Cognitive Psychology*, *24*, 837–848.

Watrous, A. J., Tandon, N., Conner, C. R., Pieters, T., & Ekstrom, A. D. (2013). Frequency-specific network connectivity increases underlie accurate spatiotemporal memory retrieval. *Nature Neuroscience*, *16*(3), 349–356.

Yi, D. J., & Chun, M. M. (2005). Attentional modulation of learning-related repetition attenuation effects in human parahippocampal cortex. *Journal of Neuroscience*, *25*(14), 3593–3600.

Zeidan, F., Johnson, S. K., Diamond, B. J., Zhanna, D., & Goolkasian, P. (2010). Mindfulness meditation improves cognition: Evidence of brief mental training. *Consciousness and Cognition*, *19*(2), 597–605.

CHAPTER 6: THE LANGUAGE AND MATH PATHWAYS

Bahrick, H. P., Bahrick, L. E., Bahrick, A. S., & Bahrick, P. E. (1993). Maintenance of foreign language vocabulary and the spacing effect. *Psychological Science*, *4*, 316–321.

Ball, P. (2012). Brain's "reading centres" are culturally universal: Whether you are reading in Chinese or French, the same brain areas light up. *Nature News*. doi:10.1038/nature.2012.11883

Banai, K., Hornickel, J., Skoe, E., Nicol, T., Zecker, S., & Kraus, N. (2009). Reading and subcortical auditory function. *Cerebral Cortex*, *19*(11), 2699–2707.

Bialystok, E., Craik, F. I., & Freedman, M. (2007). Bilingualism as a protection against the onset of symptoms of dementia. *Neuropsychologia, 45*(2), 459–464.

Bloom, K. C., & Shuell, T. J. (1981). Effects of massed and distributed practice on the learning and retention of second-language vocabulary. *Journal of Educational Research, 74*(4), 245–248.

Buchweitz, A., Mason, R. A., Tomitch, L., Just, M. B., & Adam, M. (2009). Brain activation for reading and listening comprehension: An fMRI study of modality effects and individual differences in language comprehension. *Psychology and Neuroscience, 2*(2), 111–123.

Byers-Heinlein, K., Burns, T. C., & Werker, J. F. (2010). The roots of bilingualism in newborns. *Psychological Science, 21*(3), 343–348.

Catani, M., Jones, D. K., & Ffytche, D. H. (2005). Perisylvian language networks of the human brain. *Annals of Neurology, 57*(1), 8–16.

Chandrasekaran, B., & Kraus, N. (2012). Biological factors contributing to reading ability: Subcortical auditory function. In A. A. Benasich & R. H. Fitch (Eds.), *Developmental dyslexia: Early precursors, neurobehavioral markers and biological substrates.* (pp. 83–98). Baltimore, MD: Paul H. Brookes.

Cotton, C., McIntyre, F., & Price, J. (2013). Gender differences in repeated competition: Evidence from school math contests. *Journal of Economic Behavior and Organization, 86*, 52–66.

Craik, F. I., Bialystok, E., & Freedman, M. (2010). Delaying the onset of Alzheimer disease: Bilingualism as a form of cognitive reserve. *Neurology, 75*(19), 1726–1729.

Durgunoğlu, A. Y., Mir, M., & Ariño-Martí, S. (1993). Effects of repeated readings on bilingual and monolingual memory for text. *Contemporary Educational Psychology, 18*, 294–317.

Eckert, M. A., Leonard, C. M., Richards, T. L., Aylward, E. H., Thomson, J., & Berninger, V. W. (2003). Anatomical correlates of dyslexia: Frontal and cerebellar findings. *Brain, 126*(Pt. 2), 482–494.

Engel de Abreu, P. M., Cruz-Santos, A., Tourinho, C. J., Martin, R., & Bialystok, E. (2012). Bilingualism enriches the poor: Enhanced cognitive control in low-income minority children. *Psychological Science, 23*(11), 1364–1371.

Eviatar, Z., & Just, M. A. (2006). Brain correlates of discourse processing: An fMRI investigation of irony and conventional metaphor comprehension. *Neuropsychologia, 44*(12), 2348–2359.

Friedmann, N., Kerbel, N., & Shvimer, L. (2010). Developmental attentional dyslexia. *Cortex, 46*(10), 1216–1237.

Geary, D. C., Hoard, M. K., Nugent, L., & Bailey, D. H. (2013). Adolescents' functional numeracy is predicted by their school entry number system knowledge. *PLoS One, 8*(1), e54651.

Gervain, J., & Werker, J. F. (2013). Prosody cues word order in 7-month-old bilingual infants. *Nature Communications*, *4*, art. 1490.

Glezer, L. S., Jiang, X., & Riesenhuber, M. (2009). Evidence for highly selective neuronal tuning to whole words in the "visual word form area." *Neuron*, *62*(2), 199–204.

Gold, B. T., Kim, C., Johnson, N. F., Kryscio, R. J., & Smith, C. D. (2013). Lifelong bilingualism maintains neural efficiency for cognitive control in aging. *Journal of Neuroscience*, *33*(2), 387–396.

Golestani, N., Molko, N., Dehaene, S., LeBihan, D., & Pallier, C. (2007). Brain structure predicts the learning of foreign speech sounds. *Cerebral Cortex*, *17*(3), 575–582.

Grafman, J., & Romero, S. (2001). Appearances may not be deceiving: Calculation deficits due to a brain structure abnormality in neurologically normal children. *Brain*, *124*(9), 1681–1682.

Guiso, L., Monte, F., Sapienza, P., & Zingales, L. (2008). Diversity, culture, gender, and math. *Science*, *320*(5880), 1164–1165.

Hornickel, J., & Kraus, N. (2013). Unstable representation of sound: A biological marker of dyslexia. *Journal of Neuroscience*, *33*(8), 3500–3504.

Johns, M., Schmader, T., & Martens, A. (2005). Knowing is half the battle: Teaching stereotype threat as a means of improving women's math performance. *Psychological Science*, *16*(3), 175–179.

Kaushanskaya, M., & Marian, V. (2009). Bilingualism reduces native-language interference during novel-word learning. *Journal of Experimental Psychology: Learning, Memory, and Cognition*, *35*(3), 829–835.

Kika, F. M., McLaughlin, T. F., & Dixon, J. (1992). Effects of frequent testing of secondary algebra students. *Journal of Educational Research*, *85*, 159–162.

Krizman, J., Marian, V., Shook, A., Skoe, E., & Kraus, N. (2012). Subcortical encoding of sound is enhanced in bilinguals and relates to executive function advantages. *Proceedings of the National Academy of Sciences*, *109*(20), 7877–7881 .

Lacey, S., Stilla, R., & Sathian, K. (2012). Metaphorically feeling: Comprehending textural metaphors activates somatosensory cortex. *Brain and Language*, *120*(3), 416–421.

Lawson, M. J., & Hogben, D. (1998). Learning and recall of foreign-language vocabulary: Effects of a keyword strategy for immediate and delayed recall. *Learning and Instruction*, *8*(2), 179–194.

Martensson, J., Eriksson, J., Bodammer, N. C., Lindgren, M., Johansson, M., Nyberg, L., & Lovden, M. (2012). Language growth of language-related brain areas after foreign language learning. *Neuroimage*, *63*(1), 240–244.

Mayfield, K. H., & Chase, P. N. (2002). The effects of cumulative practice on mathematics problem solving. *Journal of Applied Behavior Analysis*, *35*(2), 105–123.

Mazzocco, M. M., Feigenson, L., & Halberda, J. (2011). Preschoolers' precision of the approximate number system predicts later school mathematics performance. *PLoS One*, *6*(9), e23749.

Miller, G. A. (1956). The magical number seven, plus or minus two: Some limits on our capacity for processing information. *Psychological Review*, *63*(2), 81–97.

Moon, C., Lagercrantz, H., & Kuhl, P. K. (2013). Language experienced in utero affects vowel perception after birth: A two-country study. *ActaPaediatrica*, *102*(2), 156–160.

Morales, J., Calvo, A., & Bialystok, E. (2013). Working memory development in monolingual and bilingual children. *Journal of Experimental Child Psychology*, *114*(2), 187–202.

Murayama, K., Pekrun, R., Lichtenfeld, S., & VomHofe, R. (2012). Predicting long-term growth in students' mathematics achievement: The unique contributions of motivation and cognitive strategies. *Child Development*, *84*(4), 1475–1490.

Noël, M. P. (2005). Finger gnosia: A predictor of numerical abilities in children? *Child Neuropsychology*, *11*(5), 413–430.

Panayiotou, A. (2004). Switching codes, switching code: Bilinguals' emotional responses in English and Greek. *Journal of Multilingual and Multicultural Development*, *25*(2–3), 124–139.

Park, J., Park, D. C., & Polk, T. A. (2012). Parietal functional connectivity in numerical cognition. *Cerebral Cortex*, *23*(9), 2127–2135.

Petitto, L. A., Berens, M. S., Kovelman, I., Dubins, M. H., Jasinska, K., & Shalinsky, M. (2012). The "perceptual wedge hypothesis" as the basis for bilingual babies' phonetic processing advantage: New insights from fNIRS brain imaging. *Brain and Language*, *121*(2), 130–143.

Prior, A., & Macwhinney, B. (2010). A bilingual advantage in task switching. *Bilingualism: Language and Cognition*, *13*, 253–262.

Pugh, K. R., Shaywitz, B. A., Shaywitz, S. E., Constable, R. T., Skudlarski, P., Fulbright, R. K., & Gore, J. C. (1996). Cerebral organization of component processes in reading. *Brain*, *119*(4), 1221–1238.

Rivera, S. M., Reiss, A. L., Eckert, M. A., & Menon, V. (2005). Developmental changes in mental arithmetic: Evidence for increased functional specialization in the left inferior parietal cortex. *Cerebral Cortex*, *15*(11), 1779–1790.

Rohrer, D. (2009). The effects of spacing and mixing practice problems. *Journal for Research in Mathematics Education*, *40*, 4–17.

Rohrer, D., & Taylor, K. (2006). The effects of overlearning and distributed practice on the retention of mathematics knowledge. *Applied Cognitive Psychology*, *20*, 1209–1224.

Rohrer, D., & Taylor, K. (2007). The shuffling of mathematics problems improves learning. *Instructional Science*, *35*, 481–498.

Rubio-Fernández, P., & Glucksberg, S. (2012). Reasoning about other people's beliefs: Bilinguals have an advantage. *Journal of Experimental Psychology: Learning, Memory, and Cognition*, *38*(1), 211–217.

Schroeder, S. R., & Marian, V. (2012). A bilingual advantage for episodic memory in older adults. *Journal of Cognitive Psychology*, *24*(5), 591–601.

Shalev, R. S. (2004). Developmental dyscalculia. *Journal of Child Neurology*, *19*(10), 765–771.

Simos, P. G., Fletcher, J. M., Bergman, E., Breier, J. I., Foorman, B. R., Castillo, E. M., & Papanicolaou, A. C. (2002). Dyslexia-specific brain activation profile becomes normal following successful remedial training. *Neurology*, *58*(8), 1203–1213.

Speer, N. K., Reynolds, J. R., Swallow, K. M., & Zacks, J. M. (2009). Reading stories activates neural representations of visual and motor experiences. *Psychological Science*, *20*(8), 989–999.

Strait, D. L., Hornickel, J., & Kraus, N. (2011). Subcortical processing of speech regularities predicts reading and music aptitude in children. *Behavioral and Brain Functions*, *7*, 44.

Taylor, K., & Rohrer, D. (2010). The effects of interleaved practice. *Applied Cognitive Psychology*, *24*, 837–848.

Tierney, A., & Kraus, N. (2013). The ability to tap to a beat relates to cognitive, linguistic, and perceptual skills. *Brain and Language*, *124*, 225–231.

Tsapkini, K., & Rapp, B. (2010). The orthography-specific functions of the left fusiform gyrus: Evidence of modality and category specificity. *Cortex*, *46*(2), 185–205.

Turkeltaub, P. E., Weisberg, J., Flowers, D. L., Basu, D., & Eden, G. F. (2005). The neurobiological basis of reading: A special case of skill acquisition. In H. W. Catts & A. G. Kamhi (Eds.), *The connections between language and reading disabilities* (pp. 89–113). Mahwah, NJ: Erlbaum.

Yeatman, J. D., Dougherty, R. F., Ben-Shachar, M., & Wandell, B. A. (2012). Development of white matter and reading skills. *Proceedings of the National Academy of Sciences*, *109*(44), 3045–3053.

Zadina, J. N., Corey, D. M., Casbergue, R. M., Lemen, L. C., Rouse, J. C., Knaus, T. A., & Foundas, A. L. (2006). Lobar asymmetries in subtypes of dyslexic and control subjects. *Journal of Child Neurology*, *21*(11), 922–931.

CHAPTER 7: THE FRONTAL LOBE EXECUTIVE FUNCTION PATHWAY

Andrade, J. (2010). What does doodling do? *Applied Cognitive Psychology*, *24*(1), 100–106.

Beer, J. S., Shimamura, A. P., & Knight, R. T. (2004). Frontal lobe contributions to executive control of cognitive and social behavior. In M. S. Gazzaniga (Ed.), *The cognitive neurosciences III* (pp. 1091–1104). Cambridge, MA: MIT Press.

Butler, A. C. (2010). Repeated testing produces superior transfer of learning relative to repeated studying. *Journal of Experimental Psychology: Learning, Memory, and Cognition*, *36*, 1118–1133.

Carpenter, S. K., Pashler, H., Wixted, J. T., & Vul, E. (2008). The effects of tests on learning and forgetting. *Memory and Cognition*, *36*(2), 438–448.

Chiesa, A., & Serretti, A. (2010). A systematic review of neurobiological and clinical features of mindfulness meditations. *Psychological Medicine*, *40*(8), 1239–1252.

Elliott, R. (2003). Executive functions and their disorders. *British Medical Bulletin, 65,* 49–59.

Eslinger, P. J. (1996). Conceptualizing, describing, and measuring components of executive functioning: A summary. In G. R. Lyon & N. A. Krasnegor (Eds.), *Attention, memory, and executive function* (pp. 367–395). London: Paul H. Brookes.

Espinet, S. D., Anderson, J. E., & Zelazo, P. D. (2012). N2 amplitude as a neural marker of executive function in young children: An ERP study of children who switch versus perseverate on the dimensional change card sort. *Developmental Cognitive Neuroscience, 2*(1), S49–58.

Fisher, R. (2002). Shared thinking: Metacognitive modeling in the literacy hour. *Reading, 36*(2), 65–67.

Heckman, J. J. (2006). Skill formation and the economics of investing in disadvantaged children. *Science, 312*(5782), 1900–1902.

Lieberman, M. D., Gaunt, R., Gilbert, D. T., & Trope, Y. (2001). Reflection and reflexion: A social cognitive neuroscience approach to attributional inference. In M. Zanna (Ed.), *Advances in experimental social psychology* (pp. 199–249). New York, NY: Academic Press.

MacLeod, C. (1991). Half a century of research on the Stroop effect: An integrative review. *Psychological Bulletin, 109*(2), 163–203.

Mayer, R. E. (1983). Can you repeat that? Qualitative effects of repetition and advance organizers on learning from science prose. *Journal of Educational Psychology, 75,* 40–44.

McCutchen, D. (1988). Functional automaticity in children's writing: A problem in metacognitive control. *Written Communication, 5,* 306–324.

Meltzer, L., Katzir, T., Miller, L., Reddy, R., & Roditi, B. (2004). Academic self-perceptions, effort, and strategy use in students with learning disabilities: Changes over time. *Learning Disabilities Research and Practice, 19*(2), 99–108.

Meltzer, L., Katzir-Cohen, T., Miller, L., & Roditi, B. (2001). The impact of effort and strategy use on academic performance: Student and teacher perceptions. *Disabilities Quarterly, 24*(2), 85–98.

Merkley, D. M., & Jeffries, D. (2001). Guidelines for implementing a graphic organizer. *Reading Teacher, 54*(4), 350–357.

Moffitt, T. E., Arseneault, L., Belsky, D., Dickson, N., Hancox, R. J., Harrington, H., & Caspi, A. (2011). A gradient of childhood self-control predicts health, wealth, and public safety. *Proceedings of the National Academy of Sciences, 108*(7), 2693–2698.

Moreno, S., Bialystok, E., Barac, R., Schellenberg, E. G., Cepeda, N. J., & Chau, T. (2011). Short-term music training enhances verbal intelligence and executive function. *Psychological Science, 22*(11), 1425–1433.

Pashler, H. (1992). Attentional limitations in doing two tasks at the same time. *Current Directions in Psychological Science, 1,* 44–50.

Pashler, H., Johnston, J. C., & Ruthruff, E. (2001). Attention and performance. *Annual Review of Psychology*, *52*, 629–651.

Raney, G. E. (1993). Monitoring changes in cognitive load during reading: An event-related brain potential and reaction time analysis. *Journal of Experimental Psychology: Learning, Memory, and Cognition*, *19*(1), 51–69.

Taylor, K., & Rohrer, D. (2010). The effects of interleaved practice. *Applied Cognitive Psychology*, *24*, 837–848.

Teasdale, J. D. (1999). Metacognition, mindfulness, and the modification of mood disorders. *Clinical Psychology and Psychotherapy*, *6*(2), 146–155.

Zeidan, F., Johnson, S. K., Diamond, B. J., Zhanna, D., & Goolkasian, P. (2010). Mindfulness meditation improves cognition: Evidence of brief mental training. *Consciousness and Cognition*, *19*(2), 597–605.

CHAPTER 8: THE SOCIAL PATHWAY

Blakemore, S. J. (2008). The social brain in adolescence. *Nature Reviews Neuroscience*, *9*(4), 267–277.

Chen, Z., Williams, K. D., Fitness, J., & Newton, N. C. (2008). When hurt will not heal: Exploring the capacity to relive social and physical pain. *Psychological Science*, *19*(8), 789–795.

Chiao, J. Y., Bordeaux, A. R., & Ambady, N. (2003). Mental representations of social status. *Cognition*, *93*(2), B49–57.

Decety, J., Jackson, P. L., Sommerville, J. A., Chaminade, T., & Meltzoff, A. N. (2004). The neural bases of cooperation and competition: An fMRI investigation. *Neuroimage*, *23*(2), 744–751.

Dijksterhuis, A., & van Knippenberg, A. (1998). The relation between perception and behavior, or how to win a game of trivial pursuit. *Journal of Personality and Social Psychology*, *74*(4), 865–877.

Durlak, J. A., Weissberg, R. P., Dymnicki, A. B., Taylor, R. D., & Schellinger, K. B. (2011). The impact of enhancing students' social and emotional learning: A meta-analysis of school-based universal interventions. *Child Development*, *82*(1), 405–432.

Eisenberger, N. I., Lieberman, M. D., & Williams, K. D. (2003). Does rejection hurt? An FMRI study of social exclusion. *Science*, *302*(5643), 290–292.

Frith, U., & Frith, C. (2010). The social brain: Allowing humans to boldly go where no other species has been. *Philosophical Transactions of the Royal Society B*, *365*(1537), 165–176.

Harlow, H. F., & Zimmerman, R. R. (1959). Affectional responses in the infant monkey: Orphaned baby monkeys develop a strong and persistent attachment to inanimate surrogate mothers. *Science*, *130*(3373), 421–432.

Hughes, J., & Kwok, O. M. (2007). Influence of student-teacher and parent-teacher relationships on lower achieving readers' engagement and achievement in the primary grades. *Journal of Educational Psychology*, *99*(1), 39–51.

Iacobini, M., Molnar-Szakacs, I., Gallese, V., Buccino, G., Mazziotta, J. C., & Rizzolatti, G. (2005). Grasping the intentions of others with one's own mirror neuron system. *PloS Biology, 3*(3), 79.

Izuma, K., Saito, D. N., & Sadato, N. (2008). Processing of social and monetary rewards in the human striatum. *Neuron, 58*(2), 284–294.

Keysers, C., & Gazzola, V. (2006). Towards a unifying neural theory of social cognition. *Progress in Brain Research, 156*, 379–401.

Lieberman, M. D., Gaunt, R., Gilbert, D. T., & Trope, Y. (2001). Reflection and reflexion: A social cognitive neuroscience approach to attributional inference. In M. Zanna (Ed.), *Advances in experimental social psychology* (pp. 199–249). New York, NY: Academic Press.

Losin, E. A., Iacoboni, M., Martin, A., & Dapretto, M. (2012). Own-gender imitation activates the brain's reward circuitry. *Social, Cognitive, and Affective Neuroscience, 7*(7), 804–810.

Morton, E., Gage, H. D., & Mach, R. H. (1998). Effect of social status on striatal dopamine D2 receptor binding characteristics in cynomolgus monkeys assessed with positron emission tomography. *Synapse, 29*(1), 80–83.

Newman-Norlund, R. D., van Schie, H. T., van Zuijlen, A. M., & Bekkering, H. (2007). The mirror neuron system is more active during complementary compared with imitative action. *Nature Neuroscience, 10*, 817–818.

Nummenmaa, L., Hirvonen, J., Parkkola, R., & Hietanen, J. K. (2008). Is emotional contagion special? An fMRI study on neural systems for affective and cognitive empathy. *Neuroimage, 43*(3), 571–580.

Panksepp, J., Herman, B., Conner, R., Bishop, P., & Scott, J. P. (1978). The biology of social attachments: Opiates alleviate separation distress. *Biological Psychiatry, 13*, 607–618.

Rizzolatti, G., & Craighero, L. (2004). The mirror-neuron system. *Annual Review of Neuroscience, 27*, 169–192.

Singer, T., Seymour, B., O'Doherty, J., Kaube, H., Dolan, R. J., & Frith, C. D. (2004). Empathy for pain involves the affective but not sensory components of pain. *Science, 303*(5661), 1157–1162.

Small, G. W., Moody, T. D., Siddarth, P., & Bookheimer, S. Y. (2009). Your brain on Google: Patterns of cerebral activation during Internet searching. *American Journal of Geriatric Psychiatry, 17*(2), 116–126.

Swearer, S. M., Espelage, D., Vaillancourt, T., & Hymel, S. (2010). What can be done about school bullying? Linking research to educational practice. *Educational Researcher, 39*(1), 38–47.

Teicher, M. H., Samson, J. A., Sheu, Y. S., Polcari, A., & McGreenery, C. E. (2010). Hurtful words: Association of exposure to peer verbal abuse with elevated psychiatric symptom scores and corpus callosum abnormalities. *American Journal of Psychiatry, 167*(12), 1464–1471.

Uddin, L. Q., Iacoboni, M., Lange, C., & Keenan, J. P. (2007). The self and social cognition: The role of cortical midline structures and mirror neurons. *Trends in Cognitive Sciences*, *11*(4), 154–157.

Université de Montréal. (2012, December 18). Bullying by childhood peers leaves a trace that can change the expression of a gene linked to mood. *Science Daily*. Retrieved from http://www.sciencedaily.com /releases/2012/12/121218081615.htm

Vaillancourt, T., Duku, E., Decatanzaro, D., Macmillan, H., Muir, C., & Schmidt, L. A. (2008). Variation in hypothalamic–pituitary–adrenal axis activity among bullied and non-bullied children. *Aggressive Behavior*, *34*, 294–305.

Vaillancourt, T., Hymelb, S., & McDougall, P. (2003). Bullying is power: Implications for school-based intervention strategies. *Journal of Applied School Psychology*, *19*(2), 157–176.

Vaquero, L. M., & Cebrian, M. (2013). The rich club phenomenon in the classroom. *Scientific Reports*, *3*, 1174.

Wellcome Trust. (2012, November 8). Learning who's the top dog: Study reveals how the brain stores information about social rank. *Science Daily*. Retrieved from http://www.sciencedaily.com/releases/2012/11/121108131615.htm

Zadina, J. N., Smilkstein, R., Daiek, D. B., & Anter, N. M. (2013). *College reading: The science and strategies of expert readers*. Boston, MA: Wadsworth Cengage.

Zink, C. F., Tong, Y., Chen, Q., Bassett, D. S., Stein, J. L., & Meyer-Lindenberg, A. (2008). Know your place: Neural processing of social hierarchy in humans. *Neuron*, *58*(2), 273–283.

CHAPTER 9: THE BIG PICTURE

Benjamin, A. S., & Tullis, J. (2010). What makes distributed practice effective? *Cognitive Psychology*, *61*(3), 228–247.

Carothers, B. J., & Reis, H. T. (2013). Men and women are from Earth: Examining the latent structure of gender. *Journal of Personality and Social Psychology*, *104*(2), 385–407.

Chang, E. F., & Merzenich, M. M. (2003). Environmental noise retards auditory cortical development. *Science*, *300*(5618), 498–502.

Coe, D. P., Pivarnik, J. M., Womack, C. J., Reeves, M. J., & Malina, R. M. (2006). Effect of physical education and activity levels on academic achievement in children. *Journal of Science and Medicine in Sport*, *38*(8), 1515–1519.

Dik, M., Deeg, D. J., Visser, M., & Jonker, C. (2003). Early life physical activity and cognition at old age. *Journal of Clinical and Experimental Neuropsychology*, *25*(5), 643–653.

Fischer, K. W. (2009). Building a scientific groundwork for learning and teaching. *Mind, Brain, and Education*, *3*(1), 3–16.

Franklin, M. S., Moore, K. S., Yip, C. Y., Jonides, J., & Rattra, K. (2008). The effects of musical training on verbal memory. *Psychology of Music*, *36*, 353–365.

Gibson, C., Folley, B. S., & Park, S. (2009). Enhanced divergent thinking and creativity in musicians: A behavioral and near-infrared spectroscopy study. *Brain and Cognition, 69*(1), 162–169.

Hahn, T. T., McFarland, J. M., Berberich, S., Sakmann, B., & Mehta, M. R. (2012). Spontaneous persistent activity in entorhinal cortex modulates cortico-hippocampal interaction in vivo. *Nature Neuroscience, 15*(11), 1531–1538.

Han, S. (2012). *5-HTTLPR polymorphism moderates the association between a cultural value and the social brain network.* Paper presented at the FPR-UCLA Interdisciplinary Conference on Culture, Mind and Brain, Los Angeles, CA.

Hanna-Pladdy, B., & MacKay, A. (2011). The relation between instrumental musical activity and cognitive aging. *Neuropsychology, 25*(3), 378–386.

Hillman, C. H., Erickson, K. I., & Kramer, A. F. (2008). Be smart, exercise your heart: Exercise effects on brain and cognition. *Nature Reviews Neuroscience, 9*(1), 58–65.

Iacoboni, M., & Dapretto, M. (2006). The mirror neuron system and the consequences of its dysfunction. *Nature Reviews Neuroscience, 7*(12), 924–951.

Karpicke, J. D., & Bauernschmidt, A. (2011). Spaced retrieval: Absolute spacing enhances learning regardless of relative spacing. *Journal of Experimental Psychology, Learning Memory, and Cognition, 37*(5), 1250–1257.

Maltese, A. V., Tai, R. H., & Fan, X. (2012). When is homework worth the time? Evaluating the association between homework and achievement in high school science and math. *High School Journal, 96*(1), 52–72.

Mayfield, K. H., & Chase, P. N. (2002). The effects of cumulative practice on mathematics problem solving. *Journal of Applied Behavior Analysis, 35*(2), 105–123.

Moreno, S., Bialystok, E., Barac, R., Schellenberg, E. G., Cepeda, N. J., & Chau, T. (2011). Short-term music training enhances verbal intelligence and executive function. *Psychological Science, 22*(11), 1425–1433.

Moreno, S., Friesen, D., & Bialystok, E. (2011). Effect of music training on promoting preliteracy skills: Preliminary causal evidence. *Music Perception: An Interdisciplinary Journal, 29*, 165–172.

Moreno, S., Marques, C., Santos, A., Santos, M., Castro, S. L., & Besson, M. (2009). Musical training influences linguistic abilities in 8-year-old children: More evidence for brain plasticity. *Cerebral Cortex, 19*(3), 712–723.

Petitto, L. A. (2008). Arts education, the brain, and language. In *The Dana Consortium Report on Arts and Cognition* (pp. 93–104). New York, NY: Dana Press.

Piro, J. M., & Ortiz, C. (2009). The effect of piano lessons on the vocabulary and verbal sequencing skills of primary grade students. *Psychology of Music, 37*(3), 325–347.

Posner, M., Rothbart, M. K., Sheese, B. E., & Kieras, J. (2008). How arts training influences cognition. In *The Dana Consortium Report on Arts and Cognition,* (pp. 1–10). New York, NY: Dana Press.

Rauscher, F. H., Shaw, G. L., & Ky, K. N. (1993). Music and spatial task performance. *Nature, 365*(6447), 611.

Rose, D., Harbour, W., Johnston, S., Daley, S., & Abarbanell, L. (2006). Universal design for learning in postsecondary education: Reflections on principles and their application. *Journal of Postsecondary Education and Disability, 19*(2), 135–151.

Schellenberg, E. G. (2005). Music and cognitive abilities. *Current Directions in Psychological Science, 14,* 317–320.

Sibley, B. A., & Etnier, J. L. (2003). The relationship between physical activity and cognition in children: A meta-analysis. *Pediatric Exercise Science, 15,* 243–256.

Skoe, E., & Kraus, N. K. (2012). A little goes a long way: How the adult brain is shaped by musical training in childhood. *Journal of Neuroscience, 32*(34), 11507–11510.

Strait, D. L., & Kraus, N. (2011). Playing music for a smarter ear: Cognitive, perceptual and neurobiological evidence. *Music Perception, 29*(2), 133–146.

Taylor, K., & Rohrer, D. (2010). The effects of interleaved practice. *Applied Cognitive Psychology, 24,* 837–848.

Venner, S. A., Saper, C., & Fuller, P. (2012). *Probing the contribution of monoaminergic networks in sleep-wake regulation.* Paper presented at the Society for Neuroscience, New Orleans, LA.

Winter, B., Breitenstein, C., Mooren, F. C., Voelker, K., Fobker, M., Lechtermann, A., & Knecht, S. (2007). High impact running improves learning. *Neurobiology of Learning and Memory, 87*(4), 597–609.

The Author

Janet Nay Zadina is an educational neuroscientist who sees brain research through the eyes of a teacher and teaching through the eyes of a researcher. After twenty years of teaching experience at both high school and college levels, she became a cognitive neuroscientist and is one of the few people with experience and credentials in both neuroscience and education. Zadina bridges the fields of education and neuroscience through her work as a researcher, teacher, author, and international speaker.

She received her doctorate in the College of Education at the University of New Orleans, conducting her award-winning dissertation research on the neuroanatomy of dyslexia through collaboration with Tulane University School of Medicine. She continued her postdoctoral education with a fellowship in cognitive neuroscience in the Department of Neurology at Tulane, where she researched neuroanatomical risk factors for developmental language disorders through magnetic resonance imaging brain scans. She is currently an adjunct assistant professor at Tulane and an educational consultant, conducting presentations and workshops internationally on many aspects of the brain and learning. She also provides workshops on teaching and learning in the aftermath of trauma for educators affected by natural disaster or violence and populations with a high incidence of postraumatic stress disorder.

Zadina received a lifetime achievement award as a fellow in the College Learning and Developmental Education Association and is the winner of the 2011 Society for Neuroscience science educator award given to "an outstanding neuroscientist who has made a significant impact in informing the public about neuroscience." She has given a TEDx talk and is the author of several books. Her website, www.brainresearch.us, contains resources for teachers, as well as information about her publications and presentations.

Index

Page references followed by *fig* indicate an illustrated figure; followed by *t* indicate a table.

Case Western University, 100
Cebrian, Manuel, 204
Center for Neuroscience (UCD), 120
Center of Biomedical Imaging (Harvard University), 67
Centre for Neuroscience in Education (St. John's College), 153
Centre for Studies on Human Stress, 191
Cerebellum: description and location of the, 49, 65*fig*; dorsolateral prefrontal cortex interaction with, 54–55; emotion pathway role of the, 65; math pathway role of, 144*fig*; reading role of, 142
Chase, Philip, 156
Child abuse, 191
Child sexual abuse, 191
Christie, Deborah, 202
Chun, Marvin, 112
Chunking information, 122, 125, 126*fig*, 127*t*, 128, 155
Classroom applications: attention and memory pathways, 114–119; auditory-centered learning and, 47–48; of the brain's process of learning, 19–26; curriculum design principles, 221–227; early childhood educational investment, 230–232; emotion-centered learning, 69–72, 75–79; frontal lobe executive function pathway, 171–182; knowledge of physiology and, 216; language pathway, 139–141; math pathway, 154–160; mirror neurons, 200–203; positive emotions, 81–85; positive social interactions, 192–198; reading instruction, 141; reward pathway and, 96–106; setting the stage for achievement, 28–29; student speaking and discussion, 51–52; students with dyslexia, 147–151; technology, 205; visual-centered learning and, 40–44. *See also* Teaching
Classroom practices: activating reward, 97–98; administer a pretest, 22–23; audio input, 48; classroom emotional climate, 202–203; Concentration (game), 124–125; controlling distractions, 114–115; dual-language programs, 138; facilitate making connections, 23–24; flipped classroom format, 48; frontal lobe fatigue consideration of, 180–182; games to improve math skills, 154; to improve attention, 117–119; to improve math skills, 154–160; incorporating gestures as part of learning, 56–57; to increase motivation, 103–104; meditation, 118; using pattern detection, 98–102; pose a question or problem, 25; provide time for reflection, 25–26, 179–180; providing a sense of progress, 102–103; scaffolding, 24, 158–159, 173, 175–176, 223; setting the tone for positive interactions, 197; speaking as part of learning foreign language, 140–141; visualization, 118. *See also* Curriculum; Educational neuroscience
Classroom technology: brain research on use of, 203–204; classroom applications of, 205;

computer learning games, 204; implications for educators, 204
Classrooms: creating a positive atmosphere in the, 70–71; creating positive emotions in the, 82–85; emotional climate of, 202–203; Procedures and Consequences chart posted in, 71; providing students with sense of control in the, 77–78; reducing threats in the, 69–71, 77–79, 81; setting the tone for positive interactions, 197. *See also* Schools; Students
Cliques: example of intervention for social, 192–193; hierarchies of school, 193
Cocaine, 92*fig*
Cognitive fatigue, 130
Cognitive load: classroom practices to aid with, 176–178; description of, 130, 169; frontal lobe fatigue and, 180–182; metacognition as increasing, 178–179; multitasking increase of, 176–177; texting while driving and, 18
College Reading: The Science and Strategies of Expert Readers (Zadina, Smilkstein, Daiek, and Anter), 150
Community service projects, 197
Computer learning games, 204
Concentration (game), 124–125
Connections. *See* Making connections
Corpus callosum, 135*fig*, 153
Cortisol, 191
Cross, Emily, 55
Culturally relevant materials, 19
Curriculum: activating reward through, 95–96; addressing issues of what to incorporate into the, 7; applying learning and Hebbian law to the, 18; the arts, 217–218; earlier introduction of foreign language into, 139; including attention training in, 113–114; including multiple pathways in the, 4; increased demands for using executive functions skills with, 170–171; using multiple pathways as part of the, 182; need to include prior knowledge in the, 19; providing meaningful material as part of the, 101–102, 103–104; providing rigorous, 94, 96, 104–105; SEL (social and emotional intelligence) included in the, 80, 197–198. *See also* Classroom practices
Curriculum design: addressing learning differences, 221–222; brain research on, 217; classroom applications of principles of, 221–227; educating parents on, 220–221; implications for educators, 219–221; including the arts as part of, 217–218; multiple pathways of assessment as part of, 223–225; using music as part of the, 226–227; planning for instruction, 222–223; research application to, 220; time for unstructured play in early childhood, 232

Damasio, Antonio, 64
Dartmouth College, 55

impact on, 229; of high school and college students, 173–174; Homework Menu, 182; implications for educators, 169–171; importance of early intervention for, 170; life-span development of, 171; listed, 168–169; metacognition used to improve, 178–179; recognizing weakness in, 172–173; Reflect and Connect, 184; scaffolding and strengthening, 173, 175–176, 223; suggested strategies for improving, 182–184; teachers' modeling of, 174–175; teaching strategies to improve, 175. *See also* Thinking

Exercise: early childhood education and inclusion of, 228; importance to learning of, 215–216; physiological need and benefits of, 213–214

Exogenous attention, 111

Experience: as critical to learning, 18, 234; long-term potentiation process accompanying, 16, 18

Fail (freedom to), 174, 196

FastForward, 14

FastForWord(software), 46

Feedforward/feedbackward system, 67, 69

Fisch, A., 43

Flashbulb memories, 74

Flipped classroom format, 48

Fluid intelligence, 55

Focused attention, 112–113, 118

Food (as reward), 92*fig*

Foreign language: classroom applications for learning, 139–141; exposure to multiple speakers aiding ability to learn, 139; implications for educators on teaching a, 138–139; speaking as part of learning a, 140–141. *See also* Language; Second language

Franklin, Michael, 218

Freeze, flight, or fight responses: description of the, 73–75; how student behavior is impacted by the, 75–76; implications for educators, 75. *See also* Test anxiety

Frey, Scott, 198

Frontal cortex, 142, 144*fig*

Frontal lobe: attentional mechanisms in the, 38; description and location in the brain, 10*fig*, 167*fig*; emotion pathway role of the, 65–66; executive function of the, 165–166; executive functions centered in the, 166; fatigue of the, 180–182; Google search activation of the, 204; math pathway role of, 144*fig*; reading role of, 142; reflection as resting the, 26; reward pathway role of, 165–166; sensory motor strip, 37*fig*, 49; social pathway role of, 187; ventrolateral prefrontal, 66–67. *See also* Brain areas/regions

Frontal lobe executive function pathway: brain research on, 166–169; classroom applications, 171–182; early childhood education benefits for the, 229; Homework Menu, 182; implications for educators, 169–171; making connections, 165,

182–184; Reflect and Connect, 184; suggested strategies for making connections, 182–184

Frontal lobe fatigue, 180–182

Fuel: importance to learning of, 214–215; physiological need for, 213

Fulcher, James, 206

Furster, Joaquin, 120

Fusiform face area (FFA), 188, 189*fig*

Gabrieli, John D. E., 38, 67

Gazzaley, Adam, 110

Geary, David, 153–154, 230

Gender-imitation bias, 199

Gender similarities hypothesis, 212

Gestures: classroom applications for learning, 56–57; high fluid intelligence related to increased, 55; nonverbal language of, 42; visual-centered teaching and use of, 42–43

"Get out of jail free" card, 174

Glezer, Laurie, 146

Glucksberg, Sam, 137

Gold, Brian, 137

Goal-driven attention, 112

Goleman, Daniel, 64, 84

Golestani, Narly, 45

Gonda Multidisciplinary Brain Research Center (Israel), 146

Google Images, 42, 44

Google search, 204

Gopnik, Alison, 100, 135–136

"Gorilla video basketball" (YouTube video), 38, 113, 137

Goswami, Usha, 153

Grafman, Jordan, 204

Gray matter: changing differently in different brain areas, 13; illustration of, 14*fig*; process of learning and, 15–18; reading ability association to, 145. *See also* Neurons

Group work/activities, 193–195

Gunderson, Elizabeth, 96

Gurung, Regan, 129

Hakuta, Kenji, 136

Hampshire, Adam, 123

Handwriting (writing): brain research on process of, 52–53; classroom applications of, 53–54; educational implications of, 53

Harper, Michelle, 75

Harvard University, 39, 140, 213

Hebb, Donald, 16

Hebbian learning, 16, 18

Heckman, James, 170

Hedden, Trey, 67

Heschl's gyrus, 37*fig*, 45

High-stakes testing, 68

Hillman, Charles, 213

Hippocampus: emotion pathway role of the, 64, 65; location in the brain, 12*fig*, 65*fig*, 120*fig*; memory

and, 212; sleep and, 212–213, 214. *See also* The
    brain
Pictionary game, 44
Pictorial superiority effect, 39, 41
Piro, Joseph, 219
Pisoni, David, 139
Plasticity: of the auditory cortex, 45–46; brain
    research on the, 11–13; brain's rewiring ability
    due to, 12–13, 15; description of the, 11–12;
    educational significance of neuroscience
    discovery of, 234; implications for educators,
    13–15
Positive emotion: brain research on, 80; classroom
    applications for learning and, 81–85;
    implications for educators, 80; music to create,
    84–85; what we know about, 79
Positive psychology: description and emergence of, 64;
    on learning and positive emotions, 79–85
Posner, Michael, 218
Posterior superior temporal sulcus (pSTS), 188, 189*fig*
Posttraumatic stress disorder (PTSD): description of,
    73, 74–75; high stress situations that can cause,
    76–77; implications for educators, 75. *See also*
    Stress
Practice: long-term potentiation process through, 16,
    18; spaced repetition strategy for encoding
    memories, 126*fig*, 129
Prefrontal cortex: description and brain area of,
    90*fig*, 144*fig*, 167*fig*; metacognition skill of the,
    178–179
Preschool educational investment. *See* Early childhood
    educational investment
Pretest anxiety, 66
Pretests, 22–23
Preview, Study-Read, and Review model, 150
Price, Cathy, 137
Primary auditory area, 135*fig*
Primary motor cortex, 135*fig*
Priming study, 201–202
Princeton University, 137
Prior knowledge: as critical to learning new material,
    21–22; description of, 19; facilitating new
    connections to, 23–24; how culturally relevant
    materials build on, 19; as not being enough by
    itself for learning, 36; number system knowledge,
    153–154; pretests to assess, 22–23. *See also*
    Information
Problem-based learning, 25
Procedural memory, 120
"Process praise," 96
Progress notebook, 102
Protzko, John, 228
Purdue University, 45
Puzzles, 98–99

Qinghua, 145
Quagliariello, Grace, 193

Quellet-Morin, Isabella, 191
Questions/problems, 25
*Quiet: The Power of Introverts in a World That Can't
    Stop Talking* (Cain), 194

Radboud University, 202
Raji, Cyrus, 214
Ratey, John, 213
Razza, Rachel, 170
Reading: brain regions activated during, 145*t*; brain
    regions involved in, 143*fig*; brain research on
    dyslexia and process of, 142–146; classroom
    practices for auditory and visual instruction of,
    47–48; implications for educators, 146–147;
    language and math pathways during process of,
    141; orthographic processing of sight words,
    145–146, 148; phonologic processing of, 142,
    145, 146, 148; relationship between
    auditory-centered learning and, 45; reward
    activated by story, 93, 97; semantic processing of
    meaning when, 145, 146, 148; students with
    dyslexia and difficulties in, 148–151; suggested
    strategies for teaching, 161; thalamus role in,
    135*fig*, 142, 144
Reading comprehension: as form of thinking skill,
    149; Preview, Study-Read, and Review model of,
    150; summary concept, 177; vocabulary role in,
    149; working memory role in, 148, 149, 150
Red Rocks Community College, 155
Reflect and Connect: on attention and memory
    pathways, 131–132; on the big picture, 234–236;
    description of process, 25, 26; on emotion
    pathway and learning, 86; on language and math
    pathways, 162–163; on reward pathway and
    learning, 107–108; on sensory pathway and
    learning, 60–61; on social pathway, 208–209; on
    teaching that helps the learning process, 32
Reflection: examples of, 180; providing students with
    time for, 25–26; "reflect and connect" motto on,
    25, 26; 10/80/10 rule of, 179–180
Reward pathway: brain regions most active in,
    90*fig*–93; brain research on the, 90*fig*–94;
    classroom applications, 96–106; dopamine
    ("pleasure chemical") role in the, 91, 92*fig*, 93, 94;
    drugs of abuse hijacking the, 92*fig*; frontal lobe
    role in, 165–166; gender-imitation bias and, 199;
    Homework Menu to tie into the, 106;
    implications for educators, 94–96; making
    connections using the, 89; motivation and the,
    93–94; "process" vs. "person" praise activating
    the, 96; rigor as part of the, 94, 96, 104–105;
    suggested strategies for making connections, 107
Richland, Lindsey, 229
Right hemisphere of brain, 134, 137
Rigor: classroom practices that promote, 104–105;
    reward pathway activated by, 94, 96
Rose, Mike, 206

Rubio-Fernandez, Paula, 137
Ryan, Richard, 93

San Francisco State University, 55
Sanbonmatsu, David, 113
Saper, Clifford, 213
Sapolsky, Robert, 190–191
Sassenberg, Uta, 55
SAT scores, 168
Sathian, Krish, 93
Scaffolding: description and examples of, 24;
    development of executive functions using, 173,
    175–176, 223; math skills and, 158–159
Schema, 19
Schools: bullying in, 191, 192, 197; importance of the
    environment of, 216; making educational
    investment in preschool, 170, 227–232; offering
    healthy meals at, 214–215; providing
    opportunities for exercise, 213–214, 215–216;
    recommended faculty diversity in, 199;
    technology used in, 203–205. *See also*
    Classrooms; Teachers
Science journal, 170
The Scientist in the Crib (Gopnik), 100
Second language: brain research on language and
    acquisition of, 134–137; classroom applications
    for teaching a, 139–141; differences in how
    adults and children learn a, 136; implications for
    educators, 138–139; infant language preferences,
    136. *See also* Bilinguals; Foreign language;
    Language
Seiger, Cindy, 57, 114
Selective attention, 115
Self-efficacy, 74–75, 79, 104, 172
Semantic processing (meaning), 145, 146
Semel Institute for Neuroscience and Human Behavior
    (UCLA), 120
Sense of control, 77–78
Sensory motor pathway: auditory, 44–48; Homework
    Menu to tie into the, 57–59; making connections,
    35, 59–61; motor (or kinesthetic), 49–57, 58–59;
    Reflect and Connect on the, 60–61; suggested
    strategies for making connections, 59; visual,
    auditory, and kinesthetic (VAK) modes of the,
    36–59
Sensory motor strip, 37*fig*, 49
Service-learning projects, 197
Sex differences, 212
Shaywitz, Bennett, 142
Shaywitz, Sally, 14, 142
Shuller, Marshall, 38
Sight word reading, 145–146, 148
Sign language, 45–46
Simon, Daniel, 38
Simon, David, 113
Simos, Panagiotia, 142
Skoe, Erika, 218

Sleep: learning and importance of, 214; physiological
    need for, 212–213
Smilkstein, Rita, 21
Smith, Christine, 121
Social cognitive theory, 746
Social intelligence, 80
Social interactions: brain research on, 188–190;
    bullying, 191, 192, 197; classroom applications to
    promote positive, 192–198; rewards of, 190;
    setting the classroom tone for positive, 197; social
    status and social rejection, 190–197;
    social/emotional learning through, 197–198
Social pain/physical pain overlap theory, 190
Social pathway: classroom technology and the,
    203–205; frontal lobe role in, 187; Homework
    Menu, 206; making connections, 187, 206–209;
    mirror neurons, 198–203; Reflect and Connect,
    208–209; social status and social rejection,
    188–198; social/emotional learning, 80,
    197–198; suggested strategies for making
    connections, 206–208
Social rejection: brain research on, 188–190; bullying,
    191, 192, 197; description and responses to, 191;
    implications for educators, 192
Social status: brain research on, 188–190; classroom
    activities and, 196–197; description and
    responses to, 190–191; group work/activities and,
    193–195; implications for educators, 191–192
Social/emotional learning (SEL), 80, 197–198
Society for Neuroscience, 46
Society for Neuroscience Conference (2012), 213, 227
Socioeconomic status (SES), 138, 228
Solis, Karen, 21
Sounds: newborn recognition of language patterns
    and, 135–136; "perceptual wedge" between
    monolinguals and bilinguals to hear, 136;
    phonological subtype of dyslexia and impaired
    ability to discern, 14, 45, 46, 145; visual word
    form area (VWFA) impairment, 37, 146. *See also*
    Language
Spaced repetition strategy, 126*fig*, 129
Spatial information: London taxi drivers' experiment
    findings on, 12–13; processed in the
    hippocampus, 13
Speaking: brain research on learning role of, 50;
    classroom applications related to, 51–52;
    educational implications of, 50
Speech patterns: ability of newborns to discern,
    135–136; exposure to multiple speakers aiding
    ability to learn foreign, 139
Spelling and dyslexia, 45
Squire, Larry, 121
St. John's College (Cambridge), 153
"Stand up and explain" strategy, 51
Stanford University, 140, 190
Stanford University School of Medicine, 153, 217–218
Stickgold, Robert, 213
Stimulating environment, 227–229